# Empathy and Moral Development
*Implications for Caring and Justice*

Contemporary theories have generally focused on the behavioral, cognitive, or emotional dimensions of prosocial moral development. In this volume, Martin L. Hoffman brings these three dimensions together while providing the first comprehensive account of prosocial moral development in children. The main concept is empathy – one feels what is appropriate for another person's situation, not one's own. Hoffman discusses empathy's role in five moral situations: one harms someone, one is an innocent bystander, one blames oneself though innocent, one must choose which among several victims to help, or one is torn between contradictory caring and justice concerns. The book's focus is empathy's contribution to altruism and compassion for others in physical, psychological, or economic distress; to feelings of guilt over harming someone; to feelings of anger at others who do harm; and to feelings of injustice when others do not receive their due. Also highlighted are the psychological processes involved in empathy's interaction with certain parental behaviors that foster moral internalization in children and the psychological processes involved in empathy's relation to abstract moral principles such as caring and distributive justice. This important book is the culmination of three decades of study and research by a leading figure in the area of child and developmental psychology.

Martin L. Hoffman is Professor of Psychology at New York University. He is series editor for Cambridge Studies in Social and Emotional Development.

# Empathy and Moral Development

IMPLICATIONS FOR CARING
AND JUSTICE

*Martin L. Hoffman*

*New York University*

 CAMBRIDGE
UNIVERSITY PRESS

CAMBRIDGE UNIVERSITY PRESS
Cambridge, New York, Melbourne, Madrid, Cape Town, Singapore,
São Paulo, Delhi, Dubai, Tokyo, Mexico City

Cambridge University Press
32 Avenue of the Americas, New York, NY 10013-2473, USA

www.cambridge.org
Information on this title: www.cambridge.org/9780521012973

© Cambridge University Press 2000

First published 2000
First paperback edition 2001
Reprinted 2003, 2007 (twice)

*A catalog record for this publication is available from the British Library*

ISBN 978-0-521-58034-2 Hardback
ISBN 978-0-521-01297-3 Paperback

*This book is dedicated with love to*
*my wife, Ann,*
*my children, Amy and Jill,*
*and my grandchildren, Alison, Nicole, and*
*  Sarah*

# Contents

Contents

# Acknowledgments

This book owes much to many. If my discipline and internalization theory works, it was Amy and Jill's challenges that taught me, for instance, that power assertion can be necessary for the voice of induction to be heard. I used to think it was good for children to have developmental psychologist parents, but in fact I learned more from them than they benefited from my "using" psychology.

My graduate students were important. I remember talking to one in Ann Arbor about how different it must be to empathize with someone in distress before, and after, one has a sense of oneself as distinct from others. That discussion led me eventually to hypothesize that self-other differentiation transforms children's global empathic distress in part into sympathetic distress. In a seminar I suggested that inductions contribute to internalization because they have meaning, which makes their content more memorable than background factors such as the source of inductions being the parents. An alert student said this reminded him of the "sleeper effect" in persuasion research when the salience of the message is greater than that of its source; another said it fits with Tulving's semantic-episodic memory distinction. These comments made me think, hey, my suggestion is plausible, so I'll stay with it.

Undergraduates helped, too, especially those in my 1997 class to whom I taught the book's first draft. Their questions revealed gaps in my theories, their anecdotes enlivened some of my concepts such as empathic anger and relationship guilt, and their writing-style suggestions resulted in the final draft's being more broadly accessible.

Last but not least, I am indebted to my wife, Ann, for her support and inspiration from the time I decided to write until the book was finished.

# CHAPTER 1

# Introduction and Overview

When I tell people my field is moral development, the first response is usually silence, sometimes "Oh!" They think I mean religion, telling the truth, the decline of traditional family life, and prohibitions against drugs, alcohol, and teenage pregnancy. When I tell them my interest is people's consideration for others, they perk up at first but then say something like it must be frustrating to study that because everybody is interested in themselves; who cares about anyone else, except maybe their family? But when I say humans could not have survived as a species if everyone cared only about himself, they pause, think about it, and then say something like "You might be right." The evolution argument carries weight, as though it were self-evident that hunters and gatherers had to help each other to survive, so humans must have helping genes.

In any case, it is in this end-of-millennium, first-world context of competitive individualism and little caring for others that some of us study prosocial moral behavior – knowing full well that however much a person cares about others, when the chips are down, the individual thinks of himself first: **He or she is not the other.** People do make sacrifices for others, however, sometimes big sacrifices, and they help others in small ways all the time. This adds to the quality of life and makes social existence possible. So there is something to study. Indeed, the topic has preoccupied philosophers at least since Aristotle and has been a topic of research interest in psychology for almost a century. The topic's staying power, I think, lies in its self-evident importance for social organization and the fact that it epitomizes the existential human dilemma of how people come to grips with the inevitable conflicts between their egoistic needs and their social obligations.

Philosophy and religion have various answers to this dilemma, and their answers have parallels in contemporary psychological theory. One answer, the "doctrine of original sin," which assumes people are born egoistic and acquire a moral sense through socialization that controls egoism, is paralleled in early Freudian and social-learning theories that stressed the importance for moral development of reward and punishment by parents, especially giving and withholding affection. The diametrically opposed and more interesting "doctrine of innate purity," associated with Rousseau who viewed children as innately good (sensitive to others) but vulnerable to corruption by society, has a rough parallel in Piaget's theory, not that children are innately pure but that their relation to adults produces a heteronomous respect for rules and authority which interferes with moral development. This corruption by adults can only be overcome by the give-and-take of free, unsupervised interaction with peers, which, together with children's naturally evolving cognitive capability, enables them to take others' perspectives and develop autonomous morality. The resemblance to "innate purity" is that the free and natural interaction of **premoral** children produces moral development, whereas interaction with (socialized) adults prevents it.

Philosophers like Immanuel Kant and his followers, who attempt to derive universal, impartially applied principles of justice, helped inspire Kohlberg (and to a lesser extent Piaget) to construct an invariant sequence of universal moral stages. And the British version of utilitarianism represented by David Hume, Adam Smith, and others for whom empathy was a necessary social bond, finds expression in current research on empathy, compassion, and the morality of caring.

Contemporary theories of prosocial moral development tend to focus on one dimension, each with its own explanatory processes. Social-learning theories deal with helping behavior and specialize in the processes involved in reward, punishment, and imitation. Cognitive-developmental theorists deal with moral reasoning and employ concepts like perspective-taking, reciprocity, cognitive disequilibrium, progressive construction, and co-construction. Theories of emotional and motivational development employ concepts like parent identification, anxiety over loss of love, empathy, sympathy, guilt, and moral internalization. I have long written on the emotional/motivational dimension, especially empathy development, guilt, and moral internalization. To me, empathy is the spark of human concern for others, the glue that makes social life possible. It may be fragile but it has, arguably, endured throughout evolutionary times and may continue as long as humans exist.

In this book, I update my previous work and frame it in a comprehensive theory of prosocial moral behavior and development that highlights empathy's contribution to moral emotion, motivation, and behavior but also assigns special importance to cognition. The aim is to elucidate the processes underlying empathy's arousal and its contribution to prosocial action; to throw light on the way empathy develops, from preverbal forms that may have existed in early humans and still do in primates, to sophisticated expressions of concern for subtle and complex human emotions. My aim is also to examine empathy's contribution to the principles of caring and justice, to resolving caring–justice conflicts, and to moral judgment.

I have been working on the theory for three decades. It includes elements of the philosophical and psychological approaches mentioned earlier but also makes use of contemporary cognitive psychology – memory, information processing, causal attribution, and especially the synthesis of affect and cognition. Its primary focus is consideration for others, often called "caring" morality, but also includes "justice" and the mutually supportive though sometimes contradictory relation between caring and justice.

The theory attempts to account for human action in five types of moral encounters or dilemmas, which I believe encompass most of the prosocial moral domain. In the first, the simplest type, one is an **innocent bystander** who witnesses someone in pain or distress (physical, emotional, financial). The moral issue is: Does one help and how does one feel if one does not help? In the second type, one is a **transgressor,** who harms or is about to harm someone (accidentally, in fights, arguments). The moral issue is: Does one refrain from harming the other or at least feel guilty afterward? In the third type of moral encounter, which combines elements of the first two, one is a **virtual transgressor,** who, though innocent, believes he or she has harmed someone. The fourth type is more complex: It involves **multiple moral claimants** among whom one is compelled to make a choice. The moral issue is: Whom does one help and does one feel guilty over neglecting the others? The fifth type, **caring versus justice,** involves multiple moral claimants but also a clash between considering others and more abstract issues such as rights, duty, reciprocity. The moral issue here is: Which principle prevails, caring or justice, and does one feel guilty for violating the other? Multiple claimant and caring–justice dilemmas are especially important in societies like ours that are becoming increasingly diverse culturally.

All five types share an empathic motive base – **empathy defined as an affective response more appropriate to another's situation than one's own.** Each type features empathic distress – one feels distressed on observing someone in actual distress – and one or more motives derived from empathic distress: sympathetic distress, empathic anger, empathic feeling of injustice, guilt.

The book begins with an analysis of innocent bystanders. The bystander model attempts to answer these questions: What are the motives that predispose innocent bystanders to help victims? What are the psychological mechanisms that underlie the arousal or activation of these motives? What is the developmental course of the motives? It takes the first three chapters (part I) to answer these questions. I begin in chapter 2 by defining empathy as an affective response that is more appropriate for another's situation than one's own. Empathic **distress** is the focus, as bystanders are typically in a position to respond to someone in distress. I review the evidence from a variety of sources that empathic distress functions as a prosocial moral motive, but most of the chapter is taken up with various modes of empathic arousal.

If empathy is the product of natural selection, as I have argued elsewhere (Hoffman, 1981), it must be a multidetermined response that can be aroused by cues of distress coming from the victim or the victim's situation. Empathy is indeed multidetermined, and I discuss five distinctly different modes of empathic arousal. These include three that are preverbal, automatic, and essentially involuntary: motor **mimicry** and afferent feedback; classical **conditioning;** direct **association** of cues from the victim or his situation with one's own painful past experience. The empathy aroused by these three modes is a passive, involuntary affective response, based on the pull of surface cues, and requires the shallowest level of cognitive processing. This simple form of empathic distress is important, however, precisely because it shows that humans are built in such a way that they can involuntarily and forcefully experience another's emotion – that their distress is often contingent not on their own but someone else's painful experience. The three preverbal modes are crucial for arousing empathy in childhood especially in face-to-face situations, but they continue to operate and provide empathy with an important involuntary dimension throughout life. They not only enable a person to respond to whatever cues are available, but they also **compel** him to do it – instantly, automatically, and without requiring conscious awareness.

There are two higher-order cognitive modes: **mediated association,** that is, association of expressive cues from the victim or cues from the victim's situation with one's own painful past experience, where the association is mediated by semantic processing of information from or about the victim; and **role-or perspective-taking,** in which one imagines how the victim feels or how one would feel in the victim's situation. These modes may be drawn out over time and they may be subject to voluntary control, but if one is paying attention to the victim they can be involuntary and triggered immediately on witnessing the victim's distress. What they contribute to a person's empathic capability is scope; they also enable a person to empathize with others who are not present.

The existence of multiple arousal modes bears on my definition of empathy as not requiring, though often including, a close match between observer's and victim's affect. The many modes of empathic arousal assure a certain degree of match, even across cultures (as will be discussed), for two reasons: mimicry, which may be automatic and neurally based, assures a match when observer and victim are in face-to-face contact; conditioning and association assure a match because all humans are structurally similar and process information similarly and are therefore likely to respond to similar events with similar feelings. But there are times when empathy does not require a match and, indeed, may require a certain mismatch, as when a victim's life condition belies his feelings in the immediate situation. These are the times when verbal mediation and role-taking may take center stage.

My theoretical framework for the development of empathic distress is presented in chapter 3, which is a key chapter in the book. In it I argue for a developmental synthesis of children's empathic affect and their development of a cognitive sense of others as distinct from themselves. The synthesis results in five "stages" in the development of empathic distress: (a) **reactive newborn cry;** (b) **egocentric empathic distress,** in which children respond to another's distress as though they themselves were in distress; this happens during the developmental interval in which they can feel empathic distress (from early preverbal arousal modes) but still lack a clear distinction between self and other; (c) **quasi-egocentric empathic distress,** in which children realize the distress is the other's, not their own, but confuse the other's inner states with their own and try to help by doing for the other what would comfort themselves; (d) **veridical empathic distress,** in which children come closer to feeling what the other is actually feeling because they now realize that the other has inner states independent of their own; (e) **empathy for another's experience beyond the immediate situation** (e.g., chronic illness, economic hardship, deprivation), when children realize that others have lives that may be generally sad or happy; and a subcategory, when children can empathize with an entire group (homeless; Oklahoma City bombing victims). I also present evidence for my hypothesis that beginning with stage (c), **children's empathic distress is transformed in part into a feeling of sympathetic distress or compassion for the victim,** and from that time on when children observe someone in distress they feel both empathic and sympathetic distress. My use of the term *empathic distress* throughout the rest of the book refers to this empathic/sympathetic distress combination.

In this developmental scheme, each stage combines the gains of the previous stages. At the most advanced stage, one is exposed to a network of information about the victim's condition, which may include verbal and nonverbal expressive cues from the victim, situational cues, and knowledge of the victim's life condition. These sources of information are processed differently: empathy aroused by nonverbal cues is mediated by the largely involuntary, cognitively shallow processing modes (mimicry, conditioning, association). Empathy aroused by verbal messages from the victim, a third party's description of the victim's state or condition, or one's personal knowledge about the victim requires more complex processing (mediated association, role-taking). At the most advanced stage, observers may act out in their minds the emotions and experiences suggested by the above information and introspect on all of it. In this way they gain understanding and respond affectively to the circumstances, feelings, and wishes of the other, while maintaining the sense that this person is separate from themselves. When their information about the other's life condition contradicts the other's behavior in the immediate situation, their empathy can be as influenced, possibly more influenced, by the other's life condition than by his or her immediate behavior.

It should be clear by now that cognition plays an important role in development of empathic distress. Cognition is highlighted even more in chapter 4, where I note the human tendency to explain events causally and show how attributions about the cause of another's distress can shape empathic distress into four empathy-based moral affects. When the cause is beyond the victim's control (illness, accident, loss), observers' empathic distress is transformed at least partly into **sympathetic distress** which is like the developmental transformation of empathic into sympathetic distress discussed in chapter 3. If someone else is the cause, one's empathic distress is transformed into **empathic anger**, which consists of either empathy with the victim's anger or a dual feeling of empathic sadness or disappointment (if that, rather than anger, is how the victim feels) and anger at the culprit. The latter, dual type of empathic anger may be prevalent in societies like ours in which, owing to socialization, direct anger is not easily felt. It is also another case in which empathy involves a mismatch between observer's and victim's feelings.

When a discrepancy exists between the victim's character and the victim's fate (a good person fares badly), the apparent violation of reciprocity or justice may transform an observer's empathic distress into an **empathic feeling of injustice**. And, finally, when observers do not help, or their efforts to help fail, even for legitimate reasons, their view of themselves as causing the victim's *continuing* distress may transform their empathic distress into **guilt over inaction**. It goes without saying that people's empathic distress can be reduced by **blaming the victim** for his or her own distress.

An important point about the bystander model is that to respond with empathic distress and the various empathy-based affects does not require the victim to be physically present. Because of the human capacity to represent events and imagine oneself in another's place, and because of the power of represented events to evoke affect, to feel empathic distress one need only **imagine** victims, as when reading about someone's misfortune, arguing about economic or political issues that involve victims or potential victims, or even making Kohlberg-style judgments about hypothetical moral dilemmas. One can also turn an abstract moral question into an empathy-relevant one by imagining a victim, say, of corporate downsizing, and how he feels. The ability to represent thus expands the importance of empathic morality beyond the face-to-face encounters of children and members of primary groups, which has been the focus of most of the research. It expands the bystander model to encompass a variety of situations limited not by the victim's presence but by the observers' imagination.

As the bystander model is the prototypic moral encounter for empathy, especially empathic distress, the transgression model is the prototypic moral encounter for empathy-based **transgression guilt** (in contrast to bystander guilt over inaction). The transgression model also highlights children's early socialization at home and is the prototypic encounter for **moral internalization**. The moral issues are these: What motivates a person to avoid harming others and to consider their needs, even when their needs conflict with his or her own? When one does harm another, does one feel guilty afterward? When one contemplates acting in an instrumental, self-serving way that one realizes may end up harming someone (though that was not one's intention), does one anticipate feeling empathic distress and guilt? Exactly what is meant by moral internalization? These issues are dealt with in part II of the book, which includes chapters 5 and 6.

Guilt and moral internalization are chapter 5 topics. There I describe empathy-based transgression guilt, adduce evidence that there is such a thing and that it functions as a prosocial moral motive, and speculate about the developmental processes in its formation. I also point up the importance of moral internalization, which I define simply as follows: A person's prosocial moral structure is internalized when he or she accepts and feels obligated to abide by it without regard to external sanctions. That is, the rewards and punishments that may have previously motivated one to consider others have lost most of their force and one now experiences the motive to consider others as deriving autonomously from within oneself. The various conceptions of moral internalization – Freudian, social-learning, cognitive-developmental, attributional, information-processing – are reviewed in this chapter.

Those that I found most useful are integrated into the theory of guilt development and moral internalization presented in chapter 6. My definition of an internal moral motive is that it: (a) has a compelling, obligatory quality, (b) is experienced as deriving from within oneself, (c) makes one feel guilty when one acts or considers acting in ways that may harm others, (d) disposes one to consider another's needs even when they conflict with one's own. When such a conflict exists, the empathy arousing processes that work in bystander situations may not be powerful enough to motivate one to act prosocially. To create prosocial motives that are powerful enough to operate in conflict situations requires parents to actively socialize the child to consider others.

Parents interact with children in many ways but only in discipline encounters do they make the connections necessary for guilt and moral internalization: that is, connections between the child's egoistic motives, the child's behavior, and the harmful consequences of the child's actions for others. And only in discipline encounters do parents put pressure on children to control their behavior and consider the needs and claims of others. If parents do this right, they can give children the experience of controlling their behavior through their own active processing of information about the consequences of their actions for others, which contributes to their developing an empathy-based internal motive to consider others.

Doing it right means using **inductions** when the child harms or is about to harm another. Induction highlights both the victim's distress and the child's action that caused it and has been found to contribute to the development of guilt and moral internalization in children. My explanation is this: Most parental discipline has power-assertive and love-withdrawing components that put pressure on the child to attend to the parent: too little pressure and the child may ignore the parent; too much, and the emotions aroused (hostility, fear) may prevent children's effective processing of inductive information and direct their attention to the consequences of their action for themselves. A salient induction that fits the child's cognitive level and puts *just enough* pressure on the child to process the induction's information and attend to the consequences of the child's action for the victim may arouse empathic distress and guilt (through the arousal mechanisms described earlier). In this way parents can exploit and build upon an ally that exists within the child – his or her empathic proclivity – and create a moral motive that may compete with the child's egoistic motives.

When the child experiences, repeatedly, the sequence of transgression followed by parent's induction followed by child's empathic distress and guilt feeling, the child forms Transgression → Induction → Guilt scripts, which have motive properties due to their empathic distress and guilt components. When a script is activated for the first time in an actual situation involving conflict with others, its motive component may not be strong enough to overcome the prospect of egoistic gain. But it may become strong enough with repetition, and when combined with cognitive development and peer pressure it may be effective. That is, peer pressure *compels* children to realize that others have claims; cognition *enables* them to understand others' perspectives; empathic distress and guilt *motivate* them to take others' claims and perspectives into account.

These prosocial moral scripts are not passively acquired but actively formed by children in a continuing process of constructing, synthesizing, and semantically organizing inductive information and relating it to their own actions and the victim's condition. This active mental processing makes the child's internal cognitive and affective processes salient to the child, and the child experiences the scripts and their implicit norm of considering others as the child's own construction and part of his or her internal motive system. Parental intervention is no longer necessary and the scripts, now Transgression → Guilt scripts, can be activated by the child's own awareness of harming someone. When activated, a script's associated guilt and motivation to make amends is felt by the child as coming from within him-or herself. The script can be activated in advance by the child's thoughts and images about the harmful effects of his or her acts. The resulting anticipatory guilt is a motive against committing the act, and if the child does commit the act, he or she will feel guilty.

In short, what chapter 6 suggests are the antecedent factors that can lead to the development of an early moral motive to consider others even when one's needs conflict with theirs. Later experiences of various kinds expand this motive to areas of life not dealt with at home. These experiences also provide skills and competencies that serve the motive and help make connections between it and relatively abstract moral principles like caring and justice. The chapter also summarizes empirical evidence for the theory and takes up the issue of direction of effects.

Once a child acquires Transgression → Guilt scripts, it should perhaps not be surprising that the scripts can be activated and trigger guilt feelings in the child whenever the child *thinks* he transgressed, even when he or she did not. I call this virtual guilt, and the presumed harmful acts, **virtual transgressions**. Virtual guilt is not a new concept: A definition of guilt in *Webster's Ninth New Collegiate Dictionary* is "feelings of culpability especially for imagined offenses." In chapter 7 I describe and try to explain several variations of virtual guilt. One, **"relationship" guilt,** may be endemic to close relationships because they provide endless opportunities not only for hurting one's partner but also for *thinking* one has. That is, relationship partners become so dependent on each other that their feelings and moods depend heavily on the feelings, moods, and actions of the other. More importantly, each partner knows the other is similarly dependent on him or her, and each partner may as a result develop a keen sensitivity to the potential impact of his or her words and deeds on the other. It may therefore seem reasonable when one's partner is sad or unhappy and *the cause is unclear* not only to feel empathic distress but also to blame oneself for the partner's state. One might not feel guilty if certain of one's innocence, but that requires keeping accurate mental records of previous interactions with one's partner, a type of emotional bookkeeping rare in close relationships.

A related type of virtual guilt – **"responsibility guilt"** – stems from having responsibility for someone who is harmed, even when the facts clearly indicate that one was not at fault. What seems to happen is that one empathizes with the victim's pain, reviews the situation in one's mind, realizes that one could have acted differently and prevented the accident, shifts from *I could have* to *I should have*, blames oneself, and feels guilty.

Whereas close relationships and positions of responsibility are the context for relationship and responsibility guilt, pursuing one's normal developmental goals and interests can provide the context for virtual transgressions involving "developmental guilt." A person may feel that by leaving home for college he will damage his parents – **separation guilt;** and by achieving more than his peers he contributes to making them feel inadequate – **achievement guilt.** A person may also feel guilty over his relative affluence, that is, over benefiting from privileges that others lack – **guilt over affluence.** Though adults may feel guilt over affluence, I class it with developmental guilt because it seems more prevalent in adolescents (at least it was in the 1960s) and may be a significant part of the prosocial moral development of those who experience it.

It is known that people who experience the traumatic death, injury, or other misfortune of someone else (in war, acts of terrorism, natural disaster, corporate downsizing), while they remain unharmed, often feel guilt over surviving. The guilt is compounded by conflicting emotions of joy at surviving and empathic sorrow for the victims. Add to this the hidden relief that the worst happened to someone else, and one can have a painful case of guilt – **survival guilt.** Guilt may be the survivor's answer to the question, "Why me – why was I saved and not somebody else?" What this person is saying, and what survival guilt may have in common with guilt over affluence is that one cannot justify the advantage one has over the victim. One's advantage therefore violates the principle of fairness or reciprocity; and the awareness of being advantaged may transform empathic distress for the victim into an empathic feeling of injustice and a feeling of guilt. The prevalence of guilt over one's relative advantage, survival, and the other types of virtual guilt confirms my belief that humans, at least in our society, are "guilt machines."

In chapter 8, I shift from empathic motivation's contributions to prosocial moral action, to its limitations, which result from empathy's dependence on the intensity and salience of distress cues and the relationship between observer and victim. One limitation is that although we expect more intense empathic arousal with more salient distress cues, extremely salient distress cues can be so aversive that an observer's empathic distress is transformed into an intense personal feeling of distress. This **empathic over-arousal** can move observers out of the empathic mode, cause them to be preoccupied with their own personal distress, and turn their attention away from the victim. An exception is that for people who are committed to a helping relationship (therapist–patient; parent–child) empathic over-arousal may intensify empathic distress and motivation to help the victim.

The second limitation is empathy's vulnerability to two types of bias: **familiarity bias** and **here-and-now bias.** Although people tend to respond empathically to almost anyone in distress, they are vulnerable to bias in favor of victims who are family members, members of their primary group, close friends, and people who are similar to themselves; and to bias in favor of victims who are present in the immediate situation.

Empathy's vulnerability to over-arousal and the two types of bias may not be a significant problem in small homogeneous "primary group" societies, or in bystander, transgressor, and virtual transgressor moral encounters involving one victim. Indeed, these limitations may have a hidden virtue: If people empathized with everyone in distress and tried to help them all equally, society might quickly come to a halt. Seen in this light, empathic bias and over-arousal may be empathy's ultimate self-regulating, self-preserving mechanisms, which fits with the increasing evidence that the ability to regulate one's emotions correlates *positively* with empathy and helping behavior.

Still, empathic over-arousal and especially empathic bias may pose problems in encounters involving multiple claimants and encounters in which caring for another conflicts with the demands of justice. These problems can be reduced, I hypothesize, when empathy is "embedded" in a moral principle with which it is congruent, because this allows empathy to gain structure and stability from the principle's cognitive dimension.

Chapter 9 relates empathic affect to Western society's prevailing moral principles: caring and justice. Empathy's congruence with caring is obvious. It is also congruent with aspects of criminal justice, which involves victims, and this is briefly discussed. Most of the chapter deals with distributive justice, which pertains to how society's resources should be allocated – "equally," or according to one's "need," "effort," or "merit" (competence, productivity). Empathy is congruent with all of these justice principles, but less so with competence and productivity. My argument that empathic arousal may alter one's views of distributive justice can be summarized thus: If a person thinks about how society's resources should be distributed, a self-serving perspective will make him prefer principles that coincide with his own condition: high producers will choose merit and low producers will choose need or equality. If empathy is aroused, the welfare of others will be considered and even high producers may choose need or equality – or, more likely, merit regulated to prevent extreme poverty (need) and vast discrepancies in wealth (equality).

Regulated merit is at the heart of the philosopher John Rawls's theory of justice, notably the "difference principle," which assigns great weight to how society's "least advantaged" are treated. Rawls uses a "veil of ignorance," which compels people whom he imagines are constructing a society from a rational, totally self-serving perspective – but without knowing their place in that society – to ensure that the least advantaged's needs will be taken care of. Rawls's other purpose in using the veil of ignorance is to rule out empathy, so that the difference principle would be derived on purely rational, self-serving grounds. I applaud Rawls's approach but spend a lot time in this chapter arguing that empathy and the veil of ignorance are actually functionally equivalent, though operative in different contexts.

Owing to empathy's congruence with justice, people will empathize with victims of justice violations (someone cheated out of his earnings or whose rights are violated). When they do this they may be aware of both their empathic feeling for the victim (empathic distress, guilt, empathic anger, empathic feelings of injustice), and the activated justice principle. The resulting concurrence of empathic affect and a moral principle creates a bond between them, a bond that is strengthened by subsequent concurrences. In this way, moral principles, even when originally heard about in "cool" didactic contexts, may acquire empathy's affective and motive properties and become emotionally charged representations or prosocial "hot cognitions."

The implications of this hot-cognition concept are twofold. First, when a moral principle is subsequently activated in a moral encounter or even in didactic or research contexts, empathic affect is aroused. This empathic affect will have two components: a stimulus-driven component (victim's distress) and a principle-driven component. The principle-driven component will have a "heightening" effect or a "lowering" effect on the intensity of the stimulus-driven component. This should reduce the likelihood of empathic over-arousal (and **under**-arousal) and thereby **help stabilize the individ-**

ual's empathic affect across situations. The second implication is that the bystander and transgression models must be enlarged to include not only empathic affect aroused by a victim's distress, but moral principles that may also be activated by the victim's distress and that may help stabilize the bystander's or transgressor's empathic affect.

Reciprocity underlies most justice principles: Good deeds should be rewarded, bad acts punished; punishments should fit crimes. I suggest reciprocity is not inherently prosocial, as it encompasses "eye-for-an-eye" as well as "hard-work-should-be-rewarded" thinking. But it can become prosocial when it is associated with empathy, as when reciprocity is violated by someone's being treated unfairly. When that happens, reciprocity can intensify the observer's empathic distress and transform it into an empathic feeling of injustice.

Finally, empathy, alone or embedded in a moral principle, can play an important role in moral judgment. The basic argument for this was made over two centuries ago by David Hume: We obviously applaud acts that further our own well-being and condemn acts that may harm us; if we empathize with others we should therefore applaud or condemn acts that help or harm others; and, unless we are abnormally callous, we will feel indignant (empathic anger) when someone willfully inflicts suffering on others. I would add that most moral dilemmas in life may arouse empathy because they involve victims – seen or unseen – of one's own actions or actions by someone else whom one is judging. Empathy can influence one's moral judgment of oneself or of the other directly, or indirectly through the moral principles it activates.

The developmental research on distributive justice, in which children are asked to allocate rewards to recipients who differ in productivity and other respects, is clear on what children of different ages view as fair. The research, discussed in chapter 10, shows a developmental trend from allocating rewards based on self-interest in preschoolers, to a strong preference for equal division of rewards at 4 or 5 years; to an increasing emphasis on reward in proportion to productive output or output integrated with need (poverty) among children 8 or 9 years and older. Older children also apply different justice principles according to the context: They favor a productivity rule in reward-for-work situations, equity in voting situations, and equality combined with need in charity situations. By 11 or 12 years, they favor "productivity" over "need" for strangers but equate the two principles for friends, and they allocate as much to a needy friend as to a productive stranger – not unlike adults.

There is little developmental research on empathy's contribution to justice. I suggest that parental inductions around sharing and turn-taking start the socialization for "equality." "Equality" is also fostered by preschool and kindergarten teachers and by direct pressure from peers who want to have their share. I suggest socialization for "effort" also begins at home but is not systematic until early elementary school when children's academic performance is assessed and rewards given for self-improvement, which, above all, requires effort. Socialization for "productivity" and "competence" begins in earnest when academic performance is based on comparison with one's classmates, in grade four or five, and continues through the rest of one's education and on into the world of work.

These socialization experiences are integrated with children's direct justice-relevant experiences such as feeling distressed when treated unfairly (not rewarded for hard work), their observations that others feel distressed when similarly treated, and their empathic responses to that distress. These direct justice-relevant experiences build on the children's empathically charged transgression-guilt scripts about sharing acquired at home. The result is a network of integrated experiences that provide raw material from which children can construct an increasingly complex empathy-based sense of fairness and concern for others. With language, they can classify certain acts as morally wrong, unfair, and (eventually) form them into more general, abstract but still empathically charged principles of justice.

Language also enables children to begin, on their own and in conversations with others, to make their own moral inferences in light of the interpretations, explanations, and emotional reactions of adults and their own cognitive and emotional reactions as bystanders and victims. Each child does not construct a moral code anew, as some cognitive developmentalists claim, but is active nonetheless in reconstructing and understanding moral rules, using information communicated by adults and his own experience.

The above can be put in terms of a division of labor between parental inductions that communicate rules of fairness and carry the force of authority, children's ability to decenter and preference for reciprocity, and peer interactions which highlight equality: Peers advancing their own claims **compel** one to realize that one's desire is not the only thing that must be considered; decentering and reciprocity **enable** one to understand the basis of another's claims; inductions, acting on one's natural empathic proclivity, **make one receptive** to those claims. The resulting empathy-based fairness concepts are shaped further by the values communicated by parents, peers, teachers, religion, media. Children with these experiences are well versed in rudimentary forms of our society's caring and justice principles.

These processes are haphazard until adolescence, when children are more "formally" introduced to moral principles that are supposed to guide behavior. It is then, **if ever,** that the individual's active role in constructing a moral code, evident throughout childhood, takes center stage. The raw materials continue to be the products of socialization, as discussed. These include empathy-charged justice/fairness scripts generated in discipline encounters by inductions bearing on sharing and effort, which are enhanced by emotionally salient personal experience as bystander and victim, and by exposure to the media. One thinks and reasons about these, and in debates, especially with peers, one may analyze, interpret, compare and contrast, and accept or reject them and thus construct one's own set of general, to some extent abstract though emotionally charged moral principles.

When one has internalized and committed himself to caring or justice principles, realizes one has choice and control, and takes responsibility for one's actions, one has reached a new level. One may now consider and act fairly toward others, not only because of empathy but also as an expression of one's internalized principles, an affirmation of one's *self.* One feels it is one's *duty* or *responsibility* to consider and be fair to others. This connection between self, principle, and duty may in some cases result from an emotionally powerful "triggering event" (extreme injustice) that causes one to reexamine one's life choices and leads to a new moral perspective and sense of social responsibility.

Behaving in accordance with a moral principle is not always a simple matter of lining one's actions up with the principle. Moral encounters often involve multiple claimants, situations in which bystanders must choose which victims to help, and some encounters involve conflict between caring and justice. Both types of moral encounters are discussed in chapter 11. Multiple claimant dilemmas in the caring domain that come to mind are people drowning or caught in a burning building, when one must choose whom to help; a doctor deciding whether to perform an abortion, when the claimants are the fetus, the pregnant teenager, and the teenager's parents; a lawyer deciding whether to defend someone he believes is guilty of murder, when the claimants are the defendant who has a right to a trial, his future victims if he goes free, and the victim's family who want him punished; Kohlberg's hypothetical World War II air-raid warden who had the choice of remaining at his post or leaving to help his family whose part of town had just been bombed; the similar but real dilemma of a nurse who was helping an Oklahoma City bombing victim when she heard the second bomb blast.

The moral issue for ethics in these dilemmas is which claimant *should* one help. The issue for science is who *will* one help. Evolutionary biology's answer is simple: One helps those with whom one shares the most genes. Psychology's answer is that when there is one claimant, bystanders empathize with virtually anyone in distress (chapter 2). When there are multiple claimants, one will probably empathize with family members and others who fit empathy's familiarity and here-and-now biases (chapter 8), although one may feel guilty over those one does not help. In other words, evolutionary psychology says we choose to help those who share our genes; psychology says we choose to help those in our primary group. But we share more genes with those in our primary group, which raises certain questions. Is psychology's answer fundamentally the same as evolutionary biology's? Is empathic bias the functional equivalent of sharing another's genes? The answer to both questions may be yes, given the argument that empathy derived from natural selection pressures in human evolution (Hoffman, 1981). In any case, in multiple claimant situations empathy may not be enough.

Kant and his followers, including Rawls and Kohlberg, claim that caring is subordinate to justice because caring is usually personal and particularistic, involves decisions that are affectively rather than rationally based, and lacks the formal properties of justice. I prefer to view caring and the different types of justice as "ideal types" that may occur in varying degrees in all situations. When caring and justice co-occur they may be congruent. They may also conflict, as when a professor is convinced by a student's plea that his "life will be wrecked" if he does not get a higher grade; as when a student is asked by a friend for the questions on an exam he just took; as in Kohlberg's famous dilemma based on *Les Miserables,* in which a man steals a drug to save his wife's life. The last two examples of caring dilemmas given earlier (Kohlberg's air-raid warden and the Oklahoma City nurse) can be considered caring-versus-justice dilemmas if we classify violations of a person's duty or responsibility as criminal acts or as instances of nonreciprocity between role demands and behavior.

To illustrate multiple claimant and caring–justice encounters in depth, I use the dilemma of a professor who is asked to write a letter of recommendation for one of his students who is applying for an important job. The student is good but not outstanding. If the professor has some friendship with the student and knows other things about him (such as that there is a sick child in his family), he might write a strong letter of support. But things get complicated if the professor also empathizes with the colleague who needs an especially outstanding applicant or with the other unknown candidates who also need the job. The dilemma so far is confined to the caring domain, but justice issues are also relevant: The academic system places high value on merit (scholarly output, competence) and the integrity of the system rests on recommenders' candid assessments of job applicants, which the professor's colleague expects from him.

This caring–justice dilemma becomes acute when a professor believes his student may not be the most qualified applicant. If he writes a candid letter that reveals the student's weaknesses, in keeping with "justice," he violates "caring" and may feel empathic guilt over betraying the student. If empathy for the student prevails and his letter emphasizes the student's strengths and downplays his weaknesses, then he violates "justice" and may feel guilty over that.

If caring and justice are valued in our society and children are socialized to internalize them both, and if I am right about empathy's links to caring and most justice principles, it follows that most mature, morally internalized individuals have empathy-charged caring and justice principles in their motive system. They should therefore be sensitive to both caring and justice perspectives, and vulnerable to empathic distress, anticipatory guilt, and other empathic emotions associated with multiple claimant and caring–justice dilemmas.

Two things psychology can do that evolutionary biology cannot is experimentally investigate multiple claimant and caring–justice dilemmas and suggest answers to the question of how to reduce empathic bias. The experimental research was reviewed in this chapter, and suggestions for reducing empathic bias through moral education are made in the very last chapter of the book. In between the two is chapter 12, to which we now turn, which deals with whether the theory presented here is universal or culture bound.

Apart from the evolution argument and the brain and behavior research evidence that empathic distress is a universal prosocial motive, I argue in chapter 12 that the self, which plays a central role in my empathy development theory, is a universal self, not a Western construction as some writers suggest, and that my stages of empathy development are plausibly universal because they accord with what is known about the brain and cognitive development. I also argue that the modes of empathic arousal are universal, that is, humans in all cultures can be empathically aroused by any of them – automatically and involuntarily by the primitive modes (mimicry, conditioning, direct association) and to some extent culturally influenced in the case of the more cognitively demanding modes (mediated association and role-taking).

The universality of the transgression model – the role of induction in the socialization of empathy-based transgression guilt and guilt's functioning as a prosocial moral motive – is on less firm grounds. Adults the world over must find it necessary at times to change children's behavior against their will, but most of the empirical evidence for induction's role in transgression guilt and moral internalization is based on white middle-class Americans. I present the case for tentatively concluding, until the research says otherwise, that induction contributes positively and power assertion negatively to transgression guilt, moral internalization, and prosocial behavior – at least in nuclear-family-organized societies where discipline encounters, power assertion, and induction are frequent and transgression guilt and moral internalization are meaningful concepts.

My overall conclusion is that there is more reason to view empathic morality as universal than as not universal. Empathic morality should promote prosocial behavior and discourage aggression in cultures guided by caring and most justice principles. But it does not operate in a vacuum, and in multicultural societies with intergroup rivalry, it might, owing to empathy's familiarity bias, contribute to violence between groups.

Even within a group, empathic morality can be disrupted by power-assertive childrearing and other harsh cultural practices, as well as powerful egoistic motives within the individual that override it. Empathic morality, though a universal prosocial moral motive, is thus fragile (the Holocaust did happen). I can see nothing better on the horizon, however, unless it is empathic morality bonded to reciprocity and certain justice principles (chapter 9). The joining of empathy with reciprocity and justice is, I would expect, not universal, and how to bring it about will require cultural invention and research. In chapter 13 I discuss the theory's implications for intervention methods that socialize children in empathic morality and reduce violence in delinquent males. I also suggest ways to reduce empathic bias and help increase motivation for prosocial action across ethnic divides. Some of these methods may with modification be useful for combining empathic morality, reciprocity, and justice.

In chapter 13 I note first of all that it is empathy's amenity to cognitive influence, stressed throughout this book, that gives a significant role to socialization and empathy-based moral education. Some suggestions for intervention follow directly from the earlier chapters. These include, for parents, a blend of frequent inductions, occasional power assertions, and a lot of affection. They also include being a prosocial model who not only helps others but also occasionally explains the cause of a victim's misfortune (to reduce blaming the victim) and openly expresses empathic and sympathetic feelings. To expand children's empathic range, parents should allow children to experience a variety of emotions. Parents can also exploit children's natural tendency to engage in pretend play by injecting role-taking scenarios that provide, vicariously, emotional experiences that may otherwise be missing in their lives, including empathic responses to others in distress.

These suggestions may also work in preschool and elementary school contexts, provided discipline encounters are not too frequent and disruptive. When discipline encounters arise, teachers may be tempted to use power assertion to achieve quick compliance; induction may seem a luxury they cannot afford. Because of the many onlooking children, however, teachers can get a lot of mileage from an induction that is well worded and timed and fits the children's developmental level. How teachers discipline a child who picks on others can be an important prosocial socializing experience for the entire class (the "ripple effect").

Empathic bias may be reduced developmentally when empathy becomes embedded in moral principles, owing to the principle's stabilizing effects. But more active efforts by parents and moral educators to reduce empathic bias and create a sense of human oneness may be necessary in our contemporary, increasingly multicultural society. This may require identifying empathic bias and showing children that while it is natural to empathize more with people who share one's life experiences, a certain amount of empathic impartiality is necessary. It also requires pointing out that despite people's social, cultural, and physical differences, there are important similarities in emotional responses – responses to being treated unfairly, for example, and to life crises like separation, loss, and aging. The media

23

can help here: Films are effective ways to present larger life sequences that promote viewers' empathic identification with others' lives. Viewing others who have concerns like ours, while sharing their emotions (through mimicry and other empathy-arousing mechanisms), could foster a sense of oneness and empathy across cultures. Regarding empathy's here-and-now bias, moral educators can teach and give children experience in using a simple rule of thumb: Look beyond the situation and ask how your action will affect the other person not only now but also in the future, and whether there are others who might be affected.

Last but not least, moral educators can turn empathic bias against itself, by encouraging children to imagine how someone they care a lot about would feel in the stranger's or absent victim's place, or in the place of each claimant in a complex moral encounter. Such training in the art of "multiple empathizing" does two things: It exploits and also counteracts the individual's natural empathic bias. Multiple empathizing may reduce the tendency to attribute negative motives to people outside one's group and thus contribute to civilized living in a multicultural society.

Some of these ideas have been found useful in treating antisocial delinquents, but other methods designed specifically for increasing empathy in delinquents may be more effective. One, in the Kohlberg tradition, has the participants discuss sociomoral dilemmas or problem situations as a way of stimulating role-taking experiences and empathy; participants must justify their decisions in the face of challenges from group leaders and developmentally advanced peers. Another method tries to reduce aggression by giving participants fine-grained practice in taking others' perspectives in social situations. How to express a complaint, for example, is broken down into six steps, one of which is to "show that you understand his feelings." And still another uses "confronting," a type of induction that directs the participant's attention to the harm to others resulting from his actions in the group. Its aim is to counteract egoism, penetrate cognitive distortions, and elicit and strengthen empathic responses. Confronting compels the antisocial individual to put himself in another's position and understand the "chain of injuries," including effects on absent and indirect victims that result from his harmful actions.

The variety of these methods is impressive. What seems missing though are theoretical analyses of why the procedures, which produce empathy and other desirable effects in the "treatment" sessions, should affect behavior in life. I suggest such an analysis might begin along the lines of my discussion of long-term carryover effects of induction (chapter 6). For example, do participants who, through "confronting" and induction by peers and group leaders, are made to feel guilty over a transgression for the first time in their lives, form a transgression-guilt script? Is the script activated when they are tempted to engage in the transgression in real life? If activated, will it be powerful enough to affect their behavior?

## A NOTE ON METHODOLOGY

In this book I advance a comprehensive theory of prosocial behavior and development. The theory is multifaceted, ranging from classical conditioning to principles of justice charged with empathic affect. It touches a lot of bases not all of which have been researched, but insofar as the theory is coherent and makes sense, which I believe it does but the reader will have to judge, the scattered bits of empirical support lend it a certain credulity. To fill in the research gaps and thus add plausibility, I use a lot of anecdotes collected over the years from subjects' interviews and written responses to open-ended research questions, newspapers, magazines, literature, student reports, and my own observations. Anecdotes can be useful if they are not just isolated events but represent something that occurs often and are pertinent to the concepts under discussion. This is especially true when the anecdotes include enough details not only to describe an event but also to suggest its underlying processes. Even when there is research, anecdotes can add nuances and suggest variations due to context that can be lost in statistical analyses.

Here is an example of using anecdotes to explain observations and suggest hypotheses for research. In chapter 3 I describe a 10-month-old who responded to a peer's distress by looking sad and burying her head in her mother's lap, which she does when she is in distress, and a 12-month-old who looked sad and brought his own mother to comfort a crying friend although the friend's mother was present and equally available, a mistake older children do not make. These observations suggested that the 10-month-old felt empathic distress but could not distinguish it from personal distress; the 12-month-old made this distinction between empathic and personal distress and knowing it was the other and not himself who was in distress, was able to feel concern for the other, but he did not realize the other child preferred his own mother.

The two observations also seemed to suggest three levels of self–other differentiation: confusion of self and other, recognition of other as a separate physical entity, recognition of other as having inner states independent of one's own. And finally, going still further beyond the data, they suggested that the transition from the first to the second developmental level results, at least in part, in the transformation of empathic into sympathetic distress. Other investigators have since confirmed the observations and conducted research that supports the transformation hypothesis, not conclusively but enough to justify further research.

Good anecdotes can generate hypotheses and, as I trust the above example shows – Piaget's work certainly did – anecdotes can sometimes confirm the *plausibility* of a hypothesis. But assessing the *validity* of a hypothesis about a developmental process, like the transformation of empathic into sympathetic distress, requires experiments, correlations, and, finally, longitudinal studies employing structural equation models and the like. In this book I have chosen anecdotes with all of this in mind, although not all of them are as effective as some. I can only hope that the anecdotes and the book as a whole will stimulate research that tests and improves the theoretical formulations.

# PART I

# Innocent Bystander

# CHAPTER 2

# Empathy, Its Arousal, and Prosocial Functioning

People are innocent bystanders when they witness someone in pain, danger, or any other form of distress. The distress can involve physical pain or discomfort due to injury or disease, emotional pain over the loss or expected loss of a loved one, fear of being attacked, anxiety over failure or financial impoverishment, and the like. The moral issue in these situations is whether the bystander is motivated to help and if he is, the extent to which the motivation is self-serving or based on true concern for the victim. The bystander model is the prototypic moral encounter for empathic distress and related empathic affects. It is also the context for my theory of empathy development. In this chapter I give my definition of empathy, provide evidence that it functions as a prosocial motive, and then describe the mechanism by which it is aroused. In chapters 3 and 4, I present the theory of empathy development and discuss four empathy-based feelings that also function as prosocial motives: sympathetic distress, empathy-based anger, empathy-based feeling of injustice, and guilt over inaction. In subsequent chapters I deal with other types of moral encounters.

## DEFINITION OF EMPATHY

Empathy has been defined by psychologists in two ways: (a) empathy is the cognitive awareness of another person's internal states, that is, his thoughts, feelings, perceptions, and intentions (see Ickes, 1997, for recent research); (b) empathy is the vicarious affective response to another person. This book deals with the second type:

affective empathy. Affective empathy seems like a simple concept – one feels what the other feels – and many writers define it in simple outcome terms: One empathizes to the extent that one's feeling matches the other's feeling. The more I study empathy, however, the more complex it becomes. Consequently, I have found it far more useful to define empathy not in terms of outcome (affect match) but in terms of the processes underlying the relationship between the observer's and the model's feeling. The key requirement of an empathic response according to my definition is **the involvement of psychological processes that make a person have feelings that are more congruent with another's situation than with his own situation.** The empathy-arousing processes often produce the same feeling in observer and victim but not necessarily, as when one feels empathic anger on seeing someone attacked even when the victim feels sad or disappointed rather than angry.

This is not to deny the importance of accurate cognitive assessment of another's feelings, what Ickes (1997) calls empathic accuracy. Indeed, a certain amount of empathic accuracy is built into my theory, although, unlike Ickes, I see empathic accuracy as including awareness of the model's relevant past and probable future – the model's life condition – an awareness that contributes importantly to an observer's empathic affect. For this and other reasons, dropping the requirement of an affect match between observer and model affords empathy far more scope and has other advantages, as we shall see.

My focus is **empathic distress** because prosocial moral action usually involves helping someone in discomfort, pain, danger, or some other type of distress.

## EMPATHIC DISTRESS AS A PROSOCIAL MOTIVE

Before reviewing the evidence that empathic distress is a prosocial motive, it is necessary to state what kind of evidence is needed. First, empathic distress must correlate positively with people's helping behavior. Second, empathic distress must not only correlate with but must also precede and contribute to the helping behavior. And third, like other motives, empathic distress should diminish in intensity and one should feel better when one helps, but it should continue at a high level when one does not help. The evidence, which I now present, is supportive on all three counts.

**a.** *Empathic distress is associated with helping.* There are countless studies showing that when people witness others in distress, they typically respond empathically or with an overt helpful act, whichever is being investigated, and when data are available on both responses, subjects typically show them both. This research was reviewed by Hoffman (1981) and Eisenberg and Miller (1987). To update these reviews, fill in the gaps, and give you a feeling for the research, here are examples. Berndt (1979) found that a group of empathic sixth graders who discussed a sad incident in another person's life donated more time to making pictures for hospitalized children than did empathic children who discussed a sad event in their own lives. Davis (1983) found that college students who obtained high empathy scores on a paper-and-pencil measure donated more money to the Jerry Lewis Muscular Dystrophy Telethon than did their less empathic classmates. Empathic college students were more likely to volunteer and put in more hours of work at shelters for homeless families (Penner, Fritzsche, Craiger, & Freifeld, 1995). In a study by Otten, Penner, and Altabe (1991), psychotherapists who scored high on empathy measures were more likely to help college students with a work assignment (writing an article on psychotherapy) than psychotherapists who scored low.

In an experimental study, college students watched a confederate of the investigator working on an unpleasant task (Carlo, Eisenberg, Troyer, Switzer & Speer, 1991). The confederate became distressed and asked the subject to take his place. One group of subjects was given the alternative of sitting and watching the confederate suffer or taking his place, and another group had the option of leaving the experiment and going home. Three-quarters of the first group chose to take the confederate's place rather than continue to experience empathic distress. Remarkably, over half the subjects in the second group chose to take the confederate's place rather than go home, and those who did this were the more empathic members of the group.

Finally, it has been found that observers are quicker to help when

**31**

the victim shows more pain (Geer & Jarmecky, 1973; Weiss, Boyer, Lombardo, & Stitch, 1973) and when their own empathic distress is high rather than low (Gaertner & Dovidio, 1977). The details of these three studies can be found in Hoffman (1978).

**b.** *Empathic distress precedes helping.* The above research shows the required association between empathic arousal and helping behavior. There is also evidence from 1970s' experimental research reviewed by Hoffman (1978) that empathic arousal precedes and motivates helping. The last and most interesting of these experiments was done by Gaertner and Dovidio (1977). In that study, female undergraduate students witnessed (through earphones) a situation in which another student (a confederate of the experimenter) stopped working on an experimental task in order to straighten out a stack of chairs that she thought was about to topple over on her. A moment later the confederate screamed that the chairs were falling on her, and then was silent. The main findings were that the observers' heart rate began to accelerate an average of 20 seconds before they rose from their chair to help the victim; and the greater an observer's heart-rate acceleration the more quickly she rose from her chair. In other words, the intensity of the observer's physiological (empathic) arousal was systematically related to the speed of her *subsequent* helping action.

**c.** *Observers feel better after helping.* The most direct evidence that empathic distress diminishes in intensity after an observer helps someone can be found in Darley and Latane's (1968) study in which subjects heard sounds indicating that someone was having an epileptic seizure. The subjects who did not respond overtly continued to be aroused and upset, as indicated by their trembling hands and sweaty palms; the subjects who tried to help showed fewer signs of continued upset. A similar finding was obtained in Murphy's (1937) classic nursery school study: When children helped others their empathic distress appeared to diminish; when they did not help their distress was prolonged. These findings suggest that empathic distress acts like other motives: When it is expressed behaviorally its intensity subsides. In the case of empathic distress, there may be an additional factor: The victim's expression of relief may produce a feeling of empathic relief in the helper – a vicarious reward that is unavailable to observers who do not help.

These findings could be interpreted as showing that people learn from experience that helping others makes them feel good, so when they feel empathic distress they anticipate feeling good and help for that reason – not to alleviate the victim's distress. The counterargument is that the consequences of an action say nothing about the motivation behind it; because helping makes one feel good does not mean that one helps in order to feel good. Furthermore, there is no evidence that people help in order to feel good, and there is evidence to the contrary (Batson & Weeks, 1996; Batson & Shaw, 1991). These investigators reasoned that if observers helped only for self-reward, then it wouldn't matter to them whether or not the victim's distress was alleviated; the sheer act of helping would make them feel better. What they found was that empathic helpers continued to feel empathic distress when, despite their efforts and through no fault of their own, the victim's distress was not alleviated. This implies that empathic helpers do have their eye on the ultimate consequences of their action for the victim and it does matter to them whether their actions reduce the victim's distress. It seems reasonable to conclude that although empathy-based helping makes people feel good by reducing empathic distress and providing empathic relief, the main objective of empathy-based helping is to alleviate the victim's distress. Empathic distress is, in short, a prosocial motive.

The discussion so far might suggest that humans are saintly empathic-distress-leads-to-helping machines. Not so: Empathic distress does not always lead to helping. Why doesn't it? There are several reasons. First, as we know from the classic work of Latane and Darley (1970), the presence of other bystanders may interfere with a person's helping by activating the assumptions of "pluralistic ignorance" (no one else is reacting; it must not be an emergency after all) and "diffusion of responsibility" (I'm sure someone else has already called the police).

Second, when bystanders are alone their motive to help may be checked by powerful egoistic motives revolving around fear, energy expenditure, financial cost, loss of time, opportunities missed, and the like. The bystanders may have learned from experience that helping makes one feel good, but the prospect of feeling good may be overridden by helping's potential cost. As a dramatic case in point, consider this quote from a study comparing Germans who rescued and those who did not rescue Jews from the Nazis during the Holocaust:

> My parents were loving and kind. I learned from them to be helpful and considerate. There was a Jewish family living in our apartment building, but I hardly noticed when they left. Later, when I was working in the hospital as a doctor, a Jewish man was brought to the emergency room by his wife. I knew that he would die unless he was treated immediately. But we were not allowed to treat Jews; they could only be treated at the Jewish hospital. I could do nothing. (Oliner & Oliner, 1988, p. 187)

These are the words of a *non*-rescuer, described by Oliner and Oliner as "a kind and compassionate woman predisposed by sentiment and the ethics of her profession to help a dangerously ill man who nonetheless did not do so" (p. 187). As we shall see, those Germans who took risks and rescued Jews were kind and compassionate, but this quote shows that when the costs are high, kindness and compassion may not be enough.

Third, in view of the costs that helping may entail, we might expect people not only to refrain from helping but also to be leery of feeling empathy in the first place for fear of what it may lead them to do: It may lead them to incur the cost of helping, including the cost of experiencing the unpleasantness of empathic distress. People might, therefore, when possible try to forestall feeling for victims in order to escape the motivational consequences of that feeling. A motive to avoid empathy has been demonstrated experimentally by Shaw, Batson, and Todd (1994), who predicted the activation of such a motive when, before being exposed to a person in need, observers are warned that they will be asked to help the person and the helping will be costly. To test this prediction, college students were given the choice of hearing one of two appeals for help made by a homeless man who had lost his job and was very ill: an empathy-inducing appeal in which the man presents his needs emotionally and asks the listener to imagine how he feels and what he is going through, and an appeal in which he presents his needs calmly and objectively. As predicted, the subjects who expected to be given a high-cost opportunity to help (spend several hours meeting and giving him support) were less likely to choose the empathy-inducing appeal than subjects who expected the cost of helping to be low (an hour writing and addressing letters on his behalf).

This analysis of the observer's motives points up the complexity of the bystander model. It is not simply that observers feel empathic distress and the desire to help. Egoistic motives are also evoked that compete with empathic distress, may preclude helping, and when bystanders know the costs in advance, may even lead to efforts to avoid empathizing. **The bystander model, in short, involves conflict between the motive to help and egoistic motives that can be powerful.** This makes it all the more remarkable that empathic distress is an effective prosocial motive. The reason may be its self-reinforcing property: Helpers feel good afterward. If so, it raises the question, Is empathy-based helping prosocial? I say yes (Hoffman, 1981), because it is instigated by another's distress, not one's own, its primary aim is to help another, and one feels good only if the victim is helped.

A final note on empathy's contribution to prosocial behavior. My focus has been on helping others in distress but it is worth noting that empathy has also been found to reduce aggression (Feshbach & Feshbach, 1969; Gibbs, 1987). The aggression-reducing feature of empathy is highlighted in my discussion of the transgressor model (chapter 6) and my review of moral education methods used to reduce aggression in delinquent adolescents (chapter 13). A more subtle, less well-known finding bears on empathy's relation to the ability to manipulate people. According to Christie and Geis (1970), who conducted extensive research on the "Machiavellian" personality in the 1960s, effective manipulators are not, as some might think, effective empathizers who use empathy to read other people's motives and then use their knowledge of others' motives to take advantage of them. Indeed, they are *weak* empathizers and poor at reading people's motives. Their "advantage" is precisely that they are not empathic, and their resulting insensitivity to others permits them to "bull their way through in pursuit of their own goals." Similarly, in the novel *Blade Runner* (Dick, 1968), "androids" were deemed a menace and outlawed by society because they could be equipped with an intelligence greater than that of many human beings but were totally incapable of empathy.[1] They were viewed as epitomizing manipulators (and killers) because, lacking empathic distress or grief at another's defeat, nothing short of destroying them could stop them from having their way.

Of course, being incapable of empathy does not doom one to manipulating or killing others. O'Neil (1999) describes patients with an empathic disorder called Asperger's (a type of autism) who "realize, and regret, a gap they can cross only with extreme difficulty" (p. F1). They try to break down behavior that most people master without thinking into discrete fragments that can be memorized; they then practice taking the other's point of view. "Things like, 'Do I have to look him in the eye?' 'Yes, but just a little bit to let him know you're listening' " (p. F4). See also Sacks (1995). This contrasts with most humans whose natural empathic sensitivity keeps them from being detached enough to take full advantage of others.

In other words, empathy not only contributes to helping but it also interferes with aggression and the ability to manipulate others. We now turn to the mechanisms that underlie the arousal of empathic distress.

### AROUSAL OF EMPATHIC DISTRESS

There are five empathy-arousing modes, as I originally proposed twenty years ago (Hoffman, 1978) and update here. Three are primitive, automatic, and, most important, involuntary. I describe them first.

---

1. I thank Krin Gabbard for suggesting I read this book.

## Mimicry

Mimicry was described a century ago by Lipps (1906), although it was intuitively understood 150 years earlier by Adam Smith (1759/ 1976) who observed:

> When we see a stroke aimed, and just ready to fall upon the leg or arm of another person, we naturally shrink and draw back our own arm. . . . The mob, when they are gazing at a dancer on the slack rope, naturally writhe and twist and balance their own bodies as they see him do. (pp. 4, 10)

Lipps (1906) defined empathy as an innate, involuntary, isomorphic response to another person's expression of emotion. A close reading of his work shows that he saw the process as involving two distinct steps that operate in rapid sequence (Hoffman, 1978). The observer first automatically imitates and synchronizes changes in his facial expression, voice, and posture with the slightest changes in another person's facial, vocal, or postural expressions of feeling – which Lipps called "objective motor mimicry." The resulting changes in the observer's facial, vocal, and postural musculature then trigger afferent feedback which produces feelings in the observer that match the feelings of the victim. To avoid confusion, I refer to the two steps as "imitation" and "feedback" and the entire process as mimicry.

Mimicry has long been neglected by psychologists, probably because it seems like an instinctual explanation. It warrants our attention, however, because intuitively it appears to be the very essence of empathy – one observes another's expression of feeling, automatically imitates his expression, and then the brain takes over and makes one feel what the other feels. Though important, demonstrating mimicry empirically is difficult, and it therefore requires more attention than the other empathy-arousing modes. I note first that despite the neglect of mimicry, recent years have seen a lot of research on imitation and on feedback, though little on the combined process.

1. *Imitation.* Bavelas, Black, Lemery, and Mullett (1987) surveyed the research documenting the existence of imitation or mimicry. They

found that people imitate another's expressions of pain, laughter, smiling, affection, embarrassment, discomfort, disgust, stuttering, reaching with effort, and the like, in a broad range of situations. Developmental researchers have found that infants shortly after birth will try to imitate another's facial gestures: They stick out their tongues, purse their lips, and open their mouths (Meltzoff, 1988; Reissland, 1988). By 10 weeks of age they imitate at least the rudimentary features of their mothers' facial expressions of happiness and anger (Haviland & Lelwica, 1987). And 9-month-olds will mirror their mothers' posed expressions of joy and sadness (Termine & Izard, 1988).

Not only do infants imitate their mothers' facial expressions of emotion but mothers imitate their infants' facial expressions as well, often without being aware of what they are doing (O'Toole & Dubin, 1968). Indeed, adults appear to have a natural tendency to mirror the facial expression of children, and of other adults, without awareness.

Most of the research has employed electromyographic procedures (EMG). These procedures can measure movements of the facial skin and connective tissues (folds, lines, wrinkles; brow and mouth movement) caused by emotion-produced contraction of the facial muscles – movements that are so subtle (weak or transient) that they produce no observable facial expression. Dimberg (1990) measured the facial EMG activity of Swedish college students as they looked at photographs of people displaying happy and angry facial expressions. He found that subjects observing happy facial expressions showed increased muscular activity over the "zygomaticus major" (cheek) muscle region. When they observed angry facial expressions, they showed increased muscular activity over the "corrugator supercilia" (brow) muscle region.

In an empathy-EMG study (Mathews, 1991; Mathews, Hoffman, & Cohen, 1991), college student's faces were secretly videotaped as they viewed a 2-minute film of a young women recounting a happy event (a dinner party with her fiancé and his parents) and a sad event (being told that her parents had decided to get divorced). In the happy segment, her facial expression, voice, and gestures conveyed a feeling of extreme joy. In the sad segment, her facial expression, voice, and gestures conveyed deep sadness. The facial EMG activity of the subjects obtained from the videotapes of their faces showed increased activity over their cheek muscles and decreased activity over their brow muscles when they watched the happy account; the reverse pattern was obtained when they watched the sad account. In a later analysis of the data, trained judges who were "blind" as to which segment the subjects observed rated the subjects' faces as happier when viewing the happier segment and sadder when viewing the sad segment. Similar results were obtained by Hatfield, Cacioppo, and Rapson (1992), whose judges rated college students' facial expressions as happy or sad when observing a 3-minute filmed interview of a man recounting a happy or a sad event in his life (a surprise birthday party or his grandfather's funeral which he attended at age 6).

Although most of the research employs facial expression, people have been found to engage in increased lip activity and frequency of eye-blink responses when observing others who stutter or blink their eyes (Berger & Hadley, 1975; Bernal & Berger, 1976). More important is people's tendency to imitate aspects of another person's speech patterns: speed, pitch, rhythm, pausing, duration of utterance (Buder, 1991). Since speech patterns are associated with feelings – happy feelings with a fast tempo, large variations in pitch, and small variations in amplitude (Scherer, 1982) – vocal mimicry becomes a real possibility. The importance of vocal mimicry is that it can occur early in life, possibly in newborns as we shall see, and, unlike facial expression, one's speech pattern is extremely difficult to control, which makes deception less likely.

The evidence is clear, then, that people tend automatically to imitate the emotional expressions of people around them – their facial expression, vocal expression, and probably their posture. The next question is: What about feedback? Does the imitation-based activation of a person's facial and vocal expression lead to afferent feedback that in turn affects his or her subjective emotional experience from one moment to the next?

**2. *Feedback*.** Charles Darwin (1877) was the first to state the feedback hypothesis ("He who gives way to violent gestures will increase rage; he who does not control the signs of fear will experience fear in a greater degree," p. 365). William James (1893) went further, postulating that feedback was the key to all emotional experience. The way people know how they feel is by sensing it from their muscular as well as their glandular and visceral responses. The well-known quote is "We feel sorry because we cry, angry because we strike, and afraid because we tremble." James advanced this view a century ago, but it has only recently been put to the test.

In the first serious study of feedback, Laird (1974) told adult subjects that he was interested in studying the action of facial muscles. Laird's experimental room contained apparatus designed to convince the subjects that complicated multichannel recordings of facial muscle activity were about to be made. Silver cup electrodes were attached to their faces between their eyebrows, at the corners of their mouths, and at the corners of their jaws. The experimenter then arranged the subjects' faces into emotional expressions (smiles or angry frowns) without their realizing it, by asking them to contract various muscles. To produce angry frowns he touched the subject lightly between the eyebrows with an electrode and said, "Pull your brows down and together . . . good, now hold it like that"); he then asked the subject to contract the muscles at the corners of his jaw ("clench your teeth"). To produce happy faces the subjects were asked to contract the muscles near the corners of their mouths ("draw the corners of your mouth back and up"). Laird found that the subjects in the frown condition felt angrier and those in the smile condition felt happier than their peers. Furthermore, cartoons viewed when the subjects were "smiling" were rated by them as being funnier than cartoons they viewed when "frowning." And, in a later study, subjects in the "smile" condition were better at recalling happy events in their lives than sad events, whereas subjects in the "frown" condition were better at recalling sad events (Laird, Wagener, Halal, & Szedga, 1982). These comments by a subject in the first study show how the process may have worked:

> When my jaw was clenched and my brows down, I tried not to be angry but it just fit the position. I'm not in an angry mood but I

found my thoughts wandering to things that made me angry, which is sort of silly, I guess. I knew I was in an experiment and knew I had no reason to feel that way, but I just lost control. (p. 480)

Other equally ingenious techniques have been used to produce smiles without subjects' awareness. In one experiment, smiles were produced by requiring subjects to fill out rating forms with a pen held in their front teeth, which eases the facial muscles into a smile. These subjects found humorous cartoons funnier than did students who held the pen in their lips, forcing their faces into a frown position (Strack, Martin, & Stepper, 1988). In another experiment, the investigators wanted subjects to furrow their brows without asking them explicitly to move facial muscles. This was achieved by taping two golf tees to the subjects' forehead (inside corner of each eye) and instructing them to move the tees together, a task which gave their faces a sad look. It also made them feel sad: Looking at photographs of starving children and other sad scenes made them feel sadder than control subjects did who looked at the same scenes without tees on their foreheads. At least a dozen other studies have produced similar results: Subjects feel the specific emotions consistent with the facial expressions they adopt and have trouble experiencing emotions incompatible with these poses. Still other methods have been used, for example, asking subjects to exaggerate or try to hide any emotional reactions they might have. These studies as well as those mentioned above and others have been reviewed and the evidence is clear that people's emotional experience tends to be influenced by the facial expressions they adopt (Adelman & Zajonc, 1989; Hatfield, Cacioppo, & Rapson, 1992).

Despite the evidence it remains unclear to me whether the subjects actually felt angry or happy because the changes in their stage-managed facial expression activated afferent neural pathways that produced the particular emotion. The alternative is that they perceived the changes in facial-expression kinesthetically and associated the changes with angry or happy experiences ("When I'm angry, my jaws are clenched and my brows are down"). If the latter explanation is correct, the research cannot be said to support afferent feedback, but a weaker self-perception-and-cognitive-inference version of feedback. This issue is important because if afferent feedback exists and operates in early childhood, then mimicry becomes a particularly important mechanism because it enables infants to empathize with another's feeling even before having had their own direct experience with the same feeling; it might even explain the newborn's reactive cry (chapter 3). But if the only feedback is through self-perception and cognitive inference, which requires previous experience with the particular feeling, then empathy in early childhood can only occur through conditioning and direct association. Laird (1984) claims that people engage in both types of feedback: "Some people are happy because they smile, angry because they scowl, and sad because they pout; others define their emotional experience in terms of situational expectations." Laird also presents evidence for this claim (Laird, 1984; Laird, et al., 1994). This dual-process explanation implies, of course, that afferent feedback exists though it is not used by everyone.

An argument can be made in favor of the strong version of the afferent feedback hypothesis. It begins with psychology's long-held assumption that connections between facial expression and emotion are culturally determined. This assumption was laid to rest by the landmark study of Ekman, Sorenson, and Friesen (1969) in which preliterate New Guinea tribespeople identified a number of emotional facial expressions in the same way that subjects in Japan, Brazil, and the United States did. This finding began a new line of research, and evidence has since accumulated suggesting that there are certain innate emotions, each with its corresponding facial expressions. These innate emotions and expressions provide the foundation for differences in subjective feeling and expression of emotion that are then elaborated by culture and socialization (Ekman, Friesen, O'Sullivan, & Chan, 1987).

More important for our purposes, the evidence suggests that the connections between certain emotions and facial expressions are universal and based on neural integration. This supports the afferent feedback hypothesis. The existence of afferent feedback does not rule out self-perception-and-cognitive-inference feedback and, indeed, may explain it. That is, it may be true that we feel angry because

42

past experience tells us that anger "fits the position" of our stage-managed facial expression, but anger may fit the position in the first place because of afferent feedback. This may also explain in part why feedback based on self-perception and cognitive inference can be as quick-acting, effortless, and involuntary as it appears to be. And, finally, Laird's finding that some people use afferent feedback and others use cognitive inference may be explained by socialization that makes some people more sensitive to situational cues and others more sensitive to internal sensations.

No one to my knowledge has actually demonstrated afferent feedback resulting from imitation. To do this may require investigating imitation-produced changes in facial expression in a realistic setting and assessing the effect of these changes on the subjects' feelings. This seems like a difficult task but Bush, Barr, McHugo, and Lanzetta (1989) may have accomplished it. They asked college students to watch comic routines under different conditions and judge how funny they were. A group that was instructed to "relax and enjoy" the routines, and viewed the routines interspersed with shots focused on the studio audience's laughing faces, imitated the audience's laughing faces and found the routines funnier than a group given the same instructions without seeing the audience. This suggests that the subjects' audience-imitating smiles resulted in afferent feedback that made them feel happier and judge the routines funnier. A more parsimonious interpretation is that feedback was unnecessary: The audience's laughing faces made the subjects both smile and think the routines were funnier. Barr et al. anticipated this, however, and included a group that saw the audience's laughing faces but were instructed to inhibit all bodily and facial movements during the experiment. This group did not find the routines funny. In other words, two groups saw the audience's laughing faces but only the group that imitated the audience found the routines funnier – presumably because of afferent feedback.

A possible problem still remains, it seems to me: Only the imitation group behaved spontaneously. The no-imitation group did not, and to follow the instructions and keep from laughing they might have turned away from the audience or tried to think about non-funny things. If so, then it is possible that had they focused on the audience they would have found the routines funnier despite not imitating the audience's laughing faces, which would rule out an afferent feedback explanation. This is sheer speculation: It seems more reasonable that the authors did it right; the group focused on the audience (in keeping with their instructions) and they did not find the routines funnier because of the lack of afferent feedback.

It seems reasonable to conclude that the weight of the evidence for the universality of emotions plus the evidence for imitation and feedback favors the imitation–feedback sequence and the mimicry process as described by Lipps. This means that mimicry is probably a hard-wired neurologically based empathy-arousing mechanism whose two steps, imitation and feedback, are directed by commands from the central nervous system. This is important for two reasons. First, as noted, a hard-wired mimicry provides a quick-acting mechanism enabling infants to empathize and feel what another feels without previously experiencing that emotion. I say quick-acting, following Davis's (1985) colorful argument that mimicry is too complex and fast-acting to be done consciously. Davis points out that whereas even the lightning-fast Muhammad Ali took 190 milliseconds to spot a light and an additional 40 milliseconds to throw a punch in response, videotapes of college students in conversation show that each student's speech and body motions were synchronized to the other's in 20 milliseconds or less. A second reason for the importance of mimicry's being hard-wired is that besides being involuntary and fast, mimicry is the only empathy-arousing mechanism that assures a match between the observer's feeling and expression of feeling and the victim's feeling and expression of feeling, at least in face-to-face encounters.

This match in emotional expression looms large in the research done by Bavelas et al. (1987) and Bavelas, Black, Chovil, Lemery, and Mullett (1988), which supports their contention that mimicry is a communicative act, conveying a rapid and precise nonverbal message to another person. Specifically, they argue that people are communicating solidarity and involvement ("I am with you" or "I am like you") when they mimic. "By immediately displaying a reaction appropriate to the other's situation (e.g., a wince for the other's pain), the observer conveys precisely and eloquently both awareness of and involvement with the other's situation" (1988, p. 278). If Bavelas et al. are right, then mimicry may not just be another mechanism of empathic arousal that predisposes people to help others, but it may also be a direct means of giving support and comfort to others. That is, mimicry-based empathy may not only be a prosocial motive but also a prosocial act.

## Classical Conditioning

Classical conditioning is an important empathy-arousing mechanism in childhood especially in the early, preverbal years. It appears that young children (or anyone for that matter) can acquire empathic feelings of distress as conditioned responses whenever they observe someone in distress at the same time that they are having their own independent experience of distress. Thus Lanzetta and Orr (1986) found that presenting adults with a fear-producing danger signal (shock electrodes) along with an another adult's fearful facial expression, results in fearful faces becoming conditioned stimuli that evoke fear in the subjects even when the shock electrodes are removed from view. Using a similar procedure, happy faces and neutral tones can become conditioned fear-producing stimuli, though not as effectively as fearful faces. At the other extreme, and of greater interest to us, two decades of research have shown, contrary to previous belief, that conditioning is possible in newborns: The sucking response of 1-day-olds, for example, can be conditioned to stroking their forehead (Blass, Ganchrow, & Steiner, 1984).

This pairing of one's actual distress with expressive cues of distress in others may be inevitable in mother–infant interactions, as when the mother's feelings are transferred to the infant in the course of physical handling. For example, when a mother feels anxiety or tension, her body may stiffen and the stiffening may transmit her distress to the infant she is holding. The infant is now distressed; and the stiffening of the mother's body was the direct cause – the unconditioned stimulus. The mother's accompanying facial and verbal expressions then become conditioned stimuli, which can subsequently evoke distress in the child even in the absence of physical contact. This mechanism may explain Sullivan's (1940) definition of empathy as a form of "nonverbal contagion and communion" between mother and infant; and Escalona's finding (1945), in a woman's reformatory where mothers cared for their own infants, that the infants were most upset when their mothers were waiting to appear before a parole board. Furthermore, through generalization of the conditioned stimulus, facial and verbal signs of distress from *anyone*, not only the mother, can make the infant feel distressed.

This type of direct physical conditioning is not confined to negative affect. When a mother holds the baby closely, securely, affectionately, and has a smile on her face, the baby feels good and the mother's smile is associated with that feeling. Later, the mother's smile alone may function as a conditioned stimulus that makes the baby feel good. And, again through stimulus generalization, other people's smiles can make the baby feel good. This process is relevant here because it may contribute to the empathic relief discussed earlier when the person one has helped smiles in gratitude or relief.

Afferent feedback, an essential component of mimicry, may also play a role in conditioning, and it may contribute to a certain degree of match between the observer's and the victim's feeling. That is, changes in the observer's facial expression accompanying empathic distress aroused by conditioning may trigger afferent feedback and produce feelings in the observer that match the victim's feelings, because: (a) all humans have certain distress experiences in common (loss, injury, deprivation), (b) they are structurally similar to each other and therefore likely to process distress-relevant information similarly, and (c) they are therefore likely to respond to similar stressful events with similar feelings (Ekman et al., 1987).

Indeed, conditioning might be thought of, like mimicry, as a two-step process: conditioning of facial expression followed by afferent feedback. There is a big difference of course: Mimicry assures a match between victim's and observer's feeling because it is the only process whose first step (imitation) is a direct response to the victim's facial expression; whereas conditioning can be a response to the victim's situation.

## Direct Association

A variant of the conditioning paradigm, described some time ago by Humphrey (1922), is the direct association of cues in the victim's situation that remind observers of similar experiences in their own past and evoke feelings in them that fit the victim's situation. We have a distressing experience; later on we observe someone in a similar situation; and his facial expression, voice, posture, or any other cue in the situation that reminds us of our past experience may evoke a feeling of distress in us. A frequently cited example is the boy who sees another child cut himself and cry. The sight of the blood, the sound of the cry, or any other cue from the victim or the situation that reminds the boy of his own past experiences of pain may evoke an empathic distress response. Another example is children's past experiences of separation from the mother – short daily separation, prolonged separation, or their worrying about the mother's dying – which may facilitate their empathizing with another person whose mother is hospitalized or dies.

Direct association differs from conditioning because it does not require previous experiences in which distress in oneself is actually paired with cues of distress in others. The only requirement is that the observer has had past feelings of pain or discomfort, which can now be evoked by cues of distress from victims or situational cues that are similar to those painful experiences. Direct association thus has more scope than conditioning and provides the basis for a variety of distress experiences in others with which children may empathize. Furthermore, what I said about the possible role of afferent feedback in conditioning may also be true of direct association: Changes in an observer's facial expression resulting from direct association may, through afferent feedback, contribute to a certain degree of match between the observer's and the victim's feeling. Here is a vivid example of direct association described by a college student:

> Getting off the bus I saw a man slip and fall and hit his head on the stairs. I was shocked. An incident flashed through my mind when I slipped on the sidewalk and cracked my skull. I don't know what came over me. I didn't think of anything but to rush to help and somehow get him to feel okay. I remember yelling at the people to call 911. I must have spent over two hours making sure everything was okay. I know myself, and I know I wouldn't have felt okay just to get him up and leave it to someone else to take care of him.

To summarize, mimicry, conditioning, and direct association are important mechanisms of empathic arousal for several reasons: (a) they are automatic, quick-acting, and involuntary; (b) they enable infants and preverbal children, as well as adults, to empathize with others in distress; (c) they produce early pairings of children's empathic distress with other people's actual distress, which contributes to children's expectation of distress whenever they are exposed to another's distress; (d) they are self-reinforcing to some extent because the helping behavior they foster may produce empathic relief; (e) they contribute an involuntary dimension to children's future empathy experiences.

The question may be raised whether conditioning and direct association are empathy-arousing processes when triggered by the situation rather than by the victim's feeling. I consider them empathy-arousing processes as long as the observer attends to the victim and the feelings evoked in the observer fit the victim's situation rather than the observer's. In any case, the problem does not exist in face-to-face encounters, where mimicry defines the observer's distress as clearly empathic, and conditioning and association may contribute to the intensity of that distress. The empathy aroused in observers by the combination of mimicry, conditioning, and association is, to be sure, a passive, involuntary response, based on the pull of surface cues and requiring the shallowest level of cognitive processing. It is a potentially powerful empathy-arousing package, nonetheless, precisely because it shows that humans are built in such a way that they can involuntarily and forcefully experience another's emotion – that is, a person's distress is often contingent not on his own but on someone else's painful experience.

It is a limited empathy-arousing package, however, because of the minimal involvement of language and cognition. This limitation makes it necessary for the victim to be present and enables observers to empathize only with simple emotions. The three mechanisms that make up the package also make little or no contribution to mature empathy's metacognitive dimension – the awareness that one's feeling of distress is a response to another's distressing situation. These deficiencies are overcome by language and cognitive development, which are central to the two remaining modes of empathy arousal, mediated association and role-taking, to which we now turn.

## Mediated Association

In the fourth empathic arousal mode, verbal mediation, the victim's emotionally distressed state is communicated through language. To highlight the processes involved in mediated association, consider what happens when language provides the only cue about another's affective state, for example, when the other person is not present but we receive a letter describing what happened to him or how he feels. Language might produce an empathic response because of the physical properties of words which have become conditioned stimuli (the sound of the word *cancer* may arouse fear in children who do not know its meaning but associate the sound with adult expressions of fear and anxiety). This is not what is special about language, however.

What is special about language is not the physical properties of words but their semantic meaning. Verbal messages from victims must be semantically processed and decoded. When this happens, language is the mediator or link between the model's feeling and the observer's experience. The message may express the model's feeling (I'm worried), the model's situation (my child was just taken to the hospital), or both. Empathic affect may then be aroused in observers who decode the victim's message and relate it to their own experience. Alternatively, the decoded message enables the observer to conjure up visual (facial expression, posture) or auditory images of the victim (cries, moans) and the observer then responds empathically to these images through direct association or mimicry.

Verbally mediated empathic arousal is interesting for several reasons. First, the time it takes to process a message semantically and relate it to one's experience, though undoubtedly greater than the time required by conditioning, association, and mimicry, varies enormously. Semantic processing can be drawn out but it can also be amazingly fast: It takes less than a second to categorize words in a list (which word is a fruit?) and 2 to 3 seconds to judge whether a word is a synonym of another word (Gitomer, Pellegrino, & Bisanz, 1983); Rogers, Kuiper, & Kirker, 1977). Second, semantic processing undoubtedly requires more mental effort than conditioning, association, and mimicry.

Third, because one is not responding directly to the victim or his situation, semantic processing puts psychological distance between observers and victims due to the decoding and encoding processes that intervene. That is, the victim encodes his feelings into words (sad, afraid). But words are general categories that can only approximate the victim's feelings at the time, and words are the total input available to the observer. In decoding the message the observer must reverse the sequence, going from the general category of feeling represented by the word to his own specific feeling and the associated past events in which he had that feeling. As a result, the observer's feelings have much in common with the victim's feelings, owing to the normative, shared meaning of the victim's words, but there is always some slippage due to encoding and decoding "errors" (and memory lapses for associated past events). These errors can be reduced when victims are expert at putting feelings into words and when observers know the victim well, know how he feels in different situations and can perhaps imagine his facial expression and behavior in the immediate situation. In general, we would expect verbal mediation to reduce the intensity of observer's empathic response below what it would be when victims are present – although there are exceptions to this, which will be discussed in the next chapter.

In most bystander situations the victim *is* present and verbal communication of his distress is accompanied by visual or auditory cues. These cues may have triggered the observer's empathic response in the first place, through conditioning, association, or mimicry because these are faster-acting than semantically processing the verbal message. Semantic processing, I would hypothesize, is more likely to follow and fine-tune the observer's empathic response, although it may at times initiate the empathic process, as when the verbal message precedes the victim's arrival on the scene. Whatever the sequence, the victim's expressive cues, which are likely to be picked up through conditioning, association, and mimicry, may keep the empathic process "alive" because these cues are salient, vivid, and can therefore hold the observer's attention – in contrast to verbal messages, which are distancing and to some extent dampen empathic affect because of the encoding and decoding involved in processing them.

The victim's expressive cues may also keep observers from being misled when victims' words belie their feelings, because of the human tendency to "leak" feelings through involuntary changes in facial expression, posture, and tone of voice. These involuntary changes in expression can be picked up and communicated to the observer by conditioning, association, and mimicry. This points up a second communication function of empathic affect (see Bavelas et al., 1988, above for the first), which is to *inform* its motivational component (Hoffman, 1981). Thus empathic affect is generated both by primitive and verbally mediated mechanisms. The information from these two sources of empathic affect is usually congruent, but when it is not congruent the discrepancy can provide corrective feedback that helps observers to make a more accurate assessment of the victim's state and thus to have a more veridical empathic response.

Verbally mediated empathic distress is illustrated in a study by Batson, Sympson, and Hindman (1996). Adolescent subjects read stories in which someone of the same sex described an upsetting life experience. One story described the acute embarrassment and shame, the enduring cruel remarks and teasing, and the hating to see oneself in the mirror that resulted from having a bad case of acne.

The other story described feeling betrayed and rejected, trying to regroup and move on, and experiencing self-doubt and lingering love after being rejected by a long-term dating partner. The subjects reported feeling considerable empathic distress after reading the stories. The female subjects reported even greater empathic distress if they recalled having a similar experience themselves, which suggests verbally mediated association. Verbal mediation probably also enabled all the subjects to imagine themselves in the victim's place, an empathy-arousing mechanism to which we turn in a moment, after this quite different example of cognitively, though not verbally, mediated empathic distress which was described to me by a student.

> When dealing with someone with a terminal illness I was always taught to never discuss that illness with them, just to talk about everyday topics. About five years ago my grandma lapsed into a coma, and for a year she "lived" this way. I would often speak to her on the phone, identifying myself and talking to her about my life. It was very difficult and painful for me because there would never be a response and I could never question her. I would speak with her in the hope that she would respond some way. She never did.

In this case there were no expressive cues from the victim except silence which would have meant nothing if not for the observer's knowledge and understanding of the victim's plight.

## Role-Taking

The fifth mode of empathic arousal requires an advanced level of cognitive processing: putting oneself in the other's place and imagining how he or she feels. The idea that putting oneself in the other's place can make one feel something of what the other feels is not new. Two-and-a-half centuries ago the British philosopher David Hume suggested that because people are constituted similarly and have similar life experiences, when one imagines oneself in another's place one converts the other's situation into mental images that then evoke the same feeling in oneself (Hume, 1751/1957). Adam Smith, a contemporary, agreed with Hume about empathy's importance, and

Smith's speculations about the nature of the empathic process fore-shadowed some of today's formulations. He realized, for example, that empathy could be a response to direct expressive cues of an-other's feeling: "Grief and joy strongly expressed in the look and gestures of anyone at once affect the spectator with some degree of a like painful or agreeable emotion" (Smith, 1759/1965, p. 260). He also viewed empathy as universal and involuntary: "Even the greatest ruffian, the most hardened violator of the laws of society is not without it" (p. 257). Though involuntary, empathy is enhanced by cognitive processes.

> By the imagination we place ourselves in the other's situation, we conceive ourselves enduring all the same torments, we enter, as it were, into his body, and become in some measure the same person with him, and thence form some idea of his sensations, and even feel something which, though weaker in degree, is not altogether unlike them. (p. 261)

Despite these early beginnings, role-taking as a mechanism of empathic arousal was not investigated empirically until the mid-1960s. The most pertinent research was done by Stotland (1969). In one study, subjects were instructed to imagine how they would feel and what sensations they would have in their hands if they were exposed to the same painful heat treatment that was being applied to someone they were observing through a one-way mirror. These subjects showed more empathic distress, as measured by palmar sweat and verbal report, than subjects who were instructed to attend closely to the victim's physical movements. They also showed more empathic distress than subjects who were instructed to imagine how the victim felt while undergoing the heat treatment. The first find-ing indicates that imagining oneself in the victim's place is more empathy-arousing than focusing on his expressive movements. The second finding suggests that imagining oneself in the other's place is more empathy-arousing than focusing one's attention directly on the victim's feeling. Stotland also found that the subjects who were in-structed to imagine themselves in the victim's place did not show an increase in palmar sweat until about 30 seconds after the experimenter announced that the painful heat treatment had begun, which was longer than the time it took for subjects who were simply asked to observe the victim. The delay in empathic responsiveness could have been due to the cognitive demands of role-taking (plus the mental effort involved in following the instructions).

Stotland's research suggested to me that there may be two types of role-taking that have somewhat different effects: One is the usual conception of role-taking in which one imagines oneself in the other's place. In the second type, one focuses directly on the other's feeling. I conducted dozens of interviews asking people to describe instances in which they responded empathically to victims who were present, victims who communicated their distress in writing, and victims whose distress was communicated to them by a third person. The interviews served two purposes: They confirmed the two types of role-taking as well as a third, combined type, and they suggested the cognitive–affective interaction processes that may underlie the types, as follows.

1. *Self-focused role-taking.* When people observe someone in distress they may imagine how they would feel in the same situation. If they can do this vividly enough, they may experience some of the same affect experienced by the victim. And if they are reminded of similar events in their own past, or if they remember worrying about such events happening, then their empathic response to the victim may be enhanced through association with the emotionally charged memory of those actual or worried-about events.

2. *Other-focused role-taking.* On learning of another's misfortune, people may focus directly on the victim and imagine how he feels; and doing this may result in their feeling something of the victim's feeling. This empathic response may be enhanced by bringing in any personal information they have about the victim (his character, life-condition, behavior in similar situations), and any normative knowledge they may have of how most people feel in that situation. It may be enhanced further if they attend to the victim's facial expression, voice tone, or posture, because these nonverbal cues of distress may enlist the more primitive empathy-arousing mechanisms (conditioning, association, mimicry). This can be done

even in the victim's absence, as when observers who are closely related to the victim imagine how he looks, "hear" his cries, and respond empathically as if he were present.

Based on my interviews, I suggested that Stotland's finding that self-focused role-taking produced more intense empathic distress than other-focused role-taking could be explained as follows:

> Imagining oneself in the other's place reflects processes generated from within the observer . . . in which connections are made between the stimuli impinging on the other person and similar stimulus events in the observer's own past. That is, imagining oneself in the other's place produces an empathic response because it has the power to evoke associations with real events in one's own past in which one actually experienced the affect in question. (Hoffman, 1978, p. 180)

Such internally generated responses are less likely when one focuses on the victim.

The hypothesis that self-focused role-taking produces more intense empathic affect than other-focused role-taking has recently been confirmed in an experimental study by Batson, Early, and Salvarani (1997). Undergraduate subjects listened to a (bogus) radio interview of a young woman in serious need: Her parents and a sister had recently been killed in an automobile crash. She explained that she was desperately trying to take care of her surviving younger brother and sister while she finished her last year of college. If she did not finish, she would not be able to earn enough money to support them and would have to put them up for adoption. One group of subjects was instructed to remain objective while listening, another to imagine how the young woman "feels about what has happened to her and how it has affected her life," and another to imagine how "you yourself would feel if you were experiencing what has happened to her and how this experience would affect your life." The main finding was that both role-taking conditions produced more empathic distress than the objective condition, but the self-focused condition produced more than the other-focused condition. That is, the subjects who imagined how they would feel in the victim's situation experienced more intense empathic distress than those who imagined how the victim felt.[2] The reason, I suggest, is that imagining how oneself would feel activates one's own personal need system.

Self-focused role-taking may have its limitations, however. When people take the victim's place and bring in emotionally charged personal memories, the memories may at times take control of their response and turn their attention away from the victim toward themselves. That is, an observer feels empathic/sympathetic distress ("I feel so much of your pain. It hurts me so much to see this happen to you"), but when he starts ruminating about a similar perhaps more traumatic experience in his own past (self-focused role-taking), he begins to feel a more personal distress; the empathic pain remains, but the image of the victim recedes into the background. In other words, the observer is overwhelmed by the empathic connection with the victim, and the empathic connection is then severed, ironically, because the empathic affect resonates so effectively with the observer's own needs; and his focus, which was initially on the victim, shifts toward himself. Ruminating about his painful past, he becomes lost in egoistic concerns and the image of the victim that initiated the role-taking process slips out of focus and fades away, aborting or temporarily aborting the empathic process.

I call this loss of empathic connection "egoistic drift" (Hoffman, 1978). Egoistic drift points up empathy's fragility: It highlights the fact that **although humans can empathize with the other they are not the other.** My hypothesis is that self-focused role-taking arouses more intense empathic distress because it makes a direct connection between the victim's affective state and the observer's own need system. But this very connection makes it vulnerable to egoistic drift. The result is that self-focused role-taking produces a more intense,

---

2. The actual finding was that both the self- and other-focused conditions produced more empathic/sympathetic distress than the objective condition, but the self-focused condition produced in addition a high degree of relatively "pure" empathic distress (called "personal distress" by Batson et al., 1997). The terms *empathic/sympathetic distress* and *pure empathic distress* will make more sense after reading the next chapter, in which they are discussed at length.

but sometimes less stable empathic response than other-focused role-taking. Regardless of the explanation, the observer's affective response, though initially triggered by the victim's affective state, would no longer, in my judgment, qualify as empathy unless the observer returned to his initial focus on the victim.

The following experience, reported by an undergraduate, illustrates both the power of self-focused role-taking to evoke empathic affect and its vulnerability to egoistic drift.

> The movie *Steel Magnolias* is a poignant film focused on the life of a woman, Shelby, struggling with diabetes. Shelby marries Jackson and they have a son. One evening Jackson returns from work to find Shelby unconscious on the floor with the phone in her hand. Their 3-year-old son is crying beside his mother. Shelby goes to the hospital where she dies. Shelby's mother, M'Lynn, is comforted by her closest friends. At the burial of her only daughter, M'Lynn becomes hysterical. She cries not only about the tragic loss of her daughter but also about the grandson who will never know his mother. She wants to know why God took her Shelby; a mother is not supposed to outlive her child.
>
> I was able to keep my composure until that last scene. As M'Lynn became hysterical – her voice, her words, her facial expression – visions of my grandmother emerged. I began to remember witnessing the same actions . . . performed by my grandmother. I became hysterical. My focus was no longer on Shelby and M'Lynn but rather on my grandmother. I remember how I felt after my aunt died leaving behind her two children. I felt the pain and depression all over again. My friends who were watching the movie with me assumed I was crying because of the movie but in actuality the tears were because of my own life.

Another student contributed this incident, which shows that one need not have had an experience like the victim's but only to be worried about having one.

> A friend who is pregnant was just told the baby, her fourth, had Down's Syndrome. I felt really sorry for her. I have been thinking about having children lately. I have none and spend a lot of time worrying about what my life would be like if I had a child with a serious deformity. I imagine all the things that might happen to the child, and to me. When my friend told me that, I immediately

started thinking about what it would be like if I were just told that the child I was carrying had Down's Syndrome. When this occurred I became so engrossed in my own thoughts about what it would feel like, that I forgot all about my friend and her condition. I was completely consumed by the fear of what might happen to my future rather than what was happening to my friend in the present.

**3. Combination.** Observers can shift back and forth between "other-focused" and "self-focused" role-taking or experience them as co-occurring parallel processes. My discussion suggests that the combination may be the most powerful because it combines the emotional intensity of self-focused role-taking with the more sustained attention to the victim of other-focused role-taking. Indeed, fully mature role-taking might be defined as imagining oneself in the other's place and integrating the resulting empathic affect with one's personal information about the other and one's general knowledge of how people feel in his or her situation. It could go either way: other-focused role-taking in the service of self-focused role-taking, or self-focused role-taking in the service of other-focused role-taking.

A final word about role-taking. Although spontaneous role-taking has been found in adults and in children as young as 9 years old (Wilson & Cantor, 1985), role-taking is more cognitively demanding than the other empathy-arousing mechanisms and might therefore be expected to have a greater voluntary component. It would seem possible, for example, to avoid role-taking by thinking distracting thoughts. This might be difficult, however, in situations that demand paying attention to the victim or when distress cues from the victim are salient, owing to the pull of primitive empathy-arousing mechanisms (conditioning, association, mimicry). This could explain why a group of Stotland's (1969) subjects who were instructed to attend to the victim but avoid putting themselves in his place showed as much palmar sweat as subjects who were simply instructed to attend to the victim; try as they might, these subjects could not avoid empathizing. It may also explain why most everyone regardless of age finds it difficult to avoid empathizing with victims in the movies. That is, they find it difficult to avoid "suspending disbelief," even though they know it is all "pretend." Role-taking, in other words, may not be as voluntary a process as it first appears to be.

A final developmental hypothesis: other-focused role-taking is more cognitively demanding (one considers another's inner states) and is thus acquired later.

## IMPORTANCE OF MANY MODES

The importance of many modes of empathic arousal is that they enable observers to respond empathically to whatever distress cues are available. If the only cues are the victim's facial expression, voice, or posture, they can be picked up through mimicry. If the only cues are situational, empathic distress can be aroused through conditioning or direct association. If the victim expresses distress verbally or in writing, or someone else describes his plight, observers can be empathically aroused through verbal mediation or role-taking.

The three primitive modes – mimicry, association, and conditioning – operating together provide a powerful package that may underlie empathic arousal in children's early preverbal years. Mimicry may be particularly important in infancy because it produces a match between observers' and victims' feelings even when observers have not had a similar experience. The three primitive modes also contribute to empathy development beyond infancy by giving young children repeated experiences of feeling distressed as a co-occurring feature of another person's distress, as well as the pleasant experience of empathic relief when they help. Finally, because the three primitive modes are automatic and encompass all the available distress cues, they may account for the involuntary dimension of empathy in adults, which may, among other things, reduce the tendency toward "egoistic drift."

Ordinarily victims are present and all the arousal mechanisms are operating. When that happens there may be a certain division of labor among them. Some arousal mechanisms are more likely to intensify empathic affect or keep one's attention focused on the victim (mimicry). On the other hand, others are more likely to contribute to "egoistic drift" (especially self-focused role-taking). Some mechanisms may start the empathic process but fade away, while others take over for them. Mimicry, for example, may start the empathy-arousing process but then fade away due to facial muscle fatigue; the victim's face is still cognitively represented, however, and the representation of the face may sustain other empathy-arousing mechanisms and keep them operating. Apart from a division of labor, the modes may interact reciprocally: Empathic affect from primitive modes may trigger role-taking, which may then intensify and give broader meaning to empathic affect from the primitive modes. Which mechanism initiates the process, the primitive or the more cognitive, may be a function of personal style and the context.

The various modes should ordinarily produce the same empathic affect (with exceptions discussed in chapters 3 and 4); and the functional redundancy should assure an empathic response in most observers. Indeed, although one's empathic distress may usually be less intense than the victim's actual distress, the combined effects of the arousal modes may sometimes make one's empathic distress more intensely painful than the victim's actual distress. This may explain a phenomenon that fascinated Darwin (1862/1965, p. 216): "It is not a little remarkable that sympathy with the distresses of others should excite more tears more freely than our own distresses; and this is certainly the case." My hypothesis is that what happens is the observer's imagination runs rampant as he or she contemplates being in the victim's place (self-focused role-taking), whereas the victim has had time to accept and come to terms with his or her condition. As a result, the observer's empathic distress can be more intense than the victim's actual distress – and presumably more intense than the *observer's* actual distress would be in the victim's situation. More about this later (chapter 8).

The existence of multiple arousal modes bears on my definition of empathy as not requiring (though often including) a close match between observer's and victim's affect. On the one hand, the many modes virtually assure a certain degree of match between the feelings of observers and victims, even across cultures, for three reasons: First, mimicry, because it is automatic and neurally based, assures a close match in feeling when there is face-to-face contact between observer and victim. Second, even conditioning and association assure some degree of match because all humans are structurally similar and process information similarly; they are therefore likely to respond to similar events with similar feelings. On the other hand, as we shall see, there are occasions in which empathy does not require a match and, indeed, may require a certain *mismatch*, as when the victim's life condition belies his feelings in the immediate situation. These are occasions in which verbal mediation and role-taking are likely to be paramount.

To summarize, empathic distress is a multidetermined, hence reliable human response. The three preverbal modes are crucial in childhood especially in face-to-face situations, but they continue to operate past childhood and provide an important involuntary dimension to empathy throughout life. They not only enable a person to respond to whatever cues are available, but they also *compel* him or her to do that – instantly, automatically, and outside of conscious awareness. An example can be found in empathic avoidance: If a person tries to avoid empathy by refraining from eye contact or not listening to a description of a victim's life condition, he may still be vulnerable to empathic distress through conditioning or association. The two cognitively advanced modes – verbal mediation and role-taking – can be drawn out and subjected to voluntary control, but if one is paying attention to the victim, they too can be fast-acting, involuntary, and triggered immediately on witnessing the victim's situation. What these two cognitively advanced modes contribute is that they add scope to one's empathic capability and enable one to empathize with others who are not present. All of this fits well with the evidence presented earlier for empathy's effectiveness as a prosocial moral motive and with the argument that empathy became a basic part of human nature through natural selection (Hoffman, 1981). It is also in keeping with the finding that empathy has a hereditary component: Identical twins are more similar to each other on empathy measures than are fraternal twins of the same age (Zahn-Waxler, Robinson, Emde, & Plomin, 1992).

Before concluding this chapter, I would like to raise a fundamental question about empathy: why do the various empathy-arousing mechanisms work, that is, why do they elicit feelings in observers that approximate the feelings of those being observed? My answer, implied in the foregoing discussion of mechanisms, is first and foremost that because of the structural similarities in people's physiological and cognitive response systems, similar events evoke similar feelings – similar but not identical for the reasons already given. However, the degree of structural similarity, hence the tendency to empathize with one another, should be greater between people in the same culture who live under similar conditions, and especially between those who interact frequently, than between people from different cultures or who rarely interact. This is obviously true of the cognitive system but it is also true of the physiological system, as evidenced by Levenson and Ruef (1997) who found an increased "physiological synchrony" in humans who spend a lot of time together, for example, an increased covariation of heart-rate changes between patients and their therapists, and between mothers and their infants.

# CHAPTER 3

# Development of Empathic Distress

As I mentioned earlier, empathic distress seems like a simple response: One feels distressed when observing someone in actual distress. When we look at empathic distress in mature observers, however, its complexity is quickly apparent. First, empathic distress in mature observers includes a metacognitive awareness of oneself as responding empathically: One not only feels distressed but knows this feeling is a response to something unfortunate happening to someone else and to what one assumes to be the victim's feeling of pain or discomfort. Mature empathizers have thus passed the developmental milestone of acquiring a cognitive sense of themselves and others as separate physical entities with independent internal states, personal identities, and lives beyond the situation and can therefore distinguish what happens to others from what happens to themselves.

Second, mature observers have a sense of how they would feel and a general understanding of how most people would feel in the other's situation. Third, mature observers know that the other's outward behavior (facial expression, posture, voice tone) can reflect how he feels internally but they also know that these outward expressions of feeling can be controlled to some extent and mask the other's internal feeling. Furthermore, all of this knowledge plus any personal information a mature observer has about the victim are likely to be quickly integrated into an explanation of the cause of the victim's plight. In short, for a person to experience mature empathic distress, he must have a clear distinction between what happens to others and what happens to himself and an understanding of how feelings are expressed and how they are shaped by events.

Although infants and very young children lack many of these cognitive capabilities, they can be empathically aroused through the primitive arousal mechanisms: mimicry, conditioning, and association. The difference between infant empathy based on these mechanisms and mature empathy suggests that the development of empathic distress may reflect children's social-cognitive development, especially development of a separate and independent sense of self, a sense of others, and a sense of the relationship between self and others. Because the sense of self and others undergoes dramatic changes developmentally, it provides a framework for a developmental scheme for empathy.

I find it useful to think of four broad stages in the development of self and other: unclear or confused self/other differentiation; awareness of self and others as separate physical entities; awareness of self and others as having independent internal states; awareness of self and others as having their own personal histories, identities, and lives beyond the immediate situation. These social-cognitive stages interact with empathic affect aroused through the various arousal mechanisms, to produce the developmental scheme that follows. Before presenting the scheme I note that the age levels assigned to the stages and transitions between stages are approximate and individual differences can be enormous.

## NEWBORN REACTIVE CRY

It has long been known by students of infancy and lay people alike that when human infants hear another infant cry they start to cry. The first controlled study of this reactive cry was done by Simner (1971), who found it in 2- and 3-day-olds. Simner also established that the cause of the reactive cry is not the loudness of the other's cry, as infants do not start to cry when they hear a synthetically produced (computer simulated) wail of equal loudness. Simner's findings have been replicated in 1-day-olds by Sagi and Hoffman (1976), who report in addition that the reactive cry is not a simple imitative vocal response lacking an affective component. Rather, it is vigorous, intense, and **indistinguishable from the spontaneous cry of an infant who is in actual discomfort.** Martin and Clark (1982) replicated these findings and also showed that infants do not cry as much to the cry of a chimpanzee (which, by the way, adults find more aversive than infant cries), or even to the sound of their own cry. There thus appears to be something uniquely unpleasant about the sound of a human infant crying that throws the newborn into a state of agitated discomfort.

Why is that? The most likely explanation is that the newborn reactive cry is an innate, isomorphic response to the cry of another being of the same species, which survived natural selection and is adaptive. The primary underlying psychological mechanism could be a form of mimicry in which the newborn automatically imitates the sound of another's cry, and the resulting sound of his own cry and changes in facial muscle patterns accompanying his own cry start a feedback process that throws him into an agitated state.

The reactive cry could also be a learned response based on conditioning. In chapter 2 I mentioned the conditioning of the sucking response in 1-day-olds. It seems likely that other frequent newborn behaviors like reactive crying can also be conditioned, perhaps as follows: Reactive crying might be a conditioned distress response to a cue (sound of another's cry) that resembles cues (the infant's own cries) associated with the infant's previous pain and discomfort experiences, perhaps beginning with the birth process itself. Yet another possibility is imitation, which also occurs shortly after birth. Imitation alone, however, cannot explain the reactive cry, which, as noted, is not just an imitated cry but a more generally vigorous and agitated distress response. The most likely psychological explanation of newborn reactive crying, it seems to me, is a combination of mimicry and conditioning, with each getting an assist from imitation.

Regardless of the cause, the newborn is responding to a cue of distress in others by feeling distressed himself. The cry must therefore be considered an early, rudimentary precursor of empathic distress – precursor because the "other" to which the newborn is responding is probably sensed by the newborn as connected to the "self," that is, as part of the same global psychological entity as the self. Interestingly, the newborn reactive cry may, despite this limitation, make a contribution to more advanced stages of empathic distress by creating a condition in which a distress cue in another (sound of a cry) occurs together with the infant's own experience of distress. Such concurrences may lead infants, through conditioning and association, to experience distress in the future, whenever they witness another in distress, that is, to experience empathic distress.

From a developmental perspective, we would expect the newborn reactive cry to be confined to the early months of life and to be gone by 6 months or so, owing to infants' dawning awareness of themselves and others as separate beings. This awareness should interfere with, or at least slow down, their automatic mimicry and conditioning responses to another's cry. The infants should also be less susceptible to cry sounds because of their growing interest in other things and the ability to regulate their emotions. There is evidence for this expected decline in a study by Hay, Nash, and Pedersen (1981), who observed twelve pairs of 6-month-old infants interacting in a laboratory playroom; both mothers were present. The main finding was that when one infant was distressed, the other generally watched but rarely cried or became distressed himself. There was a cumulative effect, however: After several instances of an infant's showing distress, the other infant did become distressed and started to cry.

The 6-month-old's cry differs from the newborn's cry in another way as well: It is not instantaneous and agitated; at 6 months the infant first looks sad and puckers up his lips before starting to cry, just as infants do at that age when they are in actual distress. It is interesting that Charles Darwin (1877), who carefully observed his son's facial and emotional responses from birth, reported something similar – "empathy was clearly shown at 6 months and 11 days by his melancholy face, with the corners of his mouth well depressed, when his nurse pretended to cry" (p. 293).

The difference between the 6-month-old and the newborn suggests that as infants differentiate from others, the basis of their global empathic distress response is undermined. They no longer respond automatically to another's cry, because the other is now becoming a true "other" who is perceived, at least dimly, as physically separate from oneself. The infants now require more prolonged signs of another's distress before feeling distressed themselves. Furthermore, the infants may be preoccupied with their own projects, and for this reason it may require the more salient stimulus of a prolonged cry to grab their attention away from what they are doing. And finally, the looking sad and puckering up of their lips before crying, which they also do when actually distressed themselves, very likely reflects the early beginning of their ability to control their emotions.

## EGOCENTRIC EMPATHIC DISTRESS

Toward the end of the first year, infants still respond to a distressed peer by looking sad, puckering up their lips, and then crying, but their cry may now be accompanied by whimpering and silently watching the distressed peer (Radke-Yarrow & Zahn-Waxler, 1984). Most infants, some sooner than others, begin to react less passively to another's distress and engage in behavior clearly designed to reduce their own distress.

Three investigators have reported the same thing: When the 10-month-old daughter of a student of mine saw a friend fall down and cry, she stared at her friend, began to cry, then put her thumb in her mouth and buried her head in her mother's lap, just as she does when she herself is hurt (Hoffman, 1975b). Radke-Yarrow and Zahn-Waxler (1984) described many similar cases, this one about an 11-month-old: "Sari, on witnessing someone in physical pain, looked sad, puckered up her lips, burst out crying, and then crawled over to her mother to be picked up and comforted" (p. 89). Kaplan (1977, p. 91) observed a 9-month-old who

> had already demonstrated strong empathic responses to other children's distress. Characteristically, she did not turn away from these distress scenes though they apparently touched off distress in her-

self. Hope would stare intently, her eyes welling up with tears if another child fell, hurt themselves or cried. At that time, she was overwhelmed with her emotions. She would end up crying herself and crawling quickly to her mother for comfort.

Kaplan's description is noteworthy because it shows at once the child's intense (empathically based) personal distress, an awareness of something unpleasant happening to another child, but also a confusion about who is really in distress. The situation is distressing to her and she seeks comfort in the same way that she does when she is in distress.

My hypothesis about why these children respond to empathic and actual distress in the same way is that although they are developing a sense of self as a coherent, continuous entity separate from others, they still have a long way to go. They also remain limited to the preverbal empathy arousal mechanisms (mimicry, conditioning, association), and their behavior suggests they are still unclear about the source of their empathic distress. Sometimes they stare at the victim, reflecting a degree of self-other differentiation. Sometimes they use their newfound motor skills (crawling) to make contact with the mother and help alleviate their own empathic distress. But the fact that they do the same thing to alleviate their empathic distress that they do to alleviate their actual distress shows how difficult it must be for them to distinguish their empathic distress from the victim's distress that gave rise to it and from their own actual distress. The most parsimonious explanation is that they behave the same way in the empathic distress and actual distress situations because they are unclear about the difference between them, that is, they are unclear about the difference between something happening to the other and something happening to the self.

This explanation may seem at first to contradict Stern's (1985) research showing that infants have a "core self" by 7 months of age. I do not think there is a contradiction, and here is why. According to Stern, the core self includes a sense of controlling one's actions and having feelings related to one's experience. The core self is a coherent, physically bounded whole having continuity with one's past.

What ties the core self together and gives it coherence and continuity are the kinesthetic sensations infants receive from their muscles, bones, and joints every time they move. These kinesthetic sensations produce an invariant pattern of awareness. The core self is thus "an experiential, proprioception-based self, not the representational, reflective verbalizable self-concept that emerges around the middle of the second year [when infants can recognize themselves in the mirror, for example]" (Stern, 1985, p. 7).

The invariant pattern of self-awareness thus comes from the continuity of the infant's kinesthetic sensations. I suggest this is a fragile basis for the infant's core self because, unlike the later reflective self, it lacks the stabilizing influence of cognition. While the fragility may not normally pose a problem, **the infant's sense of continuity may break down anytime the infant "shares" distress with another, as in feeling empathic distress, because the kinesthetic bodily sensations on which the self's continuity is based are mixed with the bodily sensations arising from the infant's feeling empathically distressed (due to mimicry, conditioning, and association). The result is a temporary breakdown of the infant's self boundaries, and a feeling of confusion about where his or her distress comes from.** The infant has difficulty telling the difference between another's distress and the infant's own actual or empathic distress and responds the same way to another's distress as to the infant's own distress.

In any case, because the infant's response to another's and to his or her own distress is similar, I call it "egocentric" empathic distress. The term *egocentric empathic distress* sounds like an oxymoron, and indeed egocentric distress at this point in development has contradictory qualities. On the one hand, the child's seeking comfort for himself attests to empathic distress' egocentric nature. But the fact that the child was content beforehand and would continue to be content if not for another's misfortune – the fact that empathic distress is contingent on another's actual distress – attests to its prosocial nature. To summarize, empathic distress late in the first year is an egocentric motive but, unlike other egocentric motives, it is triggered by another's distress and this gives it prosocial properties. It is not a complete prosocial motive but is halfway there and could just as well be called a *precursor* of prosocial motivation.

## QUASI-EGOCENTRIC EMPATHIC DISTRESS

About a month or two later, still early in the second year, children's empathic cry, whimpering, and staring become less frequent and they begin making helpful advances toward the victim. The earliest advances, which involve tentative physical contact with the victim (patting, touching), soon give way to more differentiated positive interventions such as kissing, hugging, giving physical assistance, getting someone else to help, giving advice and sympathetic reassurance (Radke-Yarrow & Zahn-Waxler, 1984). By these actions children reveal that while they are still confined largely to preverbal empathy-arousing modes, they are less mired in their kinesthetic, subjective self and more cognitively anchored in external reality. Though they still lack a sense of their bodies as an object that can be represented outside their subjective selves (cannot recognize their mirror image until 18 to 24 months), they are part way there (they reach back when a moving object appears behind them in the mirror), and they know that others are separate physical entities (Baillargeon, 1987; Lewis & Brooks-Gunn, 1979). They can therefore realize that the other is in pain or discomfort, and their actions are clearly designed to help the other.

These same actions, however, reveal an important cognitive limitation: Children have inner states but do not realize that others have their own independent inner states. They do not know that their desires relate to the world around them, and they assume others see things the same way they do. They know the other is in distress but are still egocentric enough to use helping strategies that they find comforting. A 14-month-old boy responded to a crying friend with a sad look, then gently took the friend's hand and brought him to his own mother, although the friend's mother was present (Hoffman, 1978). This behavior clearly shows empathic distress functioning as a prosocial motive but it also reveals the child's egocentric confusion between his friend's needs and his own needs. Similar behavior by a 15-month-old girl was reported by a mother in Radke-Yarrow and Zahn-Waxler's (1984) longitudinal sample: "Mary watches a visiting baby who is crying: she watched him carefully. She followed him around, and kept handing him toys and also other items that were valuable to her, like her bottle or this string of beads which she's so fond of" (p. 90).

To summarize, children at this stage are aware that others are physically separate from themselves and know when another is in distress. Though still confined largely to preverbal modes, they are capable of a rudimentary form of self-focused role-taking and no longer confuse their empathic distress with the victim's or their own actual distress. Empathic distress is clearly a prosocial motive at this stage – the child tries to help, but his actions are misguided because he lacks insight into the inner states of others and assumes that what helps him will help others. This assumption is often valid (adults make it too but are not limited to it), but when it is not valid its underlying cognitive limitations are clearly evident.

## VERIDICAL EMPATHIC DISTRESS

Major developments in the sense of self occur around the middle of the second year. Children for the first time can recognize themselves in a mirror (Lewis & Brooks-Gunn, 1979). This mirror-self signifies that one has a sense of one's body as an object that can be represented in some form that exists outside of one's kinesthetically based subjective self and probably as an object that can be seen by others.

Later in the second year, children begin to show awareness that others have inner states (thoughts, feelings, wants) and that another's inner states may at times differ from one's own. This of course enables children to empathize more accurately with another's feelings and needs in different situations and to help the other more effectively. The transition from quasi-egocentric to veridical empathic distress is illustrated by 2-year-old David who brought his own teddy bear to comfort a crying friend, who was accidentally hurt when the two were struggling over a toy. When it didn't work, David paused, then ran to

**71**

the next room and returned with the friend's teddy bear; the friend hugged it and stopped crying. David's bringing his own teddy bear is a typical example of quasi-egocentric empathy, but he was able to profit from corrective feedback (his friend kept crying). I assume this means that David was cognitively advanced enough to wonder why his teddy bear did not stop his friend's crying, to reflect on the problem, and then to realize that his friend, like David himself, would want his own teddy bear. That is, the corrective feedback may have triggered role-taking, perhaps aided by David's memory of his friend's playing happily with his teddy bear and his memory of the teddy bear's being in the next room. This suggests the transition from quasi-egocentric to veridical empathy may occur when children are cognitively ready to learn from corrective feedback after making "egocentric" mistakes. Eventually, feedback becomes unnecessary (although even adults need it at times).

In a similar incident that did not involve feedback but did show a toddler's ability to bridge time, Sarah, 2 years and 3 months old, was riding in a car with her cousin (Blum, 1987). The cousin became upset when he could not find his teddy bear. Someone said it was in the trunk and could be retrieved when they got home. Ten or fifteen minutes passed and as the car approached the house Sarah said "Now you can get your bear." The same Sarah, at 3 years, showed an even more impressive ability to bridge time when she gave her friend her Donald Duck hat to keep "forever"; the hat was to replace the Boston Celtics cap that her friend had lost several days earlier. To summarize thus far, at this stage children cannot only empathize with the fact of another's distress; they can also take the victim's role and reflect on the victim's particular needs in the situation.

Veridical empathy is an important stage because, unlike the preceding stages which are short-lived and disappear as they give way to subsequent stages, this stage has all the basic elements of mature empathy and continues to grow and develop through life. In its fully developed form, children not only have a sense of their body as an object that can be represented outside one's kinesthetic subjective self (mirror-self) but they also sense their body as containing, and being guided by, an inner mental self, an "I," which thinks, feels, plans, remembers. This "reflective self" includes knowing that one is somebody separated from others not just physically but also in terms of inner experience; and that one's external image is an aspect of one's inner experience. This makes it possible for one to realize that the same holds true for others: Their external image is the other side of their inner experience. Children can now engage in other-focused as well as self-focused role-taking. They know that others have feelings and thoughts independent of theirs, and this knowledge stays with them and provides the springboard for a lifetime of learning to empathize with all manner of feelings in a dizzying variety of situations.

At first the feelings children can empathize with are simple, like those in the teddy bear examples. But, as they gain understanding of causes, consequences, and correlates of emotions, they can empathize with other people's increasingly complex feelings of distress (their disappointment at a friend's divulging a secret or in their own poor performance, their fear of losing face if they accept help). The following selective review gives an idea of the progress in emotion understanding and therefore empathic capability that children make from early childhood through adolescence. It is presented in rough developmental order; whether there are stages or sub-stages that fall into ordered sequences is a question for research. The review is based mainly on Bretherton, Fritz, Zahn-Waxler, and Ridgeway (1986), unless otherwise indicated.

*Early childhood.* Toddlers begin to understand the causes, consequences, and correlates of emotions and especially that feelings can affect a person's facial expression ("Katie not happy face, Katie sad"); feelings can result from another's action ("You sad, Mommy. What Daddy do." "I'm hurting your feelings, 'cause I was mean to you." "Grandma mad [because] I wrote on wall"); and feelings can elicit action from someone else ("I cry [so] lady pick me up and hold me").

In the preschool years, children can be articulate about subtle emotions like missing one's parents ("He's sad. He'll be happy when his Daddy comes home," said in response to a picture in a book showing a boy looking sad). They are beginning to realize that the same event can produce different feelings in different people. They are able to take into account the desires of another person in judging the emotions that person will feel in a particular situation (Harris, Johnson, Hutton, Andrews, & Cooks, 1989). But they also realize that people can control their emotional expression, that displayed emotions may not necessarily be felt, and that someone can have a desire even if he or she does not act on it (Astington & Gopnik, 1991).

*Middle childhood.* By 6 or 7 years, some children begin showing rather sophisticated understanding of the connections between their own feelings and the feelings of others. They understand that communicating their feelings can make someone feel better ("I know how you feel, Chris. When I started kindergarten I cried the first day too.") They show a dawning awareness of the meaning of friendship, for example, that friends are more likely to forgive an unintended slight ("I tried to go up to Jim to play with him again, but he won't come near me . . . when a kid really isn't your friend yet they don't know you didn't mean to do it to them.")

Given the understanding of the connection between one's own feelings and the feelings of others, it should not be surprising that at this age children start showing the self-reflective, metacognitive awareness of empathic distress that I consider a requisite of mature empathy. In a study by Strayer (1993), 5-, 7-, 8-, and 13-year-olds were shown filmed vignettes of children in highly distressing situations (child unjustly punished by parent; disabled child learning to climb stairs with a cane; child forcibly separated from family). Afterward, the subjects were asked if they felt anything while watching each vignette and why they felt that way. Most of the 7-year and older subjects and a few 5-year-olds said they felt sad because of the film-child's feelings or his situation, indicating they understood that their own sad feeling was an empathic response to what happened to the other child. The younger children did not seem to understand this. These findings suggest that before 6 or 7 years, children may respond with veridical empathic distress – they feel what is appropriate to the other's situation – but they do not realize that their distressed feeling was caused by the other's situation, that they were empathizing. It is interesting that this metaempathic awareness precedes by a year or two children's metalinguistic awareness that words are elements of language and independent of the objects and events to which they refer (Wetstone, 1977). The reason for this may be that metalinguistic awareness is more abstract and lacks empathy's personal experiential cues.

But wait! Radke-Yarrow, Zahn-Waxler, and Chapman (1983) cite a personal communication from Lois Murphy concerning a 4-year-old boy who, upon hearing about the death of his friend's mother, said solemnly, "You know, when Bonnie grows up, people will ask her who was her mother and she will have to say 'I don't know.' You know, it makes tears come to my eyes." If we take this child's words literally, they suggest a 4-year-old can be fully aware that the source of his distress lies in another person's distressing situation, which contradicts the research. How to explain the discrepancy? One answer is that young children are metacognitively aware of their empathic distress earlier in the natural state than in the laboratory, because of salient distress cues from victims that immediately preceded and clearly caused the victims' empathic distress. Furthermore, in this particular case, the child may have been a precocious, older 4-year-old – not far out of line with Strayer's few advanced five-year-olds. (But see below for another explanation of his "precocious" metacognitive empathic distress.)

By 8 or 9 years, children understand that the same event can cause opposed feelings ("He was happy that he got the present but disappointed that it wasn't what he wanted") (Fischer, Shaver, & Cornochan, 1990; Gnepp, 1989) – although they can recognize opposed feelings a year or two earlier when prompted by an adult to consider the person's emotional reaction to each component of the conflict (Peng, Johnson, Pollock, Glasspool, & Harris, 1992). Eight- or-nine-year-olds also know something about the causes and consequences of self-esteem in others, for example, that people feel worse if they fail for lack of ability than lack of effort (Weiner, Graham, Stern, & Lawson, 1982). (This may be true mainly in merit-oriented societies, where ability is a major factor in self-esteem.)

By 9 or 10, according to a study by Gnepp and Gould (1985), children's knowledge of another's recent experience may begin to affect their awareness of his feelings in a similar situation. The subjects – kindergartners, third-, fifth-, and seventh-graders – were told short stories about children (a child is bitten by a gerbil and the next day his teacher announces it is his turn to feed the class gerbil). About half the third graders and two-thirds of the fifth graders correctly used the child's prior experience (they said he would be afraid to feed the class gerbil). This, of course, also means that half the third-graders and a third of the fifth-graders were unable to use the child's prior experience even though it was recent, clearly relevant, and made salient by the teacher moments before they made their judgments. The findings suggest that children are 9 or 10 years old before they begin to realize that another's feelings are influenced by his or her recent experience. This seems late to me, given the level of knowledge about emotion that younger children have, as discussed above.

The findings obtained by Pazer, Slackman, and Hoffman (1981) may be a little closer to the mark. Children were asked to state how "mad" they would be if someone acted in a harmful manner toward them (e.g., stole their cat). The experimental subjects were then given extenuating background information about the culprit (e.g., his own cat had run away and his parents would not get him another one). The subjects in this group who were 8 years or older said they would be less mad than control subjects who were given background information of equal word length but not extenuating. Younger subjects were not affected by the background information. This brings us down to 8 years as the age at which children begin to consider another's previous experience when judging his or her feelings in a situation.

But even 8 years seems a lot when we consider Radke-Yarrow et al.'s (1983) anecdote about the 4-year-old boy, cited above: If a 4-year-old can consider another's future, he can surely consider another's past. For this reason and because that anecdote has been cited uncritically as showing more social-cognitive sophistication in 4-year-olds than the research seems to warrant – and since further details are unavailable – the anecdote deserves close scrutiny.

A possible explanation is that the boy simply parroted something he overheard: The girl's future without a mother is just the sort of thing adults might talk about at the mother's funeral. On the other hand, adults are not likely to think the girl's big problem will be not knowing who her mother is; that sounds more like a child's construction. It seems more likely that the boy did not parrot adult words but, if not for the adult conversation, his attention, like any 4-year-old's, would be captured by the salient distress cues in the immediate situation. The adult conversation about the girl's future without a mother could well have activated his concerns about his own mother, but in any case it could explain his future-oriented response. All things considered, the boy's verbal response is best interpreted, I think, as an early, rudimentary, externally stimulated, and probably temporary expansion of a young child's time perspective – a precursor to the mature, spontaneous time perspective that appears later in life. Such external stimulation was not available in the experimental studies described earlier, which may explain why the "experimental competence" seems to lag "natural competence."

Regarding the seeming metacognitive dimension of the boy's empathic distress, the adult conversation about the girl's future could have led him to make the connection between the image of the girl without a mother and the tears and empathic sadness he was feeling at the time. This would exemplify an early, externally stimulated, rudimentary form of metacognitive empathic distress.

*Adolescence.* By 12 or 13 years, children can compensate for disparities between what a person feels in a situation and the feeling that is normally expected in that situation. They know, for example, that people who look sad when they should be happy (e.g., they just won a prize) probably feel sadder than people who look sad in situations in which they should be sad (Rotenberg & Eisenberg, (1997).

People who need help may not always want to be helped. Indeed, I think most people, at least in our individualistic society, are ambivalent about being helped except when they are desperate. Race may be a factor in this ambivalence: Black subjects' self-esteem decreased when they were given unsolicited help by Whites, though not by Blacks (Schneider, Major, Luhtanen, & Crocker (1996). Young children seem oblivious to other people's ambivalence about being helped, although they feel ambivalent about being helped themselves: Eight-to-ten-year-olds were found to worry about losing face when helped by a peer tutor (Depaulo, Dull, Greenberg, & Swain, 1989), but it is not until 16 years or so that they think twice before offering help in order to avoid putting the other at a social disadvantage (Midlarsky & Hannah, 1985).

*Adulthood.* People are sometimes ambivalent about being empathized with, let alone helped. This may occur after a long illness or period of mourning.

> When it [death in the family] happened I was shocked and very upset. I took a week off from school to get myself together. And, afterwards, I just wanted to get my life back to where it was before the death. When people would call me all I could hear was sympathy and pity in their voices. But I didn't want to hear sadness and be sad. I wanted to go on with my life because I had accepted the death and was ready to move on. So I wanted to talk about other things and to laugh but I couldn't because others were still grieving around me – laughing just didn't seem right. (Undergraduate student)

A woman responded to an article I wrote on empathy as follows:

> Having spent last year battling advanced breast cancer, I have perhaps a different perspective of what I want in empathy. I greatly appreciate the outpouring of kindness of others, but I don't want pity; pity isn't constructive. During my ordeal, I valued people who, with an underlying care and concern for my dire condition, could nevertheless remain cheerful and optimistic, who could encourage me to see the positive, beautiful, and wonderful – and, yes, the humorous. . . . Should we show our empathy by approaching each person with the knowledge of his certain mortality, or should we instead keep in mind another truth – that for now at least we are alive?

Both these people are saying that just because someone is dying or has lost a loved one does not mean he or she must remain somber and forever focused on his or her illness or loss. And when one can free oneself from depression, others should celebrate life with him or her even if they are not as successful in ridding themselves of gloomy thoughts. They may both be right, and this approach to another's tragedy – remaining aware of the other's condition and yet sharing with the other whatever he or she is feeling at the moment – may mark a kind of metacognitive, veridical empathy seen only in adults. I cite two examples from my own experience. One, I know a couple who had a child with cerebral palsy. The child did not know he had a problem in his early years. The parents of course felt sad when they were with him but could suspend their sadness and whip up tremendous enthusiasm when playing with him, even forgetting for the moment his (and their) plight. Two, I visited a close friend and colleague hospitalized with an advanced, spreading cancer. We were discussing his problems when I had the feeling, probably from his voice and facial expression, that he wanted to change the topic. We talked for two hours about recent infancy research (infancy was his research topic) and its implications for theory. During that time he was vibrant and excited about the findings, and we both forgot about his illness. When I left, he said it had been the most enjoyable afternoon he had had in months. He said he was tired of everybody's sympathy and kind words and especially tired of having to put his visitors at ease. This incident illustrates not only the type of adult empathic distress under discussion, but also another type of empathic distress: Despite this person's dire condition, he was not so self-absorbed as to ignore the feelings of his visitors; and he exerted himself to help them through the awkwardness, discomfort, and sadness he could imagine they were experiencing on his behalf.

Finally, I call attention to the experience of adults in certain professions, particularly the helping professions, which can add to the sophistication of their empathic responsiveness. Psychotherapists, for example, may realize that it can be therapeutically valuable to hold back on expressing the empathic grief they feel for a patient, at least temporarily, on those occasions when expressing empathic grief would make it difficult for the patient to express any negative feelings he may have about the relative or friend who has died.[1] In these

1. The idea of therapists holding back on expressing empathic grief was suggested to me by Tatiana Friedman.

instances, the therapist's empathic grief may include empathizing with the patient's ambivalence toward the dead person.

This review and discussion should give you a rough idea of the progress individuals make as they grow up in understanding the causes, consequences, and correlates of an increasingly complex array of emotions. Future research may fill in the gaps and allow more precise delineation of the ages and possibly stages associated with each advance in emotion understanding. My main point is that people's ability to empathize fully with another is linked to their understanding of what lies behind the other's feelings, and this understanding continues to develop through adolescence and adulthood. The discussion has been confined to empathic responses to others in the immediate situation. We now turn to empathic distress for another's life condition.

## EMPATHIC DISTRESS BEYOND THE SITUATION

At some point in development, owing to the emerging conception of self and others as continuous persons with separate histories and identities, children become aware that others feel joy, anger, sadness, fear, and low esteem not only in the immediate situation but also in the context of a larger pattern of life experience. Consequently, although they continue to feel empathically distressed in response to another's immediate pain or discomfort, they can also respond with empathic distress to what they imagine to be the other's chronically sad or unpleasant life condition.

This mental representation of the other's plight – his or her typical day-to-day level of distress or deprivation, opportunities available or denied him or her, future prospects – may fall short of what one considers a minimal standard of well-being (socially determined). When that happens, I expect observers to feel empathic distress. Furthermore, this empathic distress should be enhanced when observers' representation of the other's life reminds them of similar events in their own past. The observer may re-live these events (self-focused role-taking) and/or imagine the victim's chronically sad state (other-focused role-taking). As a result, the observer's mental representation of the victim's unhappy life both generates and becomes charged with empathic affect, that is, it becomes a "hot" cognition. In this way, people may respond empathically to persons whose lives they imagine are filled with sadness and deprivation (chronically ill, emotionally deprived, economically depressed) – and this can happen even in the victim's absence.

When the victim is present, observers also respond as usual to distress cues from the victim and from the victim's situation. The question may be asked, how does empathy for another's life condition interact with empathy for his or her immediate distress? It seems reasonable that if the two are congruent, they will enhance each other: If the other is sad, one's empathic sadness is intensified by knowing the sadness is not transitory but reflects a sad life; if one knew about and empathized with the other's sad life beforehand, one would be more sensitive to his or her immediate signs of sadness.

When the two sources of empathy are contradictory, however, observers must deal with the contradiction, which can have different causes. The other may not be as sad as expected because his problem (terminal illness) has been kept secret from him; he is in denial; or he may be fully aware but accepts his plight and is trying to enjoy life. A close friend (a different one) with cancer was deciding between surgery and radiation but just wanted to talk as usual about sports and the stock market, and with the usual gusto – about anything but his condition. Had I been openly empathic it could have disrupted his denial, so I went along, got lost in conversation and enjoyed myself; empathic distress was kept under control in the back of my mind, but it returned afterward. The point is that adults do not respond in such situations by simply empathizing with the other's momentary happy state, as children might. My hypothesis is that most adults realize that another's momentary pleasure is a less compelling index of his or her well-being than a sad life; they therefore respond with empathic sadness, sadness mingled with joy, or sadness following joy.

Here are two examples from students, which show observers' unmitigated sadness despite the victim's pleasure at the time. The second also shows how empathy with others' distressed lives can motivate the choice of a helping profession.

My cousin's mom died. He was too young to understand and he just kept on playing with his toys. I tried to smile and play with him but I kept on thinking about how not having his mother would affect him. He wouldn't have the sweet hugs when he bumped his knee. Especially since his father was strict and very much a disciplinarian. And all that I could think of was that the softness of his mother was gone and he'd miss that. But he wasn't recognizing it. He thought everything was great.

It was a beautiful day and I was having fun in the park with a friend. We were joking around and laughing when I noticed a child about four years old who had a severe case of Down Syndrome. She must have been having a blast because she was laughing. I no longer was. I kept thinking how horrible it must be to live life with such a handicap, and how I would feel as the mother of such a child, or as an individual with the same impairment. I kept thinking of how she would feel when she got older and could not attend a normal school like the other children her age that lived in the neighborhood. Yet her ignorance of the situation was remarkable. She was enjoying . . . [the] life that was given to her, and whatever obstacles . . . would come in the future she would learn to defeat. For some reason this logical truth just did not ease the feeling that I was having. This child is not unique, and I often experience these same reactions to those I feel that life has dealt an unfair hand. In response to these emotions, I have decided to become a special ed teacher so that I may be able to help in some way.

There are other contradictions between a person's life and his or her immediate behavior. Someone does something that makes me angry; I find out that his harmful act was due to a sad event in his life and that knowledge arouses empathy and reduces my anger. My colleagues and I commuted to work, taking a bus to the train. We were infuriated day after day when buses that were not full passed us by. We finally complained to one of the bus drivers, who told us about the impossible schedules they had to follow to keep their jobs. That was enough to make us empathic and end our anger toward the drivers (but not the bus company). The study by Pazer et al.

(1981) discussed earlier demonstrates the same thing: Extenuating circumstances that put a harmdoer in a sympathetic light reduced subjects' anger toward the harmdoer.

My point is not that we ignore the victim's feelings in the situation, but we are thinking as well as feeling animals and cannot totally dismiss the other's general condition from our minds. Our empathic feelings inevitably involve some mixing of emotions in these situations. Some people alternate back and forth between empathizing with the victim's feelings and empathizing with his or her life condition. In general, I hypothesize that the victim's immediate stimulus value will have stronger affective pull and the knowledge of his life condition will have lower priority *at first* (unless one knows about it beforehand). With cognitive processing, however, the affective pull of the victim's immediate feelings is reduced, possibly overridden by the observer's being reminded of the victim's life condition. Empathy with the victim's feeling in the situation may then be transformed into empathy with the victim's life condition. This transformation – affective decentration (?) – presumably begins when the observer recognizes the contradiction between the victim's behavior and life condition.

In other words, I hypothesize that the mental image of the other's general life condition cannot be ignored. It operates independently of and sometimes overrides the immediate situational cues or expressive behavior of the other person. It follows that responding empathically to the image of the other's life may involve a certain amount of distancing: One responds partly to one's mental image of the other rather than to the stimulus immediately presented by the other. It may also follow, developmentally, that once a person engages in such distancing he may no longer respond only to another's immediate stimulus value; he may always assume, or wonder about the other's life beyond the situation.

It should be clear from this discussion that information about another's previous, or expected future experience may affect one's empathic distress in two ways: (a) One empathizes with the victim's life condition; (b) one empathizes with the victim's immediate distress, and this empathic distress is affected by information about the other's life condition. The first type is our focus here and is more advanced developmentally because it requires the ability to represent another's life condition and respond to the representation empathically. The second type was discussed earlier under the topic of veridical empathic distress in middle childhood and is repeated here because it frequently accompanies the first.

This discussion points up an important advantage of defining empathy as not requiring an affect match between observer and model: Requiring a match would rule out the contradictions between immediate situation and life condition as being relevant to empathy. It should be noted, however, that **there is a sort of match after all – the match between the observer's affective response to the observer's representation of the victim's life condition, and the victim's likely response to that same representation.** The victim may be defending against that representation because the reality of the life it represents is too painful for him or her to bear. The victim consequently feels less distress than the observer feels on the victim's behalf.

*When can children empathize with another's life?* When do children have the sense of others as continuous persons with their own histories and identities, which is necessary for them to respond empathically to another's life condition? There is no direct research but the research on self-identity provides a clue. In Erikson's scheme, children do not have a sense of themselves as continuous persons with a history and identity until adolescence. The gender and ethnic identity research (Ruble & Martin, 1998), however, suggests European American children understand that their gender and ethnic identity are stable, consistent, and permanent by around 5 to 6 years and 6 to 7 years respectively. It therefore seems reasonable to assume that around 5 to 8 years is the age at which children have a sense of others as having a history, an identity, and a life.

Whether they actually empathize with another's life condition at that age is another question. On the one hand, we might expect children's attention to be fixed or "centered" on the more salient personal and situational cues of another's distress in the situation.

Owing to the powerful impact of conditioning, association, and mimicry, the "pull" of these cues may be powerful enough to capture a child's attention, with the result that his empathic response is based on these cues and influenced not at all by his knowledge of the victim's unhappy life. It might thus take awhile before children can transcend the salient stimuli and empathize with another's life condition. This would fit with Gnepp and Gould's (1985) finding, noted above, that children could not use clearly relevant, recently acquired information about another child's experience to predict that child's feelings in a similar situation, until 9 or 10 years of age.

On the other hand, we must entertain the possibility that the 4-year-old boy's empathic grief over his friend's loss was actually intensified by the vision of his friend's future life without a mother. Though that vision may have been stimulated by adult conversation, it might still signify a rudimentary, though long-term future time perspective that contributes to empathic distress. Research is clearly needed on the development of a long-term time perspective, how it is influenced by context, and how it mediates the way in which children's knowledge of another's past or anticipated future influences their empathic response in the present.

*Empathy for a distressed group.* It seems likely that with further cognitive development, especially the ability to form social concepts and classify people into groups, children will eventually be able to comprehend the plight not only of an individual but also of an entire group or class of people such as those who are economically impoverished, politically oppressed, social outcasts, victims of war, or mentally retarded. This combination of empathic distress and the mental representation of the plight of an unfortunate group would seem to be the most advanced form of empathic distress, as it is hard to imagine a child being able to empathize with a group before he can empathize with the mental representation of an individual's life. The sequence from empathy with an individual's life to empathy with his or her group may show up in a single occasion, as when one empathizes with an individual and then realizes he is an exemplar of a group or category of people who share his plight. A case in point is the student quoted earlier who empathized with a Down Syndrome child as an individual but also as someone who was "not unique" but one of many "that life has dealt an unfair hand." Also, I assume that many people who saw the famous picture of a fireman carrying a dead, burned baby must have felt empathic distress for the baby and the parents, and other pictured victims, before generalizing to empathic distress for the Oklahoma City bombing victims as a group. (Should this be called media-produced or media-enhanced empathic distress for a group?)

One group of more than passing interest is that composed of society's economically least advantaged members. If one empathized with that group, this could underlie the motivation for adopting political ideologies centered around alleviation of the group's plight (Hoffman, 1980, 1990). It could also provide an internal motive base for accepting a system of distributing society's resources that helps the least advantaged even at some cost to oneself (higher taxes). This issue will be taken up in chapter 9's discussion of empathy's relation to principles of distributive justice.

If one can empathize with an individual's life condition that contradicts his immediate behavior, one should be able to do the same thing with a group. This report by a student is a good illustration of how one can empathize with both an oppressed group's life condition and its contradictory, though understandable behavior:

> When I read accounts of slaves in America who were often extremely religious and quite optimistic when in religious services, I feel somewhat happy that these people were doing something that gave them a sense of joy, even ecstasy, but I am reminded of the fact that they were oppressed and this is a false sense of joy or hope in the midst of an unpleasant, unfortunate, and unfair life. I feel happy that they are happy despite being enslaved, but I also feel bad for them in general but especially in light of the fact that this religious hope or joy is really a false sense of security. It was truly a bitter irony that they took joy from the promised salvation of this religion, given to them by the slave owners who they wanted to be liberated from.

## TRANSFORMATION OF EMPATHIC INTO SYMPATHETIC DISTRESS

Thus far I have suggested that observers' empathic distress includes both an affective component and a cognitive component derived from their cognitive sense of others as distinct from themselves. Theorists going back at least to the early 1960s have noted that how a person experiences an affect is heavily influenced by pertinent cognition ("One . . . identifies this stirred-up state in terms of the characteristics of the situation and one's apperceptive mass" [Schachter & Singer, 1962, p. 380]). These writers attempt to explain how we distinguish among different affects (anger, joy, fear) aroused directly. Quite apart from their explanation for directly aroused emotions, about which there has always been disagreement (Zajonc, 1980), the cognitive sense of oneself and others as separate, independent entities is so intrinsic to *empathically* aroused affect as to alter the very quality of the observer's affective experience. It follows that once children have a sense of themselves as separate from others, something happens to the quality of their empathic distress. One possibility is that when children discover that the pain or discomfort is someone else's, they simply turn away and respond as though the problem was not theirs. Some children do that. But the weight of the evidence – which includes the research connecting empathic distress to helping (chapter 2), the argument from human evolution (Hoffman, 1981), and the many studies and anecdotes cited here – is that most children do not turn away but respond with the same level of empathic distress as previously, and, in addition, they are motivated to help the victim.

My hypothesis, more specifically, is that once children have separate images of themselves and others, their own empathic distress, which is a parallel response – that is, a more or less exact replication of the victim's actual or presumed feeling of distress – may be transformed at least in part into a more reciprocal feeling of concern for the victim; and the motive to comfort themselves is correspondingly transformed into a motive to help the victim. This developmental transformation fits with how older children and adults report feeling when observing someone in distress: They continue to respond in a partly egoistic manner – to feel uncomfortable and highly distressed themselves – but they also experience a feeling of compassion or what I call sympathetic distress for the victim, along with a conscious desire to help.[2]

In other words, **the same advance in self–other differentiation that moves children from "egocentric" to "quasi-egocentric" empathy, produces a qualitative transformation of empathic into sympathetic distress.** From then on and continuing into adulthood, children's empathic distress always includes a sympathetic component and, insofar as it does, children want to help because they feel sorry for the victim, not just to relieve their own empathic distress.[3] The sympathetic distress component of empathic distress is thus the child's first truly prosocial motive.

It is difficult to test a hypothesis about a qualitative developmental shift, but there is convergent circumstantial evidence in favor of it. First, there is the supportive developmental research I cited showing that children progress from responding to another's distress by seeking comfort for themselves, to seeking comfort for the victim (Zahn-Waxler, Radke-Yarrow, & King, 1979; Zahn-Waxler, Radke-Yarrow, Wagner, & Chapman, 1992). Second, three groups of investigators tested the hypothesis directly by predicting that advances in self–other differentiation predate children's shift from empathic to sympathetic distress (Bischoff-Kohler, 1991; Johnson, 1992; Zahn-Waxler et al., 1979). All three studies found, as expected, that mirror-self-image–recognition predicts later sympathetic distress and helping behavior.

Demonstrating the actual steps in the transition from empathic to sympathetic distress is even more difficult but can be done with

2. This distinction between empathic and sympathetic distress is similar to Scheler's (1913/1954) distinction between "vicarious feeling" and "fellow-feeling" and his view that the first is necessary but not sufficient for the second (p. 14).
3. It is questionable whether children ever help just to relieve their empathic distress. There are easier ways to do this such as turning away from the victim, which, as the research indicates, they rarely do.

anecdotes showing the expected combination of empathic and sympathetic distress in the second year. I described one incident about a child whose typical response to his own distress, beginning late in the first year, was to suck his thumb with one hand and pull his ear with the other. Early in his second year, on seeing a sad expression on his father's face, the child looked sad and sucked his thumb, while pulling his father's ear (Hoffman, 1978). Three similar anecdotes were reported by Radke-Yarrow and Zahn-Waxler (1984): One child's first prosocial act alternated between gently touching the victim and gently touching himself; another child comforted his crying mother by wiping her tears while wiping his own eyes although there were no tears; and a third child, who saw his mother bump her elbow, did the following: rubbed her elbow, rubbed his own elbow, said "Ow," and grimaced as though in pain. And, in a study by Main, Weston, and Wakeling (1979), a child who observed an adult "clown" pretending to cry, said "man crying" very sadly, went to his father's lap and from there with a sad expression repeatedly addressed the clown as if to comfort or distract him.

In young children, especially during the transitional period, only part of their empathic distress may be transformed into sympathetic distress, as illustrated by the child who sucked his thumb and pulled his father's ear. With further advances in social cognition and a sharpened sense of the other, the transformation of empathic into sympathetic distress becomes more complete. However, a purely empathic component may remain, even in adulthood. This dual, empathic/sympathetic feature of adult empathic distress is evident in the combined self-and-other-focused role-taking mechanism described in chapter 2. It is also illustrated by the phenomena of "empathic over-arousal" and "compassion fatigue," discussed in chapter 8, and the observation that nurses early in their training may experience a conflict between feelings of sympathetic distress, which include an intense desire to help their severely ill patients, and their own empathic distress which makes it difficult at times even to stay in the same room with those patients (Stotland, Matthews, Sherman, Hansson, & Richardson, 1979).

**Insofar as the transformation of empathic into sympathetic dis-**

tress takes place, the last three stages of empathic distress (quasi-egoistic, veridical, beyond the situation) are also stages of sympathetic distress. This should be understood by the reader, even though I continue using the term empathic distress for convenience, except when to avoid confusion I refer to empathic/sympathetic distress.

When a person has advanced through the five stages and encounters someone in physical, emotional, or economic distress, he or she is exposed to a network of information about the victim's condition. The network may include verbal and nonverbal expressive cues from the victim, situational cues, and one's knowledge about the victim's life. These sources of information are processed differently: Empathy aroused by nonverbal and situational cues is mediated by the largely involuntary, cognitively shallow processing modes (mimicry, conditioning, association). Empathy aroused by verbal messages from the victim or one's knowledge about the victim requires more complex processing by mediated association and role-taking. In role-taking's most highly developed form, observers may act out in their minds the emotions and experiences suggested by the above information and introspect on all of it. In this way they gain understanding and respond affectively to the circumstances, feelings, and wishes of the other, while maintaining the sense that this is a separate person from themselves.

The various cues, arousal modes, and processing levels usually contribute to the same empathic affect, but contradictions do occur – for example, between different expressive cues, such as facial expression and tone of voice, or between expressive and situational cues. A more important contradiction is the one I discussed between one's knowledge of the other's life condition and the other's immediate behavior. In this case, the expressive and situational cues of the other's feelings may lose a lot of emotional force for observers who know they only reflect a temporary state. Imagine a poor lower-class boy, unaware of his poverty and its implications for his future life course, laughing and having fun. A child observer unaware of the boy's limited prospects feels unalloyed empathic joy. The boy's limited prospects are not easily dismissed by a mature observer, who realizes they are a more compelling index of his welfare than his immediate joy and consequently feels empathic sadness or joy mingled with sadness. The most advanced level of empathic distress thus involves distancing: It is partly an affective response to one's mental image of the victim, not just his immediate stimulus value. This fits my definition of empathy, not as an exact match of another's feelings but as an affective response more appropriate to another's situation than one's own.

## COGNITIVELY EXPANDED BYSTANDER MODEL

Though we deal with affective empathy, the role of cognition has been evident throughout – in the higher-level empathy-arousing modes of mediated association and role-taking, in the central role of self–other differentiation in early empathy development, in the importance of social cognition to veridical empathy and beyond. What I do here is highlight some key points about cognition that may be buried in the details of arousal mechanisms and developmental stages: (a) Cognitive development enables humans to form images, represent people and events, and imagine themselves in another's place; and (b) because represented people and events can evoke affect (Fiske, 1982; Hoffman, 1985), **victims need not be present for empathy to be aroused in observers.**

Empathy can thus be aroused when observers **imagine** victims: when they read about others' misfortunes, when they discuss or argue about economic or political issues, or even when they make Kohlbergian judgments about hypothetical moral dilemmas. A 13-year-old male subject gave this response to the question, "Why is it wrong to steal from a store?": "Because the people who own the store work hard for their money and they deserve to be able to spend it for their family. It's not fair, they sacrifice a lot and they make plans and then they lost it all because somebody who didn't work for it goes in and takes it." This subject seemed to turn an abstract moral question about stealing into an empathy-relevant question by hypothesizing a victim and imagining his inner states (motivation to work hard, expectation of reward, future plans, disappointment).

In other words, cognitive development expands the bystander model to encompass an enormous variety of situations, limited not by the other's physical presence but only by the observer's imagination.

# CHAPTER 4

# Empathic Anger, Sympathy, Guilt, Feeling of Injustice

To recapitulate what I have covered so far, I have defined empathy as an affective response more appropriate to another's situation than one's own, described five mechanisms of empathic arousal ranging from classical conditioning to role-taking, and delineated stages in the development of empathic distress. Despite the focus on empathic affect, I have also pointed out the important contributions of cognition to the arousal and development of empathic distress and generalizing beyond the immediate situation. In this final chapter on the bystander model, affect continues to share center stage with cognition – in this case, causal attribution.

Most people make spontaneous attributions about the cause of events (Weiner, 1985), and they surely do this when observing someone in distress. Depending on the attribution, their empathic distress may be reduced, neutralized, or transformed into other empathic affects. It may be reduced or neutralized when the victim is viewed as responsible for his own plight. Humans have a tendency, when the circumstances are ambiguous, to attribute the cause of another's action (but not their own action) to his own internal dispositions: the "fundamental attribution error" (Jones & Nisbett, 1971). They also have a tendency to blame the victim for his or her own misfortune in order to support their "belief in a just world" (I'll be safe if I don't act that way) (Lerner & Miller, 1978). But given the evidence that humans tend to empathize with and help others in distress (chapter 2), it seems clear that blaming victims is not incompatible with empathy.

Bystanders are especially likely to blame victims when causal information is ambiguous or there is a "factual" basis for doing so (rape victims who jog in dangerous places; spousal abuse victims who stay with the abusing spouse). A female undergraduate student wrote the following:

> I have seen and heard on the news on so many occasions that women are being raped or murdered during either very early or very late hours in the park. These women are usually alone. At first I am extremely saddened by the terrible news. But then I think about how many times I have heard this same event occur in the past, and I think that the women are stupid for jogging in the park under these circumstances. Even though I know nothing about the victim I assume that it is their fault that something has happened – possibly their stupidity, stubbornness, or ignorance. I lose my sympathy for them.

The discussion so far assumes that empathic distress is aroused first and causal information follows, and that the victim is not present. But what if one had advance information and blamed the victim beforehand? The only relevant research is Stotland's (1969) finding that the "set" to avoid empathizing with someone in pain does not stop subjects from empathizing. This suggests there may be a limit to the degree that advance knowledge of a victim's culpability will reduce observers' empathic distress, at least while they are attending to the victim (as were Stotland's subjects). It would be interesting to know whether observers who blame a victim can avoid empathizing by averting their gaze, plugging their ears, or thinking distracting thoughts. I suspect they can and discuss this in chapter 8.

Whether there is a factual base, and whether causal information follows or precedes empathic arousal, blaming a victim puts psychological distance between bystander and victim and reduces the bystander's empathic distress and motivation to help. Staub (1996) suggests this distancing is especially likely to occur when observers feel helpless, because it is extremely difficult to see others suffer when one can do nothing about it.

Aside from blaming the victim, observers' empathic distress may, depending on the cause of the victim's distress, be transformed into sympathetic distress, empathic anger, empathy-based feeling of injustice, or empathy-based guilt.

## SYMPATHETIC DISTRESS

Empathic distress may be transformed into sympathetic distress if the victim's pain or discomfort is clearly due to natural causes or is otherwise beyond the victim's control, as is the case with an accident, an illness, or the loss of a loved one. This is consistent with Weiner's (1982) classic analysis of the influence of causal attribution on emotion. Empathic distress may also be transformed into sympathetic distress when the victim's distress is salient and the cause is unclear, as in the developmental transformation of empathic into sympathetic distress discussed in chapter 3.

The evidence that empathic/sympathetic distress is reliably aroused and motivates bystanders to alleviate a victim's distress, and that empathic helpers focus on the ultimate consequences of their action for victims was presented in chapter 2. I also noted that when the costs are high, empathically aroused bystanders may not help. There are other, causal attributional reasons for not helping. For example, bystanders may not help if they think the person does not deserve it. Schmidt and Weiner (1988) asked college students this question: "You're walking across campus when a male student you don't know asks you to lend him your class notes from last week. Would you do it?" If the student was described as wearing an eye patch and dark glasses and needing the notes because eye problems prevented his taking his own notes, most of the subjects were sympathetic and said they would lend him their notes. But if the student was described as having gone to the beach instead of class, most of the subjects expressed anger at him and said they would not help. Some said they would help even then, which suggests, as noted earlier, that blaming the victim is not always incompatible with empathizing/sympathizing and helping ("he may have gotten himself into this mess but he still needs help").

## EMPATHIC ANGER

If someone else caused the victim's plight, one's attention may be diverted from the victim to the culprit. One may feel angry at the culprit because one sympathizes with the victim or because one empathizes with the victim and feels oneself vicariously attacked, or both. One's feelings may alternate between empathic/sympathetic distress and empathic anger. Empathic anger may crowd out empathic/sympathetic distress entirely.

Empathic anger has been neglected in the morality literature, although over two centuries ago Adam Smith (1759/1976) wrote, "The furious behavior of an angry man is more likely to exasperate us against himself than against his enemies" (p. 260). Smith claimed that we cannot identify with such a man because we are unaware of his provocation, but we plainly see the victim's situation and therefore identify with the victim.

A hundred years later, John Stuart Mill (1861/1979) made the connection between empathic anger and morality explicit when he suggested that empathic anger, which he described as "the natural feeling of retaliation . . . rendered by intellect and sympathy applicable to . . . those hurts which wound us through wounding others" (p. 469), serves as the guardian of justice. Although Mill generally stressed rationality as the basis of morality, he believed that the only way to convince someone to abide by a moral principle is not a rational argument showing it is in his long-term interest, but "sanctions" which are "private pleasures to be gained and pains to be avoided" (p. 264). The ultimate, intrinsically desirable sanction is the "feeling of unity" with others that is based largely on empathy. Mills contended further that people's response's to someone's unjust behavior – their judgment and feelings of resentment toward that person – are moral because of their empathy with the victim. In short, a moral society needs voices that are empathically angry enough to uphold the cause of justice, that is, to object to people who abuse others and be ready to punish them. Without such voices, there is nothing to stop the abusers.

Empathic anger may shift from one target to another. If I discover the victim had previously harmed the culprit, my empathic distress for the victim may decrease; I may even begin to empathize with the culprit and feel empathic anger at the victim. If I find out the victim – an abused wife – has a history of being mistreated but remains with her husband, I might assume she chooses to stay and is therefore responsible for her plight and less of a victim. This could reduce my empathic distress for the wife and empathic anger at the husband. But, if I learn that an abused wife has little choice either because she is economically dependent and her husband does not allow her to work, or because her husband threatens to kill her if she does not remain silent or if she leaves him (threats that are often carried out!), then I will likely return to feeling empathic distress for the wife and anger at the husband.

Young children often miss the nuances (when observing marital fights) and respond with empathic anger at the visible culprit. Older children may be more aware of subtleties but confused and angry at a mother who is a "floor mat" and does not "stand up" to an abusive husband. Here is a young woman who switched from empathic distress for her mother and anger at her father, to anger at her mother.

My dad is a strict disciplinarian. In the culture he was brought up in the man ruled the house. Usually this means that my mother's opinion does not count. That angers me. I feel my dad victimizes my mother, belittles her, always saying that what she says does not count. I used to feel very angry at my father and very bad for my mother. I still feel angry at my father but even more angry at my mom who does nothing to stand up for herself. She takes it all. She does nothing to defend herself or to act as a parent. When it comes to decision-making it's always "ask your father." I understand that she was brought up to live that way but because I was brought up in this country my views are different. I get more angry at her than at him, because she knows he's wrong yet chooses to remain with him and continue to allow it to happen.

*Two types of empathic anger.* There are two types of empathic anger. In the first, relatively simple type, the victim is angry at the abuser and the observer picks up that anger through the empathy-arousing mechanisms and feels empathic anger. In the second, more complex type, the victim feels sad, hurt, or disappointed but *not* angry at the abuser. The observer empathizes with these feelings, but also **feels empathy-based anger at the abuser as a result of taking the victim's perspective, even though the victim is not angry. In this case the observer's response is an empathic duality, including both an empathic-distress-for-victim component and empathy-based anger-at-aggressor component.** The two types of empathic anger are combined when the victim feels sad, hurt, disappointed, *and* angry. It should be noted that only the first type involves an affect match between observer and victim. But in keeping with my definition of empathy as a feeling that fits the other's situation, though not necessarily his feeling, I also count the second type as empathic anger.

The second type may be more prevalent in middle-class Americans and others who are socialized to inhibit aggressive behavior, because the angry feeling underlying it may also be inhibited (an unintended consequence of socialization?). The inhibition of anger, together with the emotional complexities of one's relationship with one's abuser, could make it difficult to feel angry at one's abuser. One may nevertheless be perfectly capable of feeling empathic anger when **someone else** is abused, because as an observer one may be unaware of the complexities and see the situation as a simple one involving culprit and victim, In that case one may experience anger as a **moral affect,** on behalf of the victim, not oneself.

> My friend Ellen lived next door to me since the fourth grade. Our families were close and we became like sisters. Though we went to different colleges, we both came to New York and continued the close relationship. . . . I hate to admit it but I know I can rely on her to be angry for me. For example, I recently had an argument with another close friend and for the life of me I could not get angry at him. I felt guilty that we couldn't work things out. I felt helpless and I felt like I failed. When Ellen got wind of what was happening, nothing but profanities came from her mouth. She basically said, "Joan, I'm sorry but it's not your fault. He's a &*!;@, if I ever see him again . . ." Somehow hearing her be angry made me feel better and even allowed me to feel angry.

This anecdote shows that *expressing empathic anger can help release a victim's direct anger*. It may do this by providing external validation that he is in the right, thus making angry feelings legitimate. I consider this a secondary prosocial motive function of empathic anger – secondary and subtle, but nevertheless prosocial. Empathic anger can also support a victim in the more direct sense of communicating "I am with you" (Bavelas et al., 1987). It seems reasonable to assume that if the tables were turned, the person who contributed the above anecdote, despite her difficulty in expressing direct anger, could feel empathic anger on behalf of her friend.

Empathic anger is often hard to distinguish from direct anger because it can crowd out the empathic distress that initiated it. More important, when empathic anger leads to aggressive behavior in defense of a victim it can be hard to distinguish from direct anger because the behavioral outcomes are similar: Aggression is aggression. Examples: A 17-month-old child in the doctor's office watched his brother get a shot and responded by hitting the doctor. Radke-Yarrow and Zahn-Waxler (1984) describe a toddler who hit someone who made his baby brother cry, and another toddler who tore up a newspaper that made his mother sad. Cummings, Hollenbeck, Iannotti, Radke-Yarrow, and Zahn-Waxler (1986) describe a highly aggressive toddler who learned to channel his aggression so well that by 6 years he expressed more empathic anger than any of his peers; the implication is that he was simply looking for acceptable reasons to express anger.[1]

There are times of course when the empathic basis for anger is clear: when it is accompanied by sympathetic concern for the victim. An undergraduate student wrote: "I hate the NYPD because of all the allegations of police brutality and I have a lot of sympathy towards the victims. I think I can understand why some people would riot against the police even though they weren't victims." The *New York Times* gave this account of a hero: A man pushed a woman

---

1. This child reminds me of adults who tout their own moral superiority as an excuse to punish others – a type of righteous indignation that must be distinguished from empathic anger, although doing this is not always easy.

onto the subway tracks; a bystander, age 26, who saw it happen, followed the man through the "subterranean labyrinth of escalators and corridors in the station," eventually holding the man captive in what the police called a bear hug until two officers arrived. "Call the police, call the police, this man just pushed someone under a train," the bystander yelled. He said he could not let the man get away "because that could have been my mom, because that could have been a friend of mine. . . . I know that someone is going to be lost without this person in their life" (Jan. 5, 1995, p. B8). Note that he did not do anything violent to the culprit; he just held him.

The empathic basis of anger is also evident in the finding that children from homes in which there is a lot of marital conflict often become upset, "angrily scolding the aggressor but also comforting the perceived victim" (Cummings & Davies, 1994). A 20-month-old girl "went from one parent to another saying 'hi' loudly to each while they were fighting. . . . After the mother responded with 'hi,' the child climbed up on the mother, put her arm around the mother's neck, patted the mother on the shoulder, and, finally, kissed her. . . . When the father approached, the child put up her hand and said 'go, go' to him" (p. 1279). This is not a pure bystander situation, of course, as the child's own welfare is implicated and she was clearly personally anxious as well as empathic. But empathic anger seems to be there all the same.

Finally, clinicians may feel empathic anger when patients tell of being abused. Here is a female therapist's (nonverbalized) response to a girl's highly distressed (but without any show of anger) description of being abused by her father: "What a slimy son-of-a-bitch to do that to an innocent child. How awful that no one protected her."

*Is empathic anger a prosocial motive?* A letter to the *New York Times* advanced the hypothesis that empathic anger is a more effective prosocial motive than sympathetic distress. "The pictures of starving children in Ethiopia are heart-wrenching but feeling sad isn't enough . . . we send a check, the pictures disappear from TV screens, and soon we forget that millions are dying. . . . Instead we should feel outraged that in a world of plenty hunger still exists.

Outrage produces action" (February 1985, p. D1). The John Stuart Mill quote above says the same thing: Justice requires empathic anger.

Unfortunately, there is no research on empathic anger's contribution to prosocial action. But it seems likely that, since anger in response to a threat to oneself "mobilizes energy and makes one capable of defending oneself with vigor" (Izard, 1977, p. 333), empathic anger in response to a threat to someone else would mobilize energy and make one capable of defending the victim. The examples I cited suggest that empathic anger is indeed a prosocial motive, and so do these excerpts from Oliner and Oliner's (1988) interviews of Germans who rescued Jews from the Nazis:

> "I think there was a double feeling: a feeling of compassion for Jews and anger toward the Germans." (p. 118)

> "When they started taking Jewish people, that really lit my fire. I couldn't stand it anymore. I really became full of hate because they took innocent people – especially when they took little kids. They took innocent people and I wanted to help." (p. 143)

> "Nobody was going to touch those children. I would have killed for them." (p. 148)

These quotes also illustrate the "dual" type of empathic anger.

To conclude this discussion, it should be clear that observers can at times feel empathic anger when there is no actual culprit, and they can at times not feel empathic anger when there is a culprit. Regarding the first possibility, if a person observes economically depressed people in a context in which the extravagant lifestyle of highly affluent others is salient, he might, through taking the role of the depressed group, feel empathic distress for them and empathic anger at the affluent others, even though they intended no harm, because they seemed to be flaunting their affluence. As for the second, a student wrote the following:

> I used to work with a woman who was about 70 years old. Because she was older she tended to be slower than the other (younger) girls. Her office manager would often yell at her in front of patients in the

waiting room and humiliate her for the silliest things. She would never say anything but afterwards she would go to the bathroom and cry her eyes out. I felt so sorry for her and I would often try to imagine what it would be like to be in her place. Honestly, I would hate to work in a place like that and I would hate to be humiliated in front of so many people. I often felt sorry for her – for what she had to go through daily at work.

Lots of empathic/sympathetic distress but no empathic anger.

## BYSTANDER GUILT OVER INACTION

Empathic observers who feel that the victim needs and deserves to be helped may nevertheless refrain from helping because of the competing presence of powerful egoistic motives such as avoiding involvement or fear. Oliner and Oliner (1988), as already noted, interviewed Germans who rescued Jews from the Nazis and Germans who did not; the nonrescuers who were highly empathic acknowledged fear as the major reason for their inaction. Whatever the reason, when innocent observers view themselves as allowing the victim's distress to happen or continue because of their inaction, guilt may be produced. That is, **the self-blame attribution transforms the observer's empathic distress into a feeling of guilt.** Note that this guilt is not from causing the victim's distress. Transgression guilt, where the observer is culpable, will be discussed in chapter 6. The model at this juncture of the discussion still employs an innocent bystander.

Though empathy-based guilt is, as we shall see, an effective motivator of prosocial acts like apologizing, making reparation, and becoming more considerate of others (Baumeister, Stillwell, & Heatherton, 1994), there has been little research specifically on guilt over inaction. There are enough anecdotes, however, to suggest that guilt over inaction exists and operates as a prosocial moral motive: Eighty percent of Schwartz's (1970) subjects who volunteered to contribute bone marrow said they would have felt guilty if they had not contributed; many of Eisenberg-Berg and Neal's (1979) subjects, who helped someone in need when given the opportunity to do so, explained afterward that they had helped because they would have felt bad otherwise. There is also scattered anecdotal evidence: Some of the White 1960s civil-rights activists admitted that they would have felt guilty if they had done nothing because that would have allowed the Southern Black people's victimization to continue (Keniston, 1968); a German who had saved Jews from the Nazis reported: "Unless we helped, they would be killed. I could not stand that thought. I never would have forgiven myself" (Oliner & Oliner, 1988, p. 168); and another German rescuer said: "I knew they were taking them and they wouldn't come back. I don't think I could live with that knowing that I could have done something" (p. 168).

Here are three everyday examples, closer to home. A student described a subway incident: "The woman kept hitting her kid. I felt I'd feel bad if I did nothing. So I got my keys and entertained the kid. He responded. The mother then acted better. I felt real good." Another student reported:

> Last summer I was in a swimming pool. When I got out of the pool I saw a child about 3 years old in the middle of a crowd crying. He kept saying "Mommy, Mommy." I figured he was lost. I felt so bad, all kinds of thoughts raced through my mind, like if I don't help, someone can take him and hurt him. I would feel devastated if I don't help and later find out he is dead, so I went over and helped him. I found his mother.

A high school student described an incident involving a classmate who was chronically rejected by her peers: "I'd feel bad if I didn't sit down with her though I didn't particularly want to."

In my early guilt research (Hoffman, 1970), I used a story-completion item in which a well-meaning central figure (same age and sex as the subject) is rushing to a movie with a friend and sees a child who seems lost. He suggests they help but the friend talks him out of it. The next day he hears that the child, left alone by his babysitter, ran into the street and was killed by a car. The adult version has an elderly person looking for something lost in the snow. In their completions, most subjects (fifth and seventh graders, and parents) had the central figure feeling intense guilt over doing nothing and allowing the tragedy to happen. The guilt over inaction often included empathic distress for the child or his parents and led to prosocial acts like helping the parents (mowing their lawn, running errands), going out of one's way to help children, and offering parents free baby-sitting. Older children and adults often had the hero criticize himself ("how could I be so selfish") and make a vow to reorder his priorities and think of others in the future. Besides the guilt's being followed by reparative action or reordering of one's priorities, there was another kind of evidence for its functioning as a motive: Guilt intensity dropped following a reparative act but was prolonged otherwise, which is similar to the decline in empathic distress following helping, discussed in chapter 2.

Even when bystanders try to help, they may feel guilty over not doing anything to prevent the event from happening in the first place, over not succeeding in their efforts to help, or over hesitating before helping. They may feel guilty over not doing anything to avoid the event because they assume it could have been avoided, that is, they engage in "counter-factual thinking" – they imagine alternative scripts in which an action of theirs undoes the outcome, and then they switch from "I could have" to "I should have" and feel guilty (Davis, Lehman, Silver, Wortman, & Ellard, 1996; Sanna & Turley, 1996). Bystanders who try to help may feel guilty if their efforts go for naught and they do not succeed in benefiting the victim, even if the reasons for failure are totally understandable and justified (Batson & Weeks, 1996).

Given these tendencies of bystanders to feel guilty, it seems reasonable to hypothesize that those who hesitate before helping might feel guilty because the delay allowed the victim to suffer in the interim. Assuming this is true, it then seems reasonable to hypothesize that bystanders are always vulnerable to some guilt, except in emergencies in which they act immediately and prevent harm to the victim. And the guilt that bystanders feel over hesitating, over failing in their efforts to help, and over not preventing the event in the first place may add to their motivation to help in similar situations in the future. To this extent, guilt is self-reinforcing and contributes to the further "learning" of guilt as a prosocial motive.

Guilt over inaction is cognitively demanding, as it requires not only being aware of the victim's suffering but also imagining what one might have done to help the victim or to prevent the injury. We would therefore expect guilt over inaction to increase with age, and there is some evidence that it does. Williams and Bybee (1994) asked 5th-, 8th-, and 11th-grade students to describe "things you have felt bad about not doing." Whereas only 8 percent of the 5th and 8th graders described one or more incidents in which they felt guilt over not helping, 20 percent of the 11th graders described such incidents. These findings may be misleading: the story-completion findings above showed that most 5th graders are vulnerable to extreme guilt when the consequence of their inaction was severe. And this was true even when others could be blamed (the friend who talked the "hero" out of helping, the driver of the car, the irresponsible baby-sitter, the parents who hired the baby-sitter).

*Anticipatory guilt over inaction.* We are cognitive beings, so once we experience guilt over inaction, we are more likely to anticipate feeling guilty the next time around. Anticipatory guilt should therefore accompany empathic distress in most bystander situations, as in the examples of the Germans who saved Jews cited earlier ("I knew I'd feel bad if I did nothing," "I don't think I could live with that knowing that I could have done something").

Emergency situations in which there is no time to reflect and anticipate guilt may be exceptions, as in the following example. A gasoline truck overturned and ignited on a Long Island highway. The cab of the vehicle was engulfed in flames and the driver was unconscious when a passerby stopped and pulled him from the flaming and potentially explosive wreckage. The passerby said later that the image of the man in the cab being engulfed by flames flashed through his mind, and he knew that if he were in the truck he would want someone to save him – there was no time to think. The passerby might well have felt guilty afterward if he had not helped or if he had tried but failed to save the man, but there was no time for reflection and anticipatory guilt may not have been a motive for risking his life to help.

These anecdotes say nothing about incidents in which bystanders feel no guilt over inaction or defend themselves against guilt. I mentioned Staub's suggestion that when people feel there is nothing they can do, they will often blame the victim as a way of distancing themselves and avoiding guilt. We can only guess how many of the millions of Germans who did not help Jews felt guilty, blamed the victims, or were simply unconcerned.

*Guilt and anger.* Here is an unusual example that seems to combine guilt over inaction and empathic anger; it also shows how hard it can be to distinguish empathic anger from direct anger and from a type of righteous anger that may mask direct anger.

A colleague asked her students to describe in writing *a recent situation in which you felt guilty about what you did or did not do. Be as specific as possible.* A student wrote: "I have felt guilty that I have not spoken up sooner about the needless suffering of lab animals. One hundred and ten MILLION ANIMALS ARE MURDERED ANNUALLY by so-called 'investigators' (including psychologists). However, NOW I INTEND TO FIGHT VERY STRONGLY TO STOP THESE MURDERERS. ANIMALS HAVE FEELINGS, ALSO!" In answer to the question *How often do you feel guilty?*, the student checked "very often" and added "whenever I see the evidence of torture." To the question *What were your reactions?*, the student responded "Wrote letters to congress to push HR 4805 Modernization of Primate Animals Lab Act thru congress." To the question *What are your ideas about why you felt guilty?*, "I LOVE ANIMALS." To *At the time did you have any other ideas about why you felt guilt?*, "Yes, I could imagine my cat being shocked, tortured, made to display aggressive behavior, being blinded, deprived of food and water, and I got DAMNED *ANGRY*. To *What if anything was wrong with what you did or did not do?*, "NOT ENOUGH. I MUST DO MORE TO STOP THE TORTURE. I still believe people are inwardly good (even psychologists). If they are made aware of the torture, pain, and suffering of these animals the MURDERERS WILL STOP" (underlining and uppercase in original).

I get the feeling that this person's repeated prosocial moral justifications and admissions of guilt are partly an excuse to express anger. Whether I am right or wrong, the example shows, as discussed earlier, the need for caution in interpreting someone's actions or words as empathic anger.

## EMPATHIC FEELING OF INJUSTICE

Besides causal attributions, people make inferences about whether victims deserve their plight. These inferences, which are usually about the victim's character or performance and are based on the victim's personal reputation or on stereotypes of the victim's ethnic group or social class, can affect an observer's empathic response. If the victim is viewed as bad, immoral, or lazy, observers may conclude that his or her fate was deserved and their empathic/sympathetic distress may decrease. But if the victim is viewed as basically good, observers may conclude that his or her fate was undeserved or unfair and their empathic/sympathetic distress, empathic anger, or guilt may increase. In the latter case, observers may also view him or her as a victim of injustice ("nonreciprocity" between deeds and outcomes). This may transform their empathic distress into an empathic feeling of injustice, including a motive to right the wrong. Zillman and Cantor (1977) found that fifth and sixth graders empathized with victims who were previously described in neutral terms or as benevolent, but not with victims who were previously described as malevolent.

A real-life example of empathic feeling of injustice is Coles's (1986) description of a 14-year-old Southern White schoolboy. After several weeks of joining his friends in harassing Black children trying to integrate his school, this boy, a popular athlete,

> began to see a kid, not a nigger – a guy who knew how to smile when it was rough going, and who walked straight and tall, and was polite. I told my parents, "It's a real shame that someone like him has to pay for the trouble caused by all those federal judges." Then it happened. I saw a few people cuss at him. "The dirty nigger," they kept on calling him and soon they were pushing him in a corner, and it looked like trouble, bad trouble. I went over and broke it up. . . . They all looked at me as if I was crazy.. . . .Before [everyone left] I spoke to the nigger. . . . I didn't mean to. . . . It just

came out of my mouth. I was surprised to hear the words myself: "I'm sorry." (pp. 27–28)

After this incident, he began talking to the Black youth, championing him personally while still decrying racial integration. Finally, he became the Black youth's friend and began advocating "an end to the whole lousy business of segregation." When pressed by Coles to explain his shift he attributed it to being in school that year and seeing "that kid behave himself, no matter what we called him, and seeing him insulted so bad, so real bad. Something in me just drew the line, and something in me began to change, I think" (p. 28).

The boy clearly felt sympathetic distress, empathic anger, and guilt. But what seemed to move him most was the contrast between the Black youth's admirable conduct and the way he was treated – as if he felt the victim was a fine person who deserved better. My interpretation is that the boy's empathic/sympathetic distress was transformed by the obvious lack of reciprocity between character and outcome into an empathic feeling of injustice.[2] The special importance of empathic feeling of injustice is that it may bridge the gap between empathic distress and justice principles, as will be discussed in detail in chapter 9.

## RAPID SHIFTS IN CAUSAL ATTRIBUTION

I described in chapter 2 how quickly empathic arousal occurs not only through the preverbal modes (conditioning, mimicry, association), but also through mediated association and role-taking due to the speed of cognitive processing. I assume the same is true of causal attributions and shifts among causal attributions.[3]

---

2. Gibbs (1991) and I (Hoffman, 1991) see it differently. In his view, such discrepancies between a victim's character and outcome make observers uncomfortable for two *independent* reasons: The observer empathizes with the victim, and the discrepancy violates the observer's purely cognitive motive for reciprocity. More about empathy and reciprocity in chapter 9.
3. Shifts in causal attributions can also be drawn out over time, as with the young woman described earlier who gradually shifted from empathy with

Here is an example of several causal attributions shifting back and forth in less than a minute, reported by a male graduate student whom I knew well enough to describe as an unusually empathic young man. He recounted a recent event in which he had seen the driver of an expensive sports car being wheeled on a stretcher to an ambulance. He had not seen the accident, arriving at the scene just afterward. He remembered this:

> I first assumed it was probably a rich smart-alec kid driving while drunk or on dope and I did not feel for him. I then thought this might be unfair, maybe he was rushing because of some emergency, suppose he was taking someone to the hospital, and then I felt for him. But then I thought, that was no excuse, he should have been more careful even if it was an emergency, and my feeling for him decreased. Then I realized the guy might be dying and I really felt bad for him again.

This response illustrates at once the human tendency to make causal attributions, the rapid shifts in causal attribution, and the resulting shifts in feeling that may occur in ambiguous situations. It also shows, as did some of my earlier examples, that blaming victims is not incompatible with empathic/sympathetic distress. The shifts in this person's thought processes may have been still more complex though hidden from him because of their speed. I wondered why an empathic person would blame the victim in the first place, so I asked him for details about how he felt when he first saw the accident. He suddenly remembered that his immediate response was "an intensely painful feeling of shock," quickly followed by derogatory attributions.

I suggest this was a case where "empathic over-arousal" was painful enough to transform empathic distress into personal distress; and derogating the victim was a cognitive defense that temporarily reduced his personal distress and made the situation more tolerable. This gave him time to gain control of his emotions, enabling him to respond to the stark reality of the victim's condition, *which remained*

her mother and empathic anger toward her father, to blaming her mother for not asserting herself.

*in view*, and again empathize, this time without having to derogate the victim. In other words, the derogatory attribution was as much a consequence (of empathic over-arousal) as a cause (of reducing empathy) – that is, a temporary defense against empathic over-arousal. The conflict between the painfully unpleasant empathic distress caused by the continuing presence of the victim and the observer's motivation to avoid that distress could thus have led to the series of revised causal attributions.

I find it interesting that in this person's initial report his causal attributions went back and forth and he remembered how each attribution brought about an increase or decrease in empathic distress. He remembered nothing about the influence of empathic distress on his attributions, that is, how empathic over-arousal may have led him to blame the victim. In other words, he was aware of the effect of his attributions on his feelings but not the effect of his feelings on his attributions – a cognitive-primacy bias that may reflect our society's value on rationality.

# PART II

# Transgression

# CHAPTER 5

# Guilt and Moral Internalization

We now move from the innocent bystander model to one in which the observer is a transgressive participant – transgressive because he is harming or thinking of acting in a way that may harm another. A transgression may be provoked, intentional, accidental, a by-product of conflict, or a violation of another's legitimate expectations. The moral issue is whether the transgressor is motivated to avoid the harmful act or at least feels guilty and acts prosocially afterward, and whether he or she acts in these ways even in the absence of witnesses – the hallmark of moral internalization. This chapter, then, deals with guilt and moral internalization.

Just as the bystander model is the prototypic moral encounter for the development of empathy, especially empathic distress, the transgression model is the prototypic moral encounter for empathy-based guilt, especially empathy-based transgression guilt. Transgression guilt differs from bystander guilt over inaction and from "virtual guilt" which will be discussed in chapter 7. The transgression model is also the prototypic moral encounter for moral internalization.

Empathy-based guilt is the key prosocial motive in transgressions involving harm to others and looms large in this chapter. I first introduce empathy-based guilt, give evidence for its existence and prosocial motive property, and discuss its development. The theories of moral internalization are then summarized, after which I explain the special importance of socialization, especially discipline, for guilt and moral internalization, which introduces chapter 6.

## GUILT

The first developmental account of guilt came from Freud. Strangely, Freud's guilt was not due to harming someone but was a largely unconscious throwback to early childhood based on anxiety over punishment or abandonment by parents. When this anxiety is activated by hostile feelings, first toward the parents but then toward anyone, it is transformed into guilt even if the hostile feelings are not expressed. In Freud's words, "A threatening external unhappiness, loss of love and punishment by external authority, has been exchanged for a lasting inner unhappiness, the tension of a sense of guilt." Freud recognized the pathological quality of this guilt and suggested humans also feel a more reality-based guilt but he did not come up with an alternative conception of guilt and its development, nor did his followers (Hoffman, 1970). This pathological quality may explain guilt's bad reputation and long neglect by academic psychologists.

In the late 1960s I advanced a more constructive, empathy-based theory of **interpersonal guilt, defined as a painful feeling of disesteem for oneself, usually accompanied by a sense of urgency, tension, and regret, that results from empathic feeling for someone in distress, combined with awareness of being the cause of that distress** (Hoffman, 1982c; Hoffman & Saltzstein, 1967). To keep from feeling guilty, a person can avoid carrying out harmful acts, or, having committed such an act, he can make reparation to the victim in the hope of undoing the damage and decreasing the feeling of guilt. (See Friedman, 1985, for an extension of the empathy-guilt formulation into the clinical domain.) In the intervening decades, a rather large body of research has provided support both for the existence of empathy-based guilt and for the hypothesis that it serves as a prosocial moral motive.

### Evidence for Empathy-Based Guilt

There are several lines of evidence for the existence of empathy-based guilt – narrative, correlational, and experimental. Narrative evidence is provided by Tangney, Marschall, Rosenberg, Barlow, and Wagner (1996), who found that children and adults often express empathic feelings in the course of describing personal guilt experiences. I found the same thing in my story-completion guilt research years ago, as will be discussed later in this chapter. Tangney et al. also report significant positive correlations between paper-and-pencil measures of empathy and guilt in college students, in fifth-grade children, and in the fifth-grade children's mothers, their fathers, their grandmothers, and their grandfathers (Tangney, 1991; Tangney, Wagner, Burggraf, & Fletcher, 1991). Indirect correlational support for empathy-based guilt is evident in the 1970s and 1980s parent-discipline research showing that both empathic distress and guilt in children relate positively to the same type of parental discipline (inductive discipline, discussed in chapter 6), and in the more recent finding of a positive correlation between empathy and guilt in children whose parents frequently use inductions (Krevans & Gibbs, 1996).

As for experimental evidence, Okel and Mosher (1968) induced male undergraduates to insult a fellow student (a confederate of the experimenter's), who became distressed over the insult. High-empathy subjects said later that they felt guilty over what they did and they would not have done it had they known how upset the victim would be. Thompson and Hoffman (1980) showed first-, third-, and fifth-grade children stories on slides (also narrated by the experimenter), in which a boy harms someone. The subjects in whom empathy was aroused, by asking them how the victim felt, obtained higher scores on projective guilt measures than control subjects who were not asked to think about the victim. The two studies suggest that empathic arousal contributes to transgression guilt.

There is also developmental evidence. Similarities were found between the early developmental stages of empathic distress in toddler bystanders who witnessed another's distress in natural settings (home, child-care center) and the early stages of guiltlike behavior when they caused another's distress in the same natural settings (Zahn-Waxler et al., 1979; Zahn-Waxler et al., 1992). Spontaneous helping by infants became more frequent in the second year, as did reparative acts accompanied by guiltlike expressions of concern when they caused another's distress. Examples are an 18-month-old who accidentally hit a baby-sitter and said, "Sorry, Sally," patted the sitter's forehead, and kissed her; and a 2-year-old who pulled her cousin's hair and having been told not to do that by her mother, crawled to the cousin, said "I hurt your hair, please don't cry," and gave her a kiss.

I conclude with Finnegan's (1994) quote from an adult that illustrates not only the close connection between empathy and guilt but also the long-term power of empathy-based guilt. It was a statement made by a juror on an assault-and-robbery case. The juror returned to his role as a journalist and investigated details that had not come up in court. He interviewed witnesses and the convicted man at length, over time, and came to doubt the guilty verdict that had sent the man to jail for 5 to 7 years. He reported feeling "moral horror at the now-distinct possibility that we had put him in prison for something he did not do. The comfortable gulf between juror and accused . . . had suddenly been filled with ordinary sympathy and even this referred distress was shockingly intense" (pp. 64–65).

## Guilt as a Prosocial Motive

There is considerable evidence that empathy-based transgression guilt motivates prosocial acts like apologizing and making reparations to the victim and helping other people besides the victim (see review by Baumeister et al., 1994). It also appears that guilt is especially likely to lead to prosocial action in children who are highly empathic (Krevans & Gibbs, 1996). And in close relationships empathy-based guilt may motivate people to pay increased attention to their partners, to change their behavior to suit their partners' needs and expectations, and at times to confess in a way that expresses a commitment to preserve the relationship and not repeat the transgression (Baumeister et al., 1994).

In a story-completion study, sixty subjects from preschool age to the sixth grade reacted to stories in which a child harms another

(Chapman, Zahn-Waxler, Cooperman, & Iannotti, 1987). Those subjects who attributed guilt to the story child ("She's sorry she pushed him down"), compared to children who did not attribute guilt ("He's glad she fell," "She's not really hurt"), were more likely to help others in several laboratory distress incidents. They were also more likely to express concern for the experimenter who seemed to injure her back, to look for a crying baby's lost bottle, and to help the experimenter release a kitten from a cage so it could be fed. The positive correlation between attributing guilt to the story child and these various helping indicators was obtained in all the age groups.

I mentioned in chapter 4 that some of my older subjects responded to story-completion items in which bystander inaction led to a victim's death, by producing endings in which the central figure vows to reorder his priorities and think of others in the future. I cannot think of a better real-life example of this self-transforming response to what is clearly empathy-based transgression guilt than George Orwell's (1958) autobiographical account of his feelings over being a British police officer in India as a young adult in the 1920s:

> The wretched prisoners squatting . . . the gray cowed faces of the long-term convicts, the scarred buttocks of the men who had been flogged, the women and children howling when their menfolks were led away under arrest – things like these are beyond bearing when you are in any way responsible for them. (p. 178)

> [When I came home on leave] I was haunted by an immense wave of guilt that I had got to expiate. . . . As a result, I reduced everything to the simple theory that the oppressed are always right and the oppressors are always wrong: a mistaken theory but the natural result of being one of the oppressors yourself. I felt that I had got to escape not merely from imperialism but from every form of man's domination over man. I wanted to submerge myself, to get right down among the oppressed, to be one of them and on their side against the tyrants . . . failure seemed to me to be the only virtue. Every suspicion of self-advancement, even making a few hundred a year, seemed to me spiritually ugly, a species of bullying. (p. 248)

### Development of Guilt

Empathy-based guilt is felt by mature adults when they are aware of violating an internalized moral standard or norm. The norm of interest here, one should consider the welfare of others as well as one's own, is simple but gets complicated when we realize that another's welfare includes not only the other's physical well-being but also the other's feelings and legitimate expectations regarding one's behavior toward him or her (trust, loyalty, reciprocity): "Well, there's this girl I really like. The other day at the hotel, I kind of messed around with another girl.... Now I feel sort of guilty and maybe I should tell her" (Tangney & Fischer, 1995, p. 120).

The norm gets still more complicated when we take account of the variables that determine the seriousness of violating it and therefore the intensity of a transgressor's guilt. The severity of harm done to the victim is an obvious determinant of guilt intensity. Other determinants are whether the harm done was accidental or intentional; whether the harmful act was under one's control, due to external pressure, or provoked by the victim; and whether one had a choice. Harming others intentionally when one has control or choice is a more serious transgression than harming others accidentally or under external pressure or provocation.

These variables should determine the intensity of mature guilt – the developmental end product. The developmental research does indeed show a progression from early childhood in which severity of consequences is the only determinant of guilt intensity, to later childhood in which severity of consequences shares primacy with choice and the extent to which one has control over the harmful action, to adulthood when choice and extent of control are primary and one feels most guilt from intentionally violating an abstract standard of considering others (Baumeister et al., 1994; Graham, Doubleday, & Guarino, 1984; Weiner, Graham, & Chandler, 1982).

I doubt that intentions and choice are always primary and that the severity of consequences ever loses all of its force, even in adults. Who would *not* feel guilty if he injured a child darting into his car even though he was driving carefully and well within the speed limit? Even in less extreme situations and the most extenuating of circumstances, to the extent that guilt is empathy-based I would expect some guilt to be aroused.

*Developmental prerequisites of mature guilt.* A lot must be accomplished developmentally before one is capable of mature guilt over violating the norm of considering others. One must internalize the norm and recognize when it applies. One must be able to recognize when one violates it and understand the seriousness of the harm done, which in turn requires reflecting on one's actions and understanding their present and future impact on another's well-being. One must be able to reflect on one's motives and know whether one's action was accidental or the product of choice, temptation, external pressure, or provocation. And, finally, one must not only feel guilty but also have a sense of having committed an infraction and being personally responsible for the harm done.

*"Stages" of guilt development.* Mature guilt is a far cry from the early manifestations of guilt and guiltlike behavior in childhood. The early manifestations fit the minimal criteria for empathy-based guilt: empathic distress plus awareness of causing another's distress, which implies awareness of the impact of one's action on others. In general, I would expect empathy-based guilt to follow the same developmental course as empathic distress: from guilt over causing another person physical injury and pain, to guilt over hurting another's feelings, to guilt over causing another harm beyond the situation (Hoffman, 1982). Mascolo and Fischer (1995) fleshed out this bare-bones framework, brought in the research literature on early guilt, especially that by Zahn-Waxler and her associates, and produced the following developmental scheme:

1. Beginning at 8 or 9 months, children are empathically distressed when their purposeful action (hitting) makes someone cry, although it is another year before the distress shows signs of being a feeling of guilt. They progress from guiltlike responses over causing another physical harm ("hurt Jason"); to guiltlike responses over making a hurtful remark (says "tower ugly," recognizes Jason is upset, and says "hurt Jason, make Jason sad"); to guiltlike responses over failing to respond positively to a request (refuses to share blocks

so Jason can finish his tower, recognizes Jason is upset, and says "Hurt Jason, made Jason sad" in a sad tone of voice).

Not included by Mascolo and Fischer but worth mentioning is the fact that the number of prosocial reparative acts by children who harm another rises sharply between 18 and 24 months (Zahn-Waxler & Robinson, 1995). Here is an example from one of my students:

> I was baby-sitting and playing with my cousin Ginny, 21 months old, picking her up, lifting her high, putting her gently down. I grew tired and put her down. She wanted more and jumped up while I was still bent over, so she hit my chin with the top of her head. She started to cry. I felt terrible and said "Ginny, I'm so sorry." Then I realized I had bitten my lip and split it open and it was bleeding. Ginny noticed too and immediately stopped crying and said "Ginny do that to you. Ginny give you boo-boo." I went to get a napkin and she followed me into the kitchen, patted my leg as I sat down, and she said "Ginny sorry."

It appears this child's own discomfort was overridden by her empathic distress and guilt.

At 24 months, the amount of reparative behavior correlates positively both with empathy and the child's level of mirror-self–recognition (Zahn-Waxler et al., 1992). This finding fits the hypotheses that empathy-based guilt requires the ability to reflect on one's actions and motivates reparative behavior. Now back to Mascolo and Fischer.

2. By 4 or 5 years, children start constructing more elaborate representations of others, including the demands of social reciprocity. They can now grasp the relation between another child's action and what that action implies one should do; and they can feel guilty over not reciprocating. Mark asks a friend to share his wooden blocks, which the friend does, but Mark does not share his plastic blocks when the friend requests this, and the friend cries. Mark realizes the friend is crying because Mark did not share with his friend even though the friend shared with him, and Mark feels guilty over not reciprocating. (More on reciprocity in chapters 9 and 10.)

3. By 6 to 8 years, children show guilt over not fulfilling an obli-

gation, reneging, for example, on a promise to visit a sick friend and the friend is upset. Such guilt becomes possible with the emergence of representational systems. The representational system in this case involves the ability to coordinate the friend's need, one's promise, one's failure to fulfill the promise, and the friend's distress, and to recognize that the friend's distress is due to one's failure to fulfill the promise.

4. By 10 to 12 years, children are capable of feeling guilty over violating a general abstract moral rule about how to treat other people. They are capable of generalizing across incidents and drawing conclusions such as "I have failed to live up to my promises with several friends," thus attributing a moral flaw to themselves and feeling guilty over violating the general rule of honoring agreements with friends. It is as if they say to themselves, "I let my friends down by not doing what I say I'll do." Children this age may also compare themselves to others and feel guilty over upholding the moral rule less faithfully or consistently than their friends do. In other words, children at this stage are capable of a rather mature empathy-based guilt.

Mascolo and Fischer's developmental scheme is a useful first attempt to integrate the child's empathic capability and his ability to represent increasingly complex personal and social entities (hurt feelings, reciprocity, fulfillment/nonfulfillment of obligations, abstract rules). The scheme focuses on cognitive development's impact on guilt. My theory of socialization's impact is presented in chapter 6. We now turn to moral internalization.

## MORAL INTERNALIZATION

Psychologists have long been intrigued with moral internalization, probably because it epitomizes the existential human dilemma of how people come to grips with the inevitable conflicts between personal needs and social obligations. The legacy of Freud and Durkheim is not only their concepts of "superego" and "collective representations" but also the widespread agreement among social scientists that most people do not go through life viewing society's moral norms as external, coercively imposed pressure to which they must submit. Though the norms may be initially external and often at variance with one's desires, they eventually become part of one's internal motive system, largely through the efforts of early socializers, mainly parents, and help guide one's behavior even in the absence of external authority. That is, control by others is replaced by self-control and moral action becomes the individual's attempt to achieve an acceptable balance between egoistic and moral motives, both of which reside within oneself.

Western philosophy and religion, as noted, have postulated several answers to the existential human dilemma of personal needs versus social obligations, and these answers are reflected in contemporary psychological theories. One answer is (a) the doctrine of original sin associated with early Christian theology, which states that people are born egoistic and can only acquire a sense of moral obligation through punitive socialization experiences that subordinate their egoistic drives. This doctrine is reflected in Freudian theory and certain social learning theories that stress the importance of punishment in moral development.

The opposite, more interesting answer (b), the "doctrine of innate purity" associated with writers like Rousseau who saw children as inherently good, that is, sensitive to others, though vulnerable to corruption by society, has a rough parallel in certain aspects of Piaget's theory of moral development. Piaget does not view children as innately pure, but he does view their relation to powerful adults early in life as producing a heteronomous respect for rules and authority that interferes with the child's moral development. This is a form of corruption that Piaget believes can only be overcome by the give-and-take of free, unsupervised interaction with peers: Peer interaction, together with the child's naturally evolving cognitive capability, fosters the child's taking the perspectives of others and eventually makes it possible for the child to distinguish moral norms from externally sanctioned behavior. The resemblance to "innate purity" is that the free and natural interaction of **premoral** children produces moral development, whereas interaction with (socialized) adults prevents it. More about Piaget later.

The attempt (c) by the philosopher Immanuel Kant and his followers to derive universal, impartially applied principles of justice provided part of the inspiration for Kohlberg's (and Piaget's) efforts to construct an invariant sequence of universal moral developmental stages. And (d) the British version of utilitarianism represented by David Hume, Adam Smith, and others, for whom empathy was a necessary social bond, finds expression in current research on empathy, compassion, and the morality of caring.

Perhaps the most succinct statement of moral internalization's contribution to the maintenance of society was made a century ago by a sociologist: "The tendency of society to satisfy itself as cheaply as possible results in appeals to 'good conscience,' through which the individual pays to himself the wages for his righteousness, which otherwise would have to be assured to him in some way through law or custom" (Simmel, 1902, p. 19). In other words, internalization serves the social control function of making conformity rewarding in its own right, where rewards for correct behavior and punishments for deviation are not forthcoming from society.

With this background, we move on to the theories of moral internalization advanced by psychologists. Moral internalization means different things in different theoretical contexts, and some writers do not mention the concept at all although it is implicit in their work. Most theories of what fosters moral internalization in children deal with a particular facet of morality (behavioral, affective, cognitive) and focus on a particular aspect of children's socialization experience that the other theories ignore. I now briefly update my previous review of these theories (Hoffman, 1983), discuss my own definition of moral internalization, and argue for the importance of adult intervention and socialization. In the next chapter I present my theory of moral internalization and guilt development, which highlights the role of parental discipline but also incorporates concepts from the moral internalization theories discussed here, from contemporary information processing and memory research, and from the emerging literature on the interaction of affect and cognition.

### Psychoanalytic Theory

In the traditional psychoanalytic account, young children resolve the conflict between the urge to express hostile and erotic impulses and anxiety over losing parental love if they express these impulses, by repressing the impulses and avoiding behaviors associated with parental disapproval. Furthermore, to help master anxiety and avoid punishment, as well as continue to receive parental affection, the child identifies with the parent and adopts as his own the parent's rules and prohibitions. These rules and prohibitions largely reflect the moral norms of society and in this way the child internalizes society's moral norms.

Children also adopt the parents' capacity to punish themselves when they violate or are tempted to violate a moral norm, turning toward themselves the hostility originally felt toward the parent. This self-punishment is experienced as guilt feelings that are dreaded because of their intensity and their resemblance to the earlier anxieties about being punished and abandoned. Children therefore try to avoid guilt by obeying the internalized rules and prohibitions and erecting psychological (cognitive) mechanisms of defense against the conscious awareness of any impulses to disobey the rules and prohibitions.

These basic moral internalization processes are accomplished by 5 or 6 years of age and are worked through and solidified during the remaining, relatively calm years of childhood. Moral internalization thus occurs early in life, before children are capable of complex cognitive processing of information. A person's moral norms therefore become part of a rigid, primarily unconscious, and often severe yet fragile impulse control system.

I find it difficult to understand how this largely unconscious internalized control system can be adaptive and account for the complexities of guilt and moral internalization. From the individual's standpoint, this control system or superego is a quasi-pathological concept, as noted in my discussion of guilt. Freud knew this, as do his followers, some of whom (e.g., Erikson, 1968) suggest that this quasi-pathological internal control system persists through childhood but is disrupted in adolescence due to hormonal changes, society's demands, and new information about the world that contradicts and creates disillusionment with the rigidly internalized norms. This disruption poses a threat to the child's dependent relationship with his parents, which provides the control system's main support. Due to this threat, the child must find new and more mature grounds for a moral stance, or else erect new cognitive defenses to ward off uncontrollable impulses and maintain the earlier control system (and relationship with his parents) intact. These ideas make sense to me, but unfortunately the explanations given for how the new and more mature moral stance develops are vague and unconvincing (Hoffman, 1980).

What does the research say? Freudian theory predicts that children who identify with their parents and are anxious about losing their parents' love will be more likely to feel guilty when they harm someone and show other signs of moral internalization. This hypothesis, that parent identification fosters moral behavior, is supported by positive correlations between parent identification and certain visible moral behaviors like helping people in need and making moral judgments about others; but parent identification does not correlate with using moral standards to evaluate one's own behavior or feeling guilty over harming others. The hypothesis about anxiety over loss of parental love also receives mixed support: The use of discipline in which parents try to alter children's behavior by withdrawing love contributes to children's controlling aggressive impulses, but not to their feeling guilty over harming others or using moral standards to evaluate their own behavior. In sum, the research support is mixed but for our purposes negligible: Neither parent identification nor anxiety over loss of love seems to promote guilt or moral internalization.

The above research was not done by Freudians, but some followers of Margaret Mahler (1974) have made interesting observations that may bear on an early precursor or rudimentary form of moral internalization. Parens (1979), for example, describes an 8-month-old infant who turns to look at the mother, sometimes shaking his head negatively, while at the point of doing something that the mother prohibited earlier, and then inhibits the act "in its trajectory." Parens viewed such visible self-prohibitions by infants, repeated many times, as indicating that the internalization of parental prohibitions has begun and is "exercising some influence, however weak, over the child's actions."

### Social-Learning Theory

Social-learning theory inspired an enormous amount of research in the 1960s and 1970s. The social-learning theorists generally avoided terms like moral internalization, which pertain to internal psychological states that are several steps removed from observable behavior, but they did attempt to explain a similar phenomenon: children's engaging in moral behavior (defined by social norms) or avoiding unwanted behavior in the absence of external surveillance. The most obvious social-learning theory – rewarding good behavior makes children good – was not the focus, but some attention was given to prohibitions and punishments, which might, for example, be involved in the 8-month-old's rudimentary self-control noted by Parens.

A more advanced form of the prohibition-punishment model of social-learning theory is that owing to a history of being punished for unwanted deviant acts, painful anxiety states become associated with these acts, that is, with the kinesthetic and perceptual cues produced by the acts and the cognitive cues associated with anticipating the acts. This "deviation anxiety" can be avoided by inhibiting the act, even when no one else is present. The person thus behaves in what appears to be a morally internalized manner, although he is actually behaving out of a subjective fear of punishment. When deviation anxiety becomes diffuse and detached from conscious fears of detection, as may happen, the inhibition of deviant acts becomes a primitive form of internalization: One behaves properly in order to avoid unconscious anxiety (Aronfreed, 1970; Mowrer, 1960). This conception, interestingly, resembles the psychoanalytic view of moral internalization described previously.

Social-learning theorists, notably Bandura (1969), dealt extensively with children's exposure to models who behave morally or are punished for behaving in a deviant manner. The theory was that a child learns to be moral by observing models who behave morally and imitating their behavior in similar situations even when the models are absent. When a child observes a model who deviates from a moral norm and is punished he feels vicariously punished or anticipates being punished if he misbehaves; either way, he will try to escape the model's fate by avoiding the deviant behavior.

A lot of research was done to test these ideas but, unfortunately, the research had problems. One problem was that the moral internalization index was whether the child obeyed an experimenter's arbitrary prohibition, not playing with forbidden toys when the experimenter left the room, for example. The "forbidden-toy paradigm" blurred the distinction between morally internalized behavior and self-control in the service of obeying an arbitrary request from authority; Milgram's (1963) classic research made it clear that obedience is an unacceptable moral index because it can lead to behavior that is fundamentally immoral. In any case, the findings were not promising: Children who watched a model who played with forbidden toys and was not punished were more likely to play with those toys when they thought no one was looking; but, more importantly, children who watched a model who was punished for playing with the toys, or a model who resisted the temptation to play with the toys altogether, appeared to be just as likely to play with the toys when they thought no one was looking as were children who were not exposed to a model.[1] The upshot of that research is that children imitate a model who does what they want to do and is not punished, perhaps because the absence of punishment legitimizes the behavior (Hoffman, 1970). The research tells us little about what parents or

---

1. This is my interpretation of the findings (Hoffman, 1970a, 1977). But even if seeing a model punished for playing with the toys reduced the children's playing with the toys, it might have done that only because the model's punishment signaled that the subjects would be punished for the same thing – not internalization.

other socialization agents can do to promote moral internalization, except to make sure that children are not exposed to delinquents or criminals who are not punished.

Another prominent social-learning theory pertinent to moral internalization derives from the notion that one may act in certain ways to gain self-reward (Bandura, 1977). It follows that if children are socialized to act morally and experience self-reward afterward, they will behave morally even when they are alone. This is a plausible definition of moral internalization. But it requires an explanation of how the self that is rewarded develops in the first place, and how moral actions come to reward that self so effectively that external surveillance becomes unnecessary. Unfortunately, a satisfactory theory of self-development that includes the mechanisms of self-reward has not been advanced.

## Cognitive-Developmental Theory

Cognitive-developmental theorists, notably Piaget (1932) and especially Kohlberg (1969, 1984) and his followers, have studied the development of people's ability to resolve competing moral claims and the way people invoke concepts of rights, duty, and justice to deal with these claims. These writers, like social-learning theorists, avoid the term moral internalization but for an entirely different reason: It suggests something outside the child that becomes part of his internal moral structure, that is, the child passively acquires moral norms. Cognitive-developmentalists assume children actively acquire moral norms by socially constructing them. Still, they use implicit moral internalization concepts and the end-product is a morally internalized child.

*Piaget.* According to Piaget, adults interfere with children's moral internalization because of the gross differential of power between adults and children. Parent rules are enforced without children's understanding their rationales, and they are respected only because of parental authority. "The average parent is like an unintelligent government that is content to accumulate laws in spite of the contradictions and the ever-increasing mental confusion that this accumu-

lation leads to" (Piaget, 1932, p. 192). In Piaget's view, the heteronomous morality produced by adults can only be overcome by the
give-and-take of free, unsupervised interaction among peers, together with children's naturally evolving cognitive capability. Unsupervised peer interaction is necessary for children to develop an
autonomous (internalized) morality, because it gives them the kind
of social and cognitive experiences needed to develop moral norms
based on mutual consent and cooperation among equals. These experiences, taking the role of others and participating with them in
decision making about rules and how to enforce them, are unlikely
to occur in interactions with adults, who have the power to impose
their will on children without their consent.

*Kohlberg.* In Kohlberg's scheme, each individual progresses from
a premoral level focused on the (externally determined) consequences of actions for oneself, to a conventional moral level based
on group welfare and rules, to an autonomous, principled moral
level. In this progression, the person's moral orientation expands as
he or she experiences the world, and cognitive (brain) development
permits this expansion. The underlying process, according to Gibbs
(1991), is "decentration," which pertains to the developmental shift
from (a) judgment based on the child's attention to the most salient
features of a situation, which usually fit the child's own perspective;
to (b) judgment based on a more extensive, equally distributed attention to features of a situation that fit the perspective of others; to (c)
a progressive coordination of all perspectives. In this way, children
advance from a superficial (externally bound) to a more profound,
internal understanding of a moral norm's underlying meaning.

The catalyst for these processes, according to Kohlberg, is not so
much peer interaction as the child's exposure to information that is
at an optimally higher moral level than his own – higher but not
beyond the child's cognitive reach. When exposed to an optimally
higher level, the child does not simply imitate it. The child may
instead, after experiencing some kind of cognitive disequilibrium,
engage in active mental efforts to resolve the contradiction and integrate the new information with his or her own point of view. The
resulting integration moves the child in the direction of the more

advanced moral level. This implies that children prefer the more advanced level, perhaps because they recognize it as more inclusive or otherwise superior to their own view. In any case, developmental progress is toward higher, not lower, stages: If two children at different moral stages interact, the lower-stage child will move up; the higher-stage child will **not** move down. This process of "progressively constructing" one's own moral orientation, described and first researched by Turiel (1966) and elaborated by Blasi (1983), continues until children reach their highest possible level and can be considered a type of moral internalization.

Kohlberg's followers have branched off in several directions. Most have dropped the idea of an invariant stage sequence, distinguished among moral domains (moral/conventional, caring, justice), and filled developmental gaps by studying morality in young children (e.g., Turiel, 1983, 1998; Damon, 1977, 1988).[2] But the basic theory, insofar as it pertains to internalization, remains similar to Kohlberg's: Moral internalization is an active mental process of integrating new and more comprehensive moral ideas into one's existing moral framework. The reason for the similarity with Kohlberg may be that this type of cognitive construction process is central to all cognitive theories, regardless of domain.

Some of these writers (notably Davidson & Youniss, 1995, and Turiel, 1998) have returned to Piaget and echoed his views in their own thinking about peer-interaction's contribution to moral development. Turiel (1998) summarizes this position as follows: Morality is not imposed on children; it is not framed in terms of conflict between children's needs or interests and society's requirements, and therefore it is "not regulated mainly by emotions of fear, anxiety,

---

2. Some of their views are similar to those advanced earlier by Hoffman and Saltzstein (1967), for example, this explanation by Smetana (1984) of how 2-year-olds learn the moral–conventional distinction: Mothers of 24- to 26-month-old children respond to social convention violations by focusing on the disorder the child's act creates ("Look at the mess you made"). They respond to moral transgressions by focusing on the consequences of the child's acts for another's rights and welfare or suggesting the child take the other's perspective: "Think about how you would feel if you were hit."

shame or guilt." Rather, children co-construct and "discover" moral norms, even adult norms, in the "give and take" of their social interactions, that is, in conflicts, disputes, arguments, and negotiations. Peer conflict stimulates children to take different points of view, to produce ideas on how to coordinate the needs of self and others, and to consider the rights of others – especially claims to ownership and possession of objects.[3]

The current moral cognitive-developmental theory, then, is that moral internalization occurs through a combination of Piaget and Kohlberg. This includes taking the perspective of others and actively integrating new ideas into one's existing moral framework, and doing this mainly in the course of arguing and negotiating with peers over conflicting claims (e.g., over possessions). This theory has a doubly intuitive appeal. First, it casts children as actively thinking through the ideas of people with whom they interact and accepting moral concepts on rational grounds, in keeping with Western society's rational ideal. Second, it fits with our democratic ideals as well because it highlights the importance of interaction with one's equals.[4]

But the theory seems limited precisely because of its exaggerated focus on rational, cognitive processes. It neglects affect, and it also seems to me to be vague about the role of conflict. More important for my purposes, the theory does not explain why the knowledge of other's perspectives that is gained in the context of conflicting claims should lead children to take the other's claims seriously and be willing to negotiate and compromise their own claims, rather than use the knowledge to manipulate the other. That is, why should perspective-taking serve prosocial rather than egoistic ends? Cognitive-developmental theory presupposes that children come to take the perspective of others as a natural part of cognitive development

---

3. Turiel adds the controversial claim that these moral judgments, while not innate or part of an invariant stage sequence, are "nonlocal," that is, they may have universal validity.

4. My argument for parents' positive contribution to moral development is given in chapter 6 and for unsupervised peers' *negative* contribution, elsewhere (Hoffman, 1988).

and social interaction. The theory takes for granted and ignores a central problem of early moral internalization: how children gain control of their egoistic desires and achieve an acceptable compromise between them and the moral demands of a situation.

### Attribution Theory

In Chapter 4, I said humans make causal attributions that shape and transform a person's feelings of empathic distress. The attribution theory of moral internalization is a little different. It says that one is internalized when one sees oneself as the source of one's own moral action, as opposed to seeing one's action as externally imposed. The first attributional explanation of moral internalization was that if the pressure put on a child is just enough to get the child to comply with a moral norm but not enough for the child to realize that he or she conformed under pressure, then the child will attribute his compliance to his own will. This theory is elegantly simple, but it bypasses the question of why children should subordinate their desires and alter their behavior against their will when they do not notice any pressure to do this. And, like the social-learning paradigms mentioned earlier, it equates moral internalization with compliance.

The more elaborate version of attribution theory advanced by Dienstbier (1978) gets closer to our concerns because it deals with affect. According to Dienstbier, when children are disciplined by parents, they are emotionally aroused. The aroused emotion is at first undefined, but is given meaning when the child attributes it either to the punishment the child received (if the parent makes punishment salient) or to the child's act and its harmful effects (if the parent gives an explanation that makes the act and its effects salient). Subsequently, when the child is tempted to engage in a deviant act, he will feel emotional discomfort, which he attributes either to anticipated punishment or to the deviant act and its harmful effects. If the child is alone, attributing the aroused emotion to anticipated punishment (likely if the parents made punishment salient) will give the child no reason to resist the temptation to engage in the act, since detection and punishment are unlikely. But if the child is alone and attributes his or her discomfort to the deviant act and its effects (likely if the parents made the act and its effects salient), then the child may resist temptation. Explanations that connect the child's deviant acts to their harmful effects should therefore contribute to moral internalization.

This explanation, too, is elegant and simple, but again at the cost of important details. According to the theory, if punishment is salient, the child attributes the aroused emotion to punishment; if explanation about the unwanted act and its effects is salient, the child attributes the aroused emotion to the act and its effects. In other words, the attribution the child makes is an exact copy of the aspect of the situation made salient by the parent; and the child simply labels his unpleasant emotional reaction to parental discipline according to what the parent made salient. What is missing is an explanation of how an emotion that is aroused in the child by parental discipline can remain undefined until the child makes an appropriate attribution. Another limitation is that once again internalization is equated with compliance and the child complies because he is tricked into believing he acted on his own. This may be part of moral internalization, as we shall see, but a small part.

### An Information-Processing Approach

Some writers explain moral internalization in terms of children's acquiring or learning certain behavior-control skills. Kopp (1982) proposes a three-phase process: Children move from an external-control phase in which they depend on caregivers to remind them of acceptable behaviors, to a self-control phase where they can comply with caregiver expectations in the caregiver's absence, to a self-regulation phase in which they become able to direct their own behavior and delay gratification. What enables children to reach the final phase and behave in the morally accepted fashion on their own, according to Kopp, is the development of mental representation, recall memory, and the ability to use strategies and plans to direct behavior. But Kopp does not explain what motivates children to behave in the morally acceptable way: what motivates them to give up what they wanted to do. Representation, recall, and related strategies enable children to acquire many social skills and competences, including the ability to figure out ways to "get away with it." *They are information-processing enablers which may be necessary for internalized moral action but not sufficient because they do not motivate moral action any more than egoistic self-serving action.*

While none of these theories can account for the full complexity of moral internalization, they can explain one or another aspect of it. I include some of the concepts in my own moral internalization theory, which is presented in chapter 6, but first I conclude this chapter with a definition of moral internalization and a brief argument for the importance of socialization.

## MORAL INTERNALIZATION AND MOTIVATION

I define a person's prosocial moral structure as a network of empathic affects, cognitive representations, and motives. Included are: *principles* (one should help others in distress; people should be rewarded for their efforts); *behavioral norms* (tell the truth, keep promises, help others; do not lie, steal, betray a trust, injure, hurt, or deceive others); *rules* (intentional, unprovoked harm is worse than accidental, provoked harm); *a sense of right and wrong* and of committing an infraction; *images of one's acts that have hurt or helped others and the associated self-blame and guilt.*

These components are more or less loosely tied together by the moral principles and sense of right and wrong that they share and the affects they have in common: empathic distress, sympathetic distress, empathic anger and feeling of injustice, and empathy-based guilt. The components and the structure as a whole are charged with these affects. Components can be added, dropped, recategorized, and subdivided based on experience (lies become "white lies" which are good and manipulative lies which are bad).

A person's moral structure is internalized when he or she accepts and feels obligated to abide by its organizing principles and consider others without regard to external reward or punishment. The sanctions that may have previously motivated one to consider others have lost their force and one now experiences the motive as deriving autonomously from within oneself, with little or no recollection of its origin. The socialization agents who originally did the sanctioning (usually parents) may be forgotten, but forgotten or not they are no longer a significant factor in the person's prosocial motivation.

When this internalized prosocial moral motive is activated in moral encounters, it does not assure moral action, because of competing egoistic motives. But it does have an inner, compelling, obligatory quality and therefore assures that at least a moral conflict will occur: One wants to accept an invitation to a party, but feels obligated to visit a sick friend as promised and may anticipate feeling guilty if one goes to the party. Moral acts are thus not simple behavioral expression of moral motives but attempts to achieve an acceptable balance between one's egoistic and moral motives.

The question for developmental psychology is: What prior experiences are central in developing such a complex internalized network of moral cognition, feeling, and motivation? My answer is socialization, mainly in the form of adult interventions. But before going into the details I would like to briefly argue the general case for socialization's importance.

## IMPORTANCE OF SOCIALIZATION

The empathy-arousing processes described in chapter 2 may work well as prosocial moral motives in most children when they are bystanders. They do not work as well, however, when children harm or are about to harm someone, because the emotions aroused in these situations (desire for possessions, anger, fear) can blind them to the harm done and override their empathic tendencies. The difference between bystander and transgressor is illustrated by Zahn-Waxler and Robinson's (1995) observations of a pronounced increase in children's empathic and sympathetic distress in the second year when they witnessed another's distress and a lot of repairing the damage when they caused another's distress, but *less concern, more aggression,* and more pleasure in the victim's distress when they caused the other's distress than when they witnessed it. This makes sense when we realize that children's harmful action usually serves an instrumental purpose such as getting something they want, and they can be expected to feel good when they succeed. In any case, **causing another's distress is more likely to require adult intervention than witnessing another's distress.**

In accidents, intervention is not necessary when children are aware of the harm they did, feel empathic distress and guilt, and engage in reparative action on their own. I gave an example in chapter 3 of a child who, having accidentally hurt a friend while fighting over a toy, comforted the friend by fetching his teddy bear from the next room. Here is another example, reported by Blum (1987), in which intervention was not necessary: two children, aged 22 and 24 months and close friends, are playing; one accidentally harms the other, seems concerned, apologizes, and offers the victim a toy.

Intervention *is* necessary when children are unaware of the harm they did (a child running after a playmate accidentally knocked another child down and kept on running; a child playing with a magic marker unwittingly distressed his mother by ruining her new sofa), and when they ignore or laugh at the victim's distress (a child kicked his mother in the face when she picked him up for a diaper change; another slapped a spoon in the frying pan splattering his mother with grease (Zahn-Waxler et al., 1992). Whether these children are just expressing exuberance or pleasure in their agency, they may not realize the painful consequences of their actions unless it is pointed out.

When adults harm others intentionally, it is usually for reasons like self-defense, misperceiving others' intentions, retaliation, or ideology (terrorists). Children have similar reasons (excluding ideology) but also engage in pranks like throwing stones at school windows, intentional acts that could injure others although that was not the intention. Children also harm others for reasons having more to do with their personal needs than with a deliberate attempt to inflict pain. A 5-year-old sulked over a scolding; her younger sister approached and offered her a toy; she said "Go away, I don't like you," whereupon her sister ran to the living room, buried her head in the couch, and sobbed.

Kastenbaum, Farber, and Sroufe (1989) observed "an unpopular 5-year-old playing with an African mask, growling at nearby children. One child was frightened by this, shrinking back. The masked child selected this child for intensified approach, driving her away in tears." The authors note that the same level of understanding, knowing he was scaring her, could have led him to take off the mask and reassure her, as other children his age have been observed to do. A possible explanation for his behavior, aside from sadism, is that he was so focused on the pleasure of exercising his agency that he missed the other's anxiety. The point is that in incidents like these, interventions by adults that point up the consequences of the child's action for the other can be constructive and may be necessary.

Conflicts between peers are a special challenge because of their frequency and emotionality. Shantz (1987) reviewed the research and found that most conflicts during the toddler and preschool years involve the possession and use of objects, although in some instances the goal shifts from possessing an object to aggression and retaliation (child pushes another off swing and gets on himself, gets hit by first child and hits back; child leaves toy unattended, returns to find another playing with it, grabs the toy, and they start fighting).

Next in frequency to conflicts over possession are unprovoked physical attack and interfering with a peer's ongoing activity (a child kept threatening another that he was going to throw Play-Doh at him – Shantz, 1987). According to Shantz, conflicts, though often brief, are not trivial events, as:

> the participants give every indication of being serious in their pursuits . . . and given the painful impact of some conflicts, such as being excluded from a play group or from the pleasant feeling of winning a contest or from the shared glee of the termination of conflict . . . these events appear to have substantial meaning for the children involved." (p. 287)

Conflicts may be settled by the children themselves without adult intervention. The child who fetched the teddy bear was resolving a conflict over possession as well as responding to an accident. According to Shantz, children often resolve conflicts amicably by giving reasons for their actions; children expect reasons and are responsive to them (they know one should not refuse or contradict another without a reason). But some conflicts require intervention, like the aggression-over-possession conflicts cited above.[5]

Here is a complex conflict that requires intervention: Child A says it is his turn and grabs a toy from B, who grabs it back. They argue until A pushes B away, grabs the toy and runs. B starts to cry. A ignores B's crying and plays with the toy. Intervention is necessary because it is unclear who is at fault; each child blames the other. Furthermore, powerful egoistic and angry emotions keep each child from attending both to his own behavior and the other's distress (decentering), which is necessary for each child to understand the other's perspective and realize it is like his own ("He expects to be given a reason, not a flat refusal, just as I do"). It is also necessary if each child is to empathize with the other and anticipate his disappointment at not getting what he wants, and for each child to accept his share of blame and be ready to make amends or compromise.

Blame is something children (and adults) try to avoid, because it is painful, self-deprecatory, and often associated with unpleasant memories of punishment. For these reasons, intervention is needed in conflict situations for empathy- and especially guilt-arousing processes to be set in motion. Whether empathy and guilt can actually be aroused in conflict situations has not been researched but there is suggestive evidence in a study by Camras (1977) that empathy can be aroused: A child is playing with a gerbil and another child tries to take it away; an aggressive facial expression by the first child could deter the challenger from continuing to try to take the gerbil – but so could a sad face, which suggests empathic sadness can play a role in conflicts over possessions.

---

5. Child experts know that in accidents the child helps, but in fights it is mostly bystanders who help.

When, developmentally, can adult interventions be effective, not to gain immediate compliance but to make a contribution to guilt and moral internalization? For interventions to produce an internal sense of wrongdoing and guilt (as opposed to fear) seems to require that children have acquired a sense of themselves as entities with distinct boundaries and personal characteristics that can be evaluated. This would enable them to recognize themselves both as targets of parents' disciplinary efforts and as the cause of another's distress and, therefore, to feel some rudimentary form of guilt. As noted in chapter 3, children begin acquiring a reflective sense of self in the last half of the second year. There is some evidence that this occurs before the emergence of an emotional response (guilt?) to wrongdoing (Stipek, Gralinski, & Kapp, 1990). It thus appears that parents are on schedule, as they typically begin disciplining children in earnest late in the second year, as we shall see.

Parental discipline is at the heart of a theory of moral internalization and guilt development that I began working on years ago (Hoffman & Saltzstein, 1967; Hoffman, 1970, 1983). The current version of the theory, detailed in the next chapter, is a focused, systematic information-processing account that highlights the affects and cognitions generated in discipline encounters and suggests how they are integrated and retained in children's memory and how they contribute to moral motivation and action.

# CHAPTER 6

# From Discipline to Internalization

To recapitulate, transgression situations are those in which a person harms or is about to harm another. A transgression may be provoked, intentional, accidental, a by-product of interpersonal conflict, or a violation of another's expectations. The moral issue is whether the transgressor is motivated to avoid the harmful act or at least feels guilty and acts prosocially afterward, and whether he or she does these things even in the absence of witnesses. I have long argued that the foundation for guilt and the prosocial moral internalization necessary for combating egoistic needs in conflict and other transgression situations originates in discipline encounters, especially those in which children harm someone. Discipline encounters are settings in which parents attempt to change a child's behavior against the child's will. They begin when the child's behavior diverges from the parent's wishes and end when the child complies, the parent gives up, or an external event intervenes (doorbell rings). In an intensive study of preschoolers (Hoffman, 1963), the average encounter took 2 to 3 discipline attempts (though one took 17!), and, as in Schaffer and Crook's (1980) research, the children complied in over 80 percent of them.

Why single out discipline, when parents also nurture and express affection to their children, spend time playing with them, explain and interpret the world to them, and, above all, serve as models of acceptable moral behavior? For one thing, discipline encounters are important because they are frequent. Though rare in the first year (Moss, 1967), they begin to occur regularly early in the second – one every 11 minutes when the child is between 12 and 15 months old, mostly regarding safety and keeping children away from easily broken objects (Power & Chapieski, (1986). By the end of the second year, discipline encounters involving the child's harming another are common (Parens, 1979; Tulkin & Kagan, 1972), though unfortunately there are no data on how common. In any case, by the end of the second year fully two-thirds of all parent–child interactions are discipline encounters in which parents attempt to change children's behavior against their will (Minton, Kagan, & Levine, 1971); and, in most cases children obey right away or are compelled to obey.

The same is true of preschoolers and children up to ten years of age (Lytton, 1979; Schoggen, 1963; Simmons & Schoggen, 1963; Wright, 1967). More specifically, children in the 2- to 10-year age range experience parental pressure to change their behavior every 6 to 9 minutes on average, which translates roughly into 50 discipline encounters a day or over 15,000 a year! Not all of them involve harm to others but even if only a quarter of them do – a very conservative estimate – that is a lot, especially considering that children usually end up complying. Children in the 2- to 10-year age group often attempt to negotiate parental demands and parents may enter into these negotiations (Kuczynski, Kochanska, Radke-Yarrow, & Girnius-Brown, 1987; Schaffer & Crook, 1980). But the parent calls the shots and determines how far negotiations go, as the high frequency of compliance figures indicate.

Frequency is not the only reason for discipline's special importance. Its special importance can be derived from considering how a mature, prosocial morally internalized person – the end point of our analysis – behaves when a situation's moral requirements conflict with his or her egoistic desires, that is, in a moral encounter. Internalized persons will, on their own, feel empathic concern for another, even when the other's desires conflict with theirs, anticipate the harmful effects of their actions on others, and weigh these harmful effects against the importance of fulfilling their own desires. They may then refrain from the harmful act, but if self-interest prevails and they engage in the act, they will feel guilt over the harm done. The key point is they will at least experience inner conflict.

Young children are not likely to experience inner conflict in these situations. Arsenio and Lover (1995) found that children under eight years of age who were exposed to stories about children who stole from others or refused to take turns thought the story children would be happy over their gains and oblivious to their victims' clearly expressed distress ("happy victimizers"). The finding says nothing about how children would act in the situations, but, assumimg it has some relevance to how they would act, it does suggest that socialization is necessary for moral internalization in children. The question is what settings and what types of interventions will contribute to the child's capacity for inner moral conflict.

An obvious answer is the kind of socialization settings that compel children to deal with the same conflict, that is, conflict between others' interests and their own interests, and the kind of interventions that help children resolve the conflict in the same way that internalized adults do. The settings that can accomplish this – discipline encounters in which children harm or are about to harm others whose interests conflict with theirs – occur often in the home, as noted above. But why, other than that discipline encounters are frequent, should they be more important than other things parents do? My answer is this: **Whether the harm done by the child is accidental or intentional and whether the victim is a parent or a peer, it is only in discipline encounters that parents are likely to make the connection, necessary for guilt and moral internalization, between children's egoistic motives, their behavior, and their behavior's harmful consequences for others – and put pressure on children to control their behavior out of consideration for others.**

Parents' behavior outside discipline encounters can contribute by providing a prosocial role model that reinforces children's empathic proclivity and legitimizes helping in bystander situations. Examples are expressing compassion toward and helping the homeless, verbally linking a television protagonist's feelings or situations with the child's own experience (Eisenberg et al., 1992), explaining one's own sadness (Denham & Grout, 1992), and pointing up similarities among all humans. In discussing social-learning theory (chapter 5), I pointed out that prosocial models are good at getting children to do what they are predisposed to do, probably because modeling the behavior legitimizes it. This may be what happens when parents act as prosocial models in bystander situations: Given children's empathic predisposition, children may naturally emulate the parent's prosocial action in similar situations. But, as I noted, prosocial models alone do not appear to be to be good at motivating children to act against their self-interest, and this is what is required in conflict and other transgression situations.

What prosocial role models can do, in sum, is to have an indirect effect: *They can reinforce children's empathic dispositions – especially the sympathetic component of empathic distress (chapter 3) – and make children more receptive to parental inductions which as we shall see, elicit empathic distress and guilt. And, together with induction, prosocial role models can make children more receptive to the claims of a peer with whom they are in conflict (chapter 10).*

What remains is to specify the type of discipline that can take advantage of the child's empathic proclivities and induce the child to feel empathic distress and guilt, realize the harm his or her behavior may do to another, and weigh that harm against his or her desires – as a morally internalized person does. The type of discipline that can do this is **induction, in which parents highlight the other's perspective, point up the other's distress, and make it clear that the child's action caused it.** Most of this chapter will be taken up with my theory of how inductions work and evidence for the theory, but first a brief summary of the argument, and a primer on discipline.

*Summary of the theory.* Children's experience in discipline encounters involving harm to others in which parents use inductions contributes to children's behavior in moral encounters in which, without external intervention, they experience inner conflict between their desires and another's needs. That is, their behavior in these discipline encounters, unlike in other socialization settings, resembles their later behavior in moral encounters: In each case they hold back their desires to avoid harming another or feel guilty afterward. The difference is that intervention is necessary in discipline encounters but not in moral encounters.

For inductions to work, their message must get through to the child despite the child's involvement in pursuing his or her own goals and the emotionality of the situation. This requires a certain amount of external pressure – enough to get the child to stop what he or she is doing, attend, and process the induction but not enough to arouse undue anger and fear, which can disrupt the processing.

When children process and understand an induction's message, this can produce in them an empathic response to the victim's distress, an awareness of their action's being the cause of that distress, and a feeling of empathy-based transgression guilt. Over the years the child builds up a discipline-encounter schema or script, and it is in this successive integration of inductive messages and scripts that children construct an internalized norm of considering others – a norm that is charged with the empathic distress and guilty affect elicited by the inductions. Later, in moral encounters in which they harm or are about to harm someone, this norm is activated internally (by empathic distress or anticipatory guilt) and becomes the prosocial motive component of the individual's inner moral conflict.

Inductions, no longer necessary, have in a sense "created the seeds of their own destruction" (or at least dispensability). It is as if discipline encounters involving inductions are rehearsals for moral encounters. The processes that mediate the developmental shift from discipline encounters to moral encounters – from compliance to internalization – is the focus of the theory to which I will turn after a few words about discipline in general.

### A PRIMER ON DISCIPLINE

I have found it useful to define discipline in terms of the power structure of the parent–child relationship. Parents have enormous power over all aspects of children's lives. They control children's material supplies and, being stronger at least in the early years, they can punish children physically. They can force children to do anything, with few limitations. Furthermore, how they treat the child, outside of extreme neglect and cruelty, is subject to little if any legal restraint.

Some writers claim parents do not have that much power (Kuczynski, Marshall, & Schell, 1997): Unlike the power between unre-

lated adults and children, "parents and children interact in an interdependent, intimate relationship where each is both vulnerable and
powerful with regard to the other" (p. 27). I agree up to a point:
Parents do operate under psychological and cultural constraints –
they love their children and want them to succeed and be happy.
But they can ignore the constraints whenever they feel it necessary,
which they often do. Furthermore, the power structure seems to be
lopsidedly in favor of parents, as evidenced by Schoggen's (1963)
observations of mother–child pairs, cited in my earlier article on
parental power (Hoffman, 1975a). He found that parents made attempts to change children's behavior against their will (indicated by
the child's resisting or responding with negative feeling to the parent's initial attempt) four or five times as often as children tried to
change parents' behavior; and the children submitted to these parental pressures over two-thirds of the time. These observations are
significant because they were done without any guiding hypothesis
and agree remarkably with the child-compliance findings I described
at the beginning of this chapter. As Minton et al., (1971) note, "The
event that elicits the mother's reprimand is often a minor misde-
meanor ... and the mother's modal reaction is to tell the child 'stop
it,' occasionally explaining why the prohibition is necessary. The
child typically obeys. If he does not, she does not ignore the action
but initiates stronger treatment procedures, which are usually successful" (p. 1886).

The evidence thus seems clear that parents usually have their way
with children: They are the ones who set the agenda and make the
demands. Children's resistance and attempts to negotiate may have
a delaying effect but even this depends on parents' willingness to be
influenced by children's requests for more time or other concessions.
The research is limited to children's first ten years and to Kansas,
Michigan, and Massachusetts samples; it was done in the 1960s. It
may seem reasonable to assume that the power differential diminishes as children get bigger, smarter, and subject to influences outside the home, and that times have changed and parents have or at
least assert less power nowadays. But there is no evidence for this
and to judge from news accounts parents still wield a lot of power:

Physical abuse of children by parents is commonplace, though it varies with gender, income, parents' educational level, and ethnicity.[1]

All of this is to say that parents are free to choose discipline methods that assert their power in varying degrees or not at all. I coined the term *power-assertion* almost four decades ago to describe discipline methods that assert parent power. (Hoffman, 1960). Parents also control children's emotional supplies and can threaten to withdraw love as a means of controlling children's behavior. This adds to their power.

It follows that once children become aware of the power structure, all parental discipline attempts have a "background" power-assertive and love-withdrawing dimension that puts a certain minimal amount of pressure on children to comply. Beyond that, parental discipline may have explicit power-assertive and love-withdrawing properties that add to the pressure. Parental discipline may also include a reasoning or induction component, whereby the parent explains the required behavior change by pointing up the consequences of the child's ongoing action for the child or someone else. Parental discipline is thus multidimensional. The categories power

---

1. An article in the *New York Times* (February 29, 1996) described parent immigrants from the Caribbean who favored power assertion (including physical force) and complained bitterly about American parents' permissiveness. Many of my New York University students' parents are recent immigrants from traditional cultures and with few exceptions they assert a lot of power, usually successfully, even when they cannot speak English and are heavily dependent on their children because of this. Children's getting older may thus not always signify a drop in parental power assertion, at least in some of our subcultures. There may be fewer discipline encounters per day than with younger children, but the proportion of them that assert power may be just as high.

   Nor is spanking all that rare in the less traditional West. European countries, including Austria, Denmark, Finland, Norway, and Sweden, have found it necessary to ban corporal punishment; in England, "smacking" children has long been a political as well as domestic issue; and despite a 3-decade decline in spanking in the United States, a 1995 Harris poll found that 80% of the 1250 parents surveyed said they had spanked their children (Collins, 1995).

assertion, love withdrawal, and induction are "ideal types" that rarely occur in isolation but instead, in various strengths and combinations. They contribute differently to guilt and moral internalization, however, and so I discuss them separately.

### Power Assertion

The power-assertive component of parental discipline may be "silent," in the background, as mentioned above. It can also be explicit. Explicit power assertion includes demands, threats of physical force or deprivation of possessions or privileges, and actual force or deprivation. There are two types of physical force – punitive (spanking, hitting) and constraining (holding, picking up and moving the child) – that can be quite different in their effects. The most arbitrary, coercive power-assertive techniques use force or threat to change the child's behavior, without qualification or explanation. From the child's standpoint, these unqualified power assertions violate his need for task completion, his freedom of action, and, past a certain age, his expectation that demands will be explained. They also arouse anger, the motive to restore freedom – "reactance" (Brehm, 1972) – and fear. Their frequent use produces children who obey out of fear but express their anger and oppositional tendencies toward less powerful figures like peers and nursery-school teachers; they also give children a power-assertive model of how to behave when one wants to change another's behavior (Bandura & Walters, 1959; Hoffman, 1960).

Power assertion is less coercive and arbitrary when accompanied by reasons or "cushions." Reasons justify demands in terms of something outside the parent's control. Here is a sample of reasons from my study of mothers of preschool children (the power-assertion portion is usually omitted). Some point up the physical, temporal, or spatial demands of the situation ("If you run so fast, you'll drop it and it will break"; "We don't wear shoes in bed, it dirties the sheets"; "Don't play with your food, now the baby wants to do it and she won't eat"). Others refer to the child's welfare ("Don't walk where it's muddy, you'll slip and fall"; "If you're not nice to her, she won't be nice to you"). Last but not least, reasons may point up the parent's or someone else's welfare ("Don't ever hit anyone in the face! You can really hurt them"; "You must stay in your room until you learn to come out and play and be a good girl and be nice to your baby sister and not make her cry").

"Cushions" reduce a power-assertion's coercive dimension not by explaining the demand but by allowing children some partial gratification or closure. Reasons and cushions are often the parent's response to children's attempts to negotiate an unqualified power-assertive demand. A frequent scenario in my study of preschoolers was one in which parents began with an unqualified power-assertive demand ("Stop that!" "Drink your milk!" "Turn off the TV!"). They then responded to the child's negotiation attempt either by standing firm and giving a reason or, more interestingly, by softening the blow with any of a variety of cushions. For example, they provided a substitute ("Here, hit it with this hammer, not with your dolly"), allowed partial closure ("Okay, you can watch until the next commercial and then the TV goes off"), or reduced the demand ("Okay, then drink half the glass"). Other types of cushion are remaining firm but expressing understanding of the child's desire to continue what he or she was doing, and making the required behavior change more attractive to the child (A father responded to his son's resistance to going to bed by turning off the TV, lifting his son up on his shoulders, and carrying him upstairs shouting "March! March!").[2]

Unqualified power assertion is sometimes necessary, as in emergencies when there is no other choice. Unqualified power assertion can also be used constructively, especially by parents who rarely use it. It may, for example, be the most effective way to control a child who is acting in a particularly obnoxious or openly defiant manner (Hoffman, 1970; Zahn-Waxler et al., 1979). More important for our

2. The power-assertion-and-cushion scenario occurred frequently with parents who usually used inductions. In a different, less-frequent scenario, these parents begin with induction, resist the child's negotiation attempt, and repeat the induction; if the child resists again, they introduce a mild power assertion (demand, insist) and escalate to a threat or use force if necessary to get the child to comply.

purposes, **unqualified power assertion may also be the best way at times for parents who usually use induction to communicate, loud and clear, their strong positive value on considering others and their particularly intense feeling about certain harmful acts** ("It is **not** okay to kick your mother or anyone else in the face even if it seems like fun") – although this same loud and clear message can be sent if an inductive reason is included ("Give me that stick! You know better, I told you before not to play with these sticks because you can hurt somebody with them; now give me that stick"). In any case, if parents do *not* express themselves strongly (power-assertively) in these situations it could be perceived by children as legitimizing the harmful act; the power assertion makes it unmistakably clear to the child that what he or she did or is about to do is wrong and unacceptable.

## Love Withdrawal

The love-withdrawing component of parental discipline may also be "silent" or explicit. Explicit instances of love withdrawal are those in which parents give direct but nonpower-assertive expression to their anger or disapproval of the child for engaging in an unwanted, harmful act. For example, they may ignore the child, turn their back on the child, refuse to speak or listen to the child, say they dislike the child, isolate or threaten to leave the child. Here are examples of love withdrawal by parents of preschool children: "I don't like you when you talk like that." "All right, if that's the way you're going to be, don't ask me to help you any more." "If you keep that up, Momma will go away and leave you alone." "You won't get your goodnight kiss if you keep on whining."

Love withdrawal uses the affectionate relationship between parent and child to a greater degree than power assertion but in a way that is just as likely produce a disruptive anxiety response – not anger and fear so much as anxiety over whether the parent still cares about the child. Love withdrawal also communicates the parent's strong negative feeling about the behavior at issue and makes it clear the behavior is wrong. Love withdrawal is often used when children express anger toward the parent (Hoffman, 1970), which may explain why it contributes to children's inhibition of anger (Hoffman, 1963; Hoffman & Saltzstein, 1967).

As with power assertion, love withdrawal's effects on children may be attenuated by an explanation. For example, a parent's emotional expression of moral outrage over a child's action may be received by the child as pure rejection and may arouse considerable anxiety. This is less likely if the parent's emotional outburst is accompanied by an explanation (that the child can understand) which pinpoints the aspect of his or her behavior that is disapproved of by the parent.

### Induction

When children harm or are about to harm someone – the parent, a sibling, a friend – parents may take the victim's perspective and show how the child's behavior harms the victim. These are **inductions**, as noted. The earliest inductions point up direct, observable physical consequences of the child's action ("If you push him again, he'll fall down and cry"; "It's uncomfortable when you walk on me, please let me lie here a few more minutes"; "If you have to defend yourself that's all right but you may not hit anybody with anything in your hand, you could really hurt them"; "If you throw snow on their walk they will have to clean it up all over again"). Later, the victim's hurt feelings may be pointed up – at first simple feelings ("He feels bad when you don't share your marbles with him, just as you would feel bad if he didn't share his marbles with you"; "You really hurt Mary and made her feel sad when you pushed her down and took her dolly" [said with conviction and emotion] [Zahn-Waxler et al., 1979]). And still later, more subtle feelings ("He feels bad because he was proud of his tower and you knocked it down").

The harmful effects of the child's action may be mentioned indirectly ("He's afraid of the dark so please turn the light back on"; "Try to be quiet, if he can sleep a while longer he'll feel better when he wakes up"). The victim's perspective may be implied by stating his intentions or legitimate desires in a way that indicates the child's antisocial behavior was unjustified ("Don't yell at him. He was only trying to help"; "Couldn't you let him have it for a few minutes just so he can look inside? He wants so much to look inside and I don't think he'll do it any harm"; "He was only taking his turn and he has a right to a turn, just as you do"; "I won't allow you to hit her when she does something by accident. You must understand that it was an accident. She is too young to know what she is doing. She did not mean to hurt you"). And, finally, reparative acts may be suggested ("Would you tell your sister that you are sorry and try to make her feel better about it?"; "Go over and pat him so he'll feel better"; "Now I would like you to help him put it [the tower the child knocked down] back together").

In using inductions, parents do several things. First of all, like any attempt to change the child's behavior, inductions communicate the parent's disapproval of the child's act and indicate implicitly or explicitly that the act is wrong and that the child has committed an infraction ("Saying nasty things to people is not nice. It makes people feel bad. That's not the way we behave in this family").[3] **But inductions do two important things that other discipline techniques do not do: (a) They call attention to the victim's distress and make it salient to the child, thus tapping into the child's empathic proclivity (using it as an ally) by activating any or all of his or her empathy-arousing mechanisms and producing empathic distress, and (b) inductions point up the role of the child's action in causing that distress. This creates the condition for feeling empathy-based guilt, which is a feeling of intense disesteem for oneself for wrongfully harming another.**

3. You may wonder why the focus is on the negative consequences of children's actions. The reason is that helpful, kindly acts are not targets of parental discipline. Parents do occasionally ask children to engage in considerate behaviors that have nothing to do with their ongoing action ("There's the bell. Please answer the door and tell Aunt Bessie that you're glad to see her, it will make her feel good"; "My feet are tired. Please take off my shoes and rub them, it will feel so good") I classify these as inductions and consider them potentially important additions to prosocial moral socialization, although I have found them to be rare.

Highlighting the child's causal role is essential because very young children could empathize and cry along with the victim without realizing they caused the victim's distress, or they might just turn away or leave, thus avoiding empathy and guilt. Older children can turn away and leave too. They can also be oblivious to their causal role – in fights and arguments, or when victims of their action are angry and retaliate rather than feeling sad or hurt – because of ambiguities in these situations that allow them to project or rationalize blame. To overcome these obstacles, as well as capitalize on children's empathy and guilt capabilities, requires that parents make the role of the child's action in causing the other's distress clear.

For inductions to accomplish all of this, they must be cast in terms that are within the child's cognitive and linguistic reach and, especially with a young child, they must be clearly related to his own experience. Common sense says that parents would normally do this and there is evidence that they do: They begin using simple inductions in the child's third year, just when children are making rapid strides in language; and they increase the ratio of inductions to power assertions as children grow older (Chapman, 1979). For inductions to be effective also requires that children not remain passive. They must stop what they are doing and attend to the parent. They must actively process the inductive message, that is, they must make the connection between their actions and the victim's distress, thus allowing empathy and guilt to be generated from within themselves. To motivate children to do this, given their involvement in their own agenda, their motivation to pursue their own goals, and the emotionality of the situation, requires a certain amount of external pressure – enough to get them to attend and process the inductive message but not enough to produce undue anger, fear, or anxiety over losing parental love, any of which could disrupt cognitive processing.

The pressure to attend and process an induction may come from the power-assertive component of a power-assertion-with-reason. Or, if induction is used alone, there may be enough "background" power-assertive and love-withdrawing pressure, due to the power structure, as discussed earlier. Either way, processing the induction can persuade the child that the parent's suggestion is reasonable.

And whether he ends up complying voluntarily or under pressure, he should feel empathic distress, guilt, and a sense of doing wrong – to a far greater degree than in any other socialization setting. A few words about the optimal amount of pressure.

*Optimal pressure.* Too little pressure obviously gives children no reason to stop, attend, and process inductive messages. Too much pressure, as long known by information-processing researchers, directs a person's attention to the physical features of a verbal message, to the relative neglect of deriving meaning from its semantic content (Kahneman, 1973; Mueller, 1979). We may likewise assume that too much power assertion or love withdrawal directs children's attention to the consequences of their action for themselves. Discipline having a salient inductive component directs children's attention to the consequences of their action for the victim. Furthermore, induction's explanatory feature reduces the arbitrary quality of the parent's demand, and by focusing the parent's disapproval on the act and its harmful effects rather than on the child, it makes a high-anxiety, cognitively disruptive response less likely. Inductions are therefore better equipped than other discipline methods to accomplish the dual objective of focusing children's attention on their own actions and the effects of their actions on others, and allowing external pressure from parents to remain in the background.

When power assertion is necessary, what is the type and optimal amount? This would seem to depend on the situation. A mild directive may do the trick when the child is simply unaware of the harm done ("Don't you see you hurt Mary? Don't pull her hair"). But highly charged conflicts between the child and a parent or friend may require the parent to hold the child firmly and insist that he or she listen (to the induction), or to physically remove the child and calm him or her down, or even to send the child to his or her room so that the child (and the parent) can calm down. Once the child is calmed down, he or she is in a better position to process and benefit from an induction.

It can be different when both parents are involved in a sort of division of labor in which one is power-assertive and the other inductive, as in this example given by a student:

My father used his belt. I cried. My mother felt sorry for me. She would come to my room and try to explain to me why I was punished. I remember one time in particular. I was home with my mom and she said something to me. I blurted out to her to shut up. She didn't do anything to me or say anything when this happened. She just waited for my father to come home. When he came home and she told him what I said he went through the roof. I was punished and sent to my room crying and in pain because he had hit me in the rear with his belt. By doing this he taught me to fear and even hate him. My mom came into my room, sat me down, made me stop crying, and explained that I had been disrespectful of her when I told her to shut up. She also said I had hurt her feelings when I spoke to her in such a rude manner. She also said that I should never speak to anyone that way because it was rude and disrespectful. So when she sat me down and told me that I had hurt her feelings I realized that what I did was indeed wrong. I also realized that I shouldn't do it again. Not because I would be punished but because it would hurt my mom, or somebody else that I was speaking to.

When a mother defers to the father like this, children often lose respect for the mother or see her as expressing power assertion through the father, but apparently not in this case, probably because of the nature of the mother–daughter relationship. Whatever the reason, it appears that the father's administering physical punishment was a catalyst that set the stage for the mother's using induction and for its apparent effectiveness in the daughter's prosocial moral development. It also appears that the mother followed the "rule" of calming her daughter down before administering the induction.

Two final points about the optimal amount of power assertion. The first is that what is optimal may be influenced by the child's temperament: Kochanska (1995) found that fearful children require relatively little power assertion, and I would assume that willful children require relatively more. The second point is that however much power assertion is needed in particular instances, I would expect judiciously used power assertions to carry over and play a background role in motivating children to attend to inductions in future situations in which power assertion is not used.

When I talk about the positive effects of inductions from now on, I assume the pressure to attend to them is within the optimal range.

*Expressing disappointment.* Parents often say "I'm disappointed in you," which seems to communicate either induction ("You let me down"; "You don't love me") or love withdrawal ("I think less of you"; "I love you less") or both. Krevans and Gibbs (1996) found expressing disappointment to function statistically like induction, not love withdrawal, but they suggest treating expressions of disappointment separately from other inductions. I have another suggestion. When disappointment is combined with induction ("What you said makes me feel unhappy") or love withdrawal ("I can't trust you anymore"; "You're not my child when you act that way"), there is no ambiguity; it is clearly one or the other. When an expression of disappointment stands alone, the context should be considered. If the context does not help, the expression should be treated as uncodeable or called induction or love withdrawal depending on how the parent usually responds in similar situations. I have found that the context usually favors inductions, that is, although the parent is expressing disapproval, the primary message is that the child's words or actions have hurt the parent or let him or her down. This may explain why disappointment behaves statistically like induction. It certainly behaves like an induction in the following example:

> When I was about 18–19 years old, I was still living at home with my parents and I stayed out all night at a party – got home 8–9 A.M. the next day. I didn't call – it didn't even cross my mind to call home. When I did get home, kind of hung-over, tired – my mother was waiting for me with the biggest guilt trip known to man. She started the "You don't love me, you make me worry so much, I thought you were dead" routine. She told me – worst of all – that she was disappointed in me! This is my mother, who fawned over every little achievement I had from kindergarten to getting my driver's license. The way she made me feel stuck with me. We made up of course, after lots of crying and explaining. But, to this day I can still picture the look of disappointment on her face and the tone of her voice. I hope to God I never make her feel like that again. (Baumeister, Stillwell, & Heatherton, 1995, p. 267)

It is unclear whether this mother is withholding love ("Your lack of consideration makes me love you less"). But the primary message is clearly inductive ("Your lack of consideration hurts me") – "You don't love me" rather than "I don't love you" – and that is the way it seems to have been received by the son, as witness his "guilt trip" comment.

To summarize, all discipline techniques put pressure on children to change their behavior, and for that reason alone they communicate disapproval of children's harmful actions. Consequently, they may all arouse some anxiety over parental disapproval and motivate children to change their behavior to regain approval. When the power-assertive or love-withdrawal component is pronounced, this anxiety is heightened and the child's attention is focused on the consequences to him-or herself of complying or resisting. When induction is salient, the anxiety over disapproval is lower; but the power-structure context alone may be enough to motivate the child to attend and process the induction, thus making the child aware of the victim's distress and the child's role in causing it and producing empathic distress and guilt. Changes in children's behavior in response to inductions are thus not due to obedience or compliance in the sense of submitting to another's will, but at least to some extent to changes in perspective and feeling resulting from the processing of relevant information.

## A THEORY OF INDUCTION'S ROLE IN MORAL DEVELOPMENT

What follows is a review of the theory's central concepts, cast in terms of *generic event memories* or *scripts* that pertain to the cognitive and affective processes in discipline encounters and how they contribute over time to guilt and moral internalization in children. I use the script concept for several reasons. As Nelson (1993) notes, scripts are derived from experience and sketch the general outline of a familiar event, including behavior interaction sequences, without providing details of the specific time or place when such an event happened. Scripts are useful because young children form them to organize behavior and guide action: 3- and 4-year-olds are quite good at telling what happens in general in a familiar event such as having lunch at the preschool or going to the beach, the zoo, or MacDonald's (Hudson & Nelson, 1983; Nelson, 1981). It therefore seems reasonable to assume that children form scripts of discipline-interaction sequences (discipline encounters) in which they harm others and that these scripts get more complex with each repetition through a process of progressive integration of new information and details.

I assume further that discipline-encounter scripts, like other "emotional scripts" (Lewis, 1989) – or any mental representation for that matter – can be charged with the affects that accompany the event. In this case the affects are empathic distress, sympathetic distress, guilt, which I assume, confer their motive properties on the script. In this way, children's scripts of discipline encounters in which they harm or are about to harm others can become the affective-cognitive-behavioral units of children's prosocial motivational structure. Here is how I think it happens.

## Affective and Cognitive Processes in Discipline Encounters

1. To review so far, inductions, like all discipline attempts, communicate parental disapproval of the child's harmful acts. This makes it clear that the child has done something wrong and arouses a certain amount of concern over parental approval. But unlike other types of discipline, inductions do two additional things: First, they call attention to the victims' distress, and by making the victims' distress salient they exploit an ally within the child, the child's empathic proclivity. That is, inductions activate certain empathy-arousing mechanisms – mimicry if they get the child to look at the victim, role-taking if they encourage the child to imagine how he or she would feel in the victim's place, and mediated association if they bring up the child's relevant past experience. In this way inductions elicit empathic distress for the victims' pain, hurt feelings, and (if

relevant) suffering beyond the situation. Second, inductions are verbal communications that make the child's causal role in the other's distress salient. The child's processing that information under the proper conditions (optimal pressure) results in a self-blame attribution that transforms his or her empathic distress, at least partly, into guilt, that is, *transgression guilt*, in contrast to bystander guilt over inaction. In short, children's cognitive processing of inductions arouses empathic distress and transforms it into guilt.

2. In explaining how children form their first scripts, Nelson (1993) suggests that a new experience alerts the child to set up a new schema for that experience. This schema exists in memory for awhile as a single, "episodic" memory (Tulving, 1972), but with further experience with events of the same kind it comes to be more and more scriptlike; and as it becomes a script, relevant new information is integrated into it. Research on novel and repeated events with preschool children found this process of script building to occur when events were experienced five or more times (Hudson & Nelson, 1983).

I suggest the same thing happens in children's earliest discipline encounters when inductions are used. The conditions for script formation are met: The event is repeated many times and inductions supply information and create the conditions for semantically integrating this information into scripts. As in Nelson's model, I suggest the sequence – child's transgression, followed by parent's induction, followed by child's feeling empathic distress and guilt – is representated first as an "episodic" memory or schema. But with further experience in discipline encounters, the sequence is represented in a scriptlike fashion. Once a discipline-encounter script is formed, relevant information and details from subsequent discipline encounters are integrated into it. The full script may include reparative acts suggested by the parent (apologizing, comforting, hugging, kissing the victim), the parent's and victim's positive responses to these acts, and the empathic relief and guilt reduction the child may experience afterward. These additions are important: They give children a repertoire of reparative acts for future use and reinforce the acts' connection to guilt arousal and guilt reduction. The full script is thus

Transgression → Induction → Empathic Distress and Guilt → Reparation, but since my focus is motivation, especially empathy-based guilt, and also for convenience, I call it a **Transgression → Induction → Guilt script. It has motive properties due to its empathic distress and guilt components** (Chapter 3).

Before moving on, a historical note: The moral script idea, in broad outline, was anticipated by Piaget many years ago when he claimed that emotions are not simply experienced and then forgotten but are stored as part of our basic representations and understandings of various social and moral events. "Affects, by being represented, last beyond the presence of the object that excites them. This ability to conserve feelings makes interpersonal and moral feelings possible and allows the latter to be organized into normative scales of values" (Piaget, 1954/1981, p. 44). Put in my terms, Piaget is saying that script formation keeps empathic distress and guilt feelings from being experienced and immediately forgotten. The feelings are embedded in scripts that are encoded in memory and can be evoked later. (More about cognition's role in stabilizing empathic affects later, in chapter 9).

3. Children may start forming these scripts early in the third year when parents begin disciplining in earnest and when, according to the research, inductions begin contributing to children's consideration for others (Zahn-Waxler et al., 1979). For inductive information to be understood well enough to arouse empathic distress and guilt at that age, it must simply and clearly point up the victim's distress and make the child's role in causing it salient ("You pushed him and he fell down and started to cry").

In processing their very earliest inductions, children probably integrate the cause–effect relation between their act and the victim's distress into the simple, nonmoral physical cause–effect scripts that they have previously formed and brought to these discipline encounters. **Through this process, those simple physical cause–effect scripts are enriched and given a moral dimension (my actions can harm others). Furthermore, the scripts can be infused with empathic distress and a (rudimentary) guilt feeling, which gives them the properties, including the motivational properties of affectively** charged representations, or hot cognitions. These may be the earliest, most rudimentary Transgression → Induction → Guilt scripts.

I would imagine that in the beginning each harmful act – at first simple acts like kicking, hitting, pushing, spitting, pulling hair, teasing, and name-calling and later more complex behaviors like betraying a confidence, reneging on a promise, staying out late and worrying parents – has its own script. These specific scripts continue to operate and develop individually while also being combined into more generalized scripts that bear on physically injuring others, hurting their feelings, not meeting their expectations, and, eventually, an all-inclusive more abstract and highly delineated script for all actions that harm others.

4. When these early scripts are activated in children in conflict situations, they are at first no match for the pull of the prospect of egoistic gain. In time, however, cognitive development enables children to "decenter," that is, to transcend the egoistic pull, free themselves from the grip of their own perspective, and take another's perspective as well. But the newly acquired cognitive ability to decenter is not enough to keep children's own viewpoint from capturing most of their attention in a conflict situation, unless they are compelled to exercise this newly acquired cognitive ability. What compels them to do this?

Piaget's answer, that it is peers' advancing their own desires, is not supported by the research: Hay (1984) found that preschoolers often resolved their conflicts without adult intervention, but the outcome typically favored the initiators, who used force, threats, and intimidating gestures. This suggests that *conflicting peer perspectives are a reflection of the problem, not the solution.* A better formulation might be that there is a division of labor between decentering, peer conflict, and parent inductions: Peer conflict *compels* children to move out of their egocentric mode and attend to others; decentration is the cognitive structural quality that *enables* them to attend to multiple claims; but the empathy and guilt produced by inductions *motivates* them to take the claims of others into account.

In any case, the child's potential joy at having his own way can be tempered by empathic distress. That is, the force of the child's egoistic motives can be weakened by knowing the other's needs and their accompanying sadness, and it can be reduced to the level of his emerging and countervailing empathy-based motives. In other words, the motive force of the child's previously weak prosocial moral scripts is now on a par with, and may at times exceed, the force of his egoistic motives.

5. The child's first scripts may contain kinesthetic representations and visual images of the body movements involved in the child's harmful actions and visual images and sounds associated with the victim's distress, as well as the meanings the child derives from simple inductions. I assume **these scripts are encoded in memory and activated in the next discipline encounter, and that they semantically integrate the inductive information in that encounter, and so on.** With language, cognitive development, and more sophisticated ways of harming others, the inductive content of parental discipline becomes more complex. **The scripts become less kinesthetic-imagistic and more semantic-"propositional."** They continue to change and develop by progressively integrating the information in literally thousands of inductions over the childhood years.[4] Through this process, children's early, physical, nonmoral causal scripts are gradually transformed into complex, generalized, affectively charged scripts pertaining to the effects of one's actions on others – scripts that have the moral-cognitive dimension of a moral norm to consider others, while retaining their empathic and guilt-motivational components.

6. These prosocial moral scripts are not passively acquired but

4. I previously noted the research suggesting children may be exposed to as many as 15,000 discipline attempts a year. I do not know how many were inductions, but over a third of the discipline attempts by my middle-class sample of preschoolers' parents, and a sixth of the lower-class sample, were inductions. There is also evidence that middle-class parents use "reasoning" half the time (Chapman & Zahn-Waxler, 1982; Ross, Tessla, Kenyon & Lollis, 1990; Smetana, 1989; etc.). If half of these instances were inductions, which seems reasonable, then something like a quarter of the discipline attempts in those samples could have been inductions. That means "thousands of inductions over the childhood years" is not an exaggeration for parents who prefer inductions.

actively formed by children in a continuing process of constructing, synthesizing, and semantically organizing inductive information and relating it to their own actions and the victim's condition. Children have ownership of their thoughts and feelings during the processing of inductions, assuming of course the optimal amount of external pressure, discussed earlier. *The active mental processes make the child's internal cognitive and affective processes salient to the child and the child experiences the scripts, hence the moral norm of considering others – which is always implicit and often explicit in inductions – as the child's own construction and part of his or her internal motive system, despite having originated externally in discipline encounters.*

As a result, parental intervention becomes less necessary. The induction component begins to fade from the script and the child is motivated to consider others even in the parents' absence. **At some point, parental intervention really is unnecessary, and the Transgression → Induction → Guilt script becomes for all practical purposes a Transgression → Guilt script, which can be activated by the child's own awareness of harming another. When the script is activated, its associated guilt feeling and the motivation to make reparation is experienced by the child as coming from within himself.**[5]

*7. Anticipatory script activation and guilt.* The value of scripts and empathy-based guilt as a prosocial moral motive would be limited if the scripts were activated and guilt experienced only after the fact. But it seems reasonable that Transgression → Guilt scripts, like other representations, can be activated in advance by relevant stimuli, which in this case are the thoughts and images a child has when

5. I assume this activation is automatic and preconscious. Outside discipline encounters, when children are asked to reflect back on their parents' discipline methods, they may remember the relatively few instances in which their parents used power assertion to communicate how strongly they felt and how highly they valued considering others. I would hypothesize, in keeping with Nelson's theory of autobiographical memory (Nelson, 1993), that these may be among the "episodic memories" that define one's autobiographical self, even though they may rarely be activated in moral encounters (one more likely helps because of activation of scripts, not memories of parent-expressed values). But this is a topic for research.

contemplating action that may harm someone. When these anticipatory thoughts and images activate a Transgression → Guilt script, the script's associated guilt feeling should be experienced as "anticipatory guilt," which can operate as a motive against committing the harmful act. Anticipatory guilt may prevail, but when it does not and the child engages in the harmful act, he should feel guilty.

Anticipatory guilt has certain cognitive and behavior-control prerequisites: One must be able, under fire, to connect one's intentions to actions and their consequences before these have occurred, consider another's perspective, and control the urge to carry out the action. It should, therefore, follow transgression guilt developmentally. In any case, the effect of anticipatory guilt is that instead of feeling guilty after harming someone, one feels guilty at the thought of harming someone. Instead of thinking about ways to undo a harmful act, one may, in a sense, "undo" it in advance – by not doing it.

There is some research on anticipatory guilt as a motive against committing a transgression. Okel and Mosher (1968) induced male undergraduates to insult a fellow student (a confederate of the experimenter's), who became distressed as a result of the insult. High-empathy subjects said they felt guilty about what they had done and would not have done it had they known how upset the victim would be. Malinowski and Smith (1985) asked undergraduates how guilty they would feel if they cheated; those who said they would feel guilty were found in fact not to cheat on an experimental task. In chapter 4, I summarized the evidence that bystanders anticipate feeling guilty if they do not help someone in distress; it seems reasonable that they would anticipate feeling just as guilty at the thought of actually harming someone.

8. *Integration of new experience.* Once a child's scripts for considering others and capacity for anticipatory guilt are in place, the child can integrate into the scripts his or her experiences of harming others outside discipline encounters. These experiences may be new because they are associated with growing up and happen among peers but not in the presence of parents. One's experiences of *being* the victim in these new settings may also be integrated into the script

because it helps one to know how it feels to be a victim. In this way, children's internalized Transgression → Guilt scripts can grow and expand by integrating new experiences outside discipline encounters.

Though the theory's focus is parent discipline, the child's interactions with adults and peers outside the home may also contribute to moral internalization. Given the early motive base from discipline encounters, children may be receptive to induction-like communications from teachers and other adults. Interactions with peers from homes in which inductions are frequently used may have the constructive effects hypothesized by Piaget, especially in the context of indirect adult supervision or inductive "coaching" (Hoffman, 1980). Such peer interactions may reinforce the positive effects of parental inductions and help expand the domain in which children's motive to consider others is applied (e.g., keep promises, don't betray a trust, don't embarrass). This domain is also expanded as children acquire language and role-taking skills of increasing sophistication, so that the effects of actions on others can be comprehended long after, or anticipated ahead of, the situation. Although language and role-taking are neutral skills that can be used to manipulate as well as help others, a child who is motivated to consider others should employ these skills more often in the service of helping others.

To conclude, what I have suggested are the antecedent factors that may lead to the development of an early moral motive to consider others even when one's needs conflict with theirs. Later experiences of various kinds may expand this motive to other areas of life and provide the skills and competencies that serve the motive and build upon it to create complex moral ideational structures (as discussed in chapter 9).

## EVIDENCE FOR THE THEORY

The evidence for the theory is by no means ironclad, but there is support for some of its main concepts; and insofar as these concepts are part of an interconnected network, support for them can be considered as support for the theory. The research on parent discipline's contribution to guilt and moral internalization was done mainly in the 1960s and 1970s (reviewed by Hoffman, 1988) but has continued into the present (Brody & Shaffer, 1982; Crockenberg & Litman, 1990; De Veer, 1991; Hart, DeWolfe, Wozniak, & Burts, 1992; Krevans & Gibbs, 1996); Rollins & Thomas, 1979). This research supports, with a high degree of consistency (some findings are not significant statistically but none are negative), the generalization that mothers (the father findings are mixed) who use induction produce children whose moral orientation is characterized by independence of external sanctions and guilt over harming others. These findings also fit real-life observations, as exemplified by Oliner and Oliner's (1988) report that parents of Germans who rescued Jews from the Nazis were caring individuals who were more likely to use induction than power assertion. The research also shows that a moral orientation based on fear of external detection and punishment is associated with the frequent use of power assertion, especially unqualified power assertion. There appears to be no consistent relationship between moral orientation and love withdrawal, although there is some evidence that love withdrawal relates to inhibition of anger.

Most of the research is correlational, but there is experimental evidence that induction contributes to moral internalization (Kuczynski, 1983; Sawin & Parke, 1980). In Kuczynski's study, 9- to 10-year-olds, divided into three groups, played with some very attractive toys. They were then told that they had some work to do and were seated with their backs to the toys. They were all instructed not to look at the toys until the adult said they could, a mild form of power assertion. One group was told nothing more than that – mild though unqualified power assertion; another group was told that they would be unhappy if they looked at the toys because if they did not work hard enough they would have to do the work later and would have little time to play with the toys – mild power assertion with child-centered reason (child would be unhappy and deprived); a third group was instructed not to look and told they would make the adult unhappy if they looked at the toys because if they didn't work hard enough the adult would have to do the work later and have little time to do what he wanted to do – power assertion with induction (the adult would be unhappy and deprived).

The findings were as follows. When the adult remained in the room there was no difference between the three manipulations: Most of the subjects in each group complied. But when the adult left the room, saying that he would be gone longer than expected and would therefore understand if they did not work the whole time, and added, for good measure, that he would not be angry if they looked at the toys, the induction group was far more likely to continue working and not look at the toys than the other two groups; and the induction group's performance was no different than when the adult remained in the room.

I give the details of this experiment because the prosocial moral internalization measure comes close to prosocial moral internalization in life: One does something for another at cost to oneself without expecting reward for doing it or punishment for not doing it. The measure may at first appear to resemble the "forbidden toy paradigm" criticized in chapter 5, but it is a better moral internalization measure because the subjects in the induction group resisted temptation not for themselves but for the benefit of someone else.

The study by Sawin and Parke was similar except the subjects were kindergartners and second graders, the experimenter was a female, and the three manipulations were: (a) mild unqualified power assertion: "You must not touch the toys while I'm gone"; (b) the same mild power assertion plus saying the adult would be "very angry" if the children touched the toys (mild power assertion plus love withdrawal); (c) the same power assertion plus saying the adult would be "very sad" if they touched the toys (mild power assertion plus induction). As in the Kuczynski study, the induction group was less likely to touch the toys with the adult out of the room than the other two groups, although this was only true of the second graders, who were close in age to Kuczynski's subjects (the kindergartners showed no effect).

Both of these experimental studies support induction's contribution to internalization, Kuczynski's in particular, because the children were moved to act prosocially to a greater degree when they were told the unhappy consequences of their action for someone other than for themselves. The induction manipulations in both experiments highlight the other person's feelings (unhappy, sad) and how he or she is affected by the child's action. The studies therefore provide implicit support for the hypothesis that inductions work by taking advantage of children's empathic capabilities, that is, that empathy mediates induction's contribution to internalization. This hypothesis was also supported in a recent correlational study by Krevans and Gibbs (1996). They replicated the previous finding in the literature of a positive correlation between induction and prosocial behavior, but they also collected data on empathy. They found that induction relates to empathy, and when empathy is controlled, the relation between induction and prosocial behavior disappears, as they predicted from the empathy-as-mediator hypothesis.

Apart from the research findings, the theory gains plausibility because it focuses on discipline encounters involving inductions, and what it says about children's affective and cognitive responses in these discipline encounters fits well with a morally internalized person's affective and cognitive responses in moral encounters. The theory also fits well with recent findings on children's long-term memory processes: the use of scripts, and the fact that autobiographical memory begins at about 2 years (Howe & Courage, 1997), when parent discipline begins in earnest. This lends plausibility to the hypothesis that children abstract sequences of interactions in discipline encounters – child harms others, followed by inductive information from parent, followed by empathy-based guilt in child – and progressively integrate these sequences into meaningful cognitive-affective scripts.

To summarize, there is correlational and experimental support for induction's contribution to guilt and moral internalization and for empathy as mediating induction's effects. The memory research is consistent with induction's long-term cumulative effects. And the theory makes sense, because the hypothesized cognitive and emotional responses in discipline encounters in which parents use inductions closely parallel a morally internalized person's response in moral encounters.

## Direction of Effects

A few words about direction of effects, about which much has been written in recent years. No one can seriously doubt that the effects go both ways; parents affect children and children affect parents. Most would agree that parent effects are greater early in the child's life, become less important as the child becomes socialized, and are eventually unnecessary or necessary only in "maintenance dosages." But to say this is to say very little: The question is where does the child begin developmentally, where does the child end up, and, above all, how does he or she get there? Insofar as the parent is important, what are the processes that mediate parental behavior's effects on the child especially in the early years? This is what my theory is all about. I believe the parent's use of inductions is necessary for guilt and moral internalization in children, for reasons given earlier. But induction's importance rests on its ability not only to elicit empathy but also to to take advantage of the empathic predisposition that children can bring to discipline encounters. This is the assumption that led to the hypothesis that empathy mediates induction's effects and that inductions therefore work better with high-empathy children, which was supported by the Krevans and Gibbs (1996) research described above.

Empathy as mediator of induction thus assumes children have an empathic capability **before** they are exposed to inductions. This seems a safe assumption, because some empathy-arousing mechanisms (conditioning, association, mimicry) appear shortly after birth (chapter 2). Furthermore, empathy's possible evolutionary roots and hereditary component (Hoffman, 1981; Zahn-Waxler et al., 1992) argue for individual differences in children's empathic predispositions that predate the use of inductions. **Individual differences in empathy may therefore contribute to individual differences in the parent's use of inductions.** Highly empathic children may require less power assertion, like the fearful children discussed earlier, though for entirely different reasons. Highly empathic children may be more responsive to inductions, for example, because they are more likely to notice a victim's downcast look, attend to aspects of the situation mentioned by the parent, or take seriously the parent's suggestion that they put themselves in the victim's place. Their parents may discover this about their children, possibly through trial and error, and then use inductions, in part, because inductions have the desired effects. It may be more than trial and error if empathy has a hereditary component, because the parents of empathic children may be more empathic themselves and more likely to use inductions as an expression of their own empathic orientation. To the extent that all this is true, empathy and induction feed each other, but in complex, interlocking ways.

As of now, this is all conjecture. The evidence for the primacy of child effects on parental discipline is mixed: Grusec and Kuczynski (1980) and Kuczynski, Marshall, and Schell (1997) conclude from their research that disciplinary strategies are determined "more by what the child did than by some consistent childrearing approach on the mother's part"; but Dowdney and Pickles (1991) conclude on the basis of their research that "maternal style seems consistent across contexts and relatively impervious to the child's behavior." See also my discussion of parental power and the evidence that parents can determine the extent to which their discipline is influenced by the child's behavior (chap. 6, "A Primer on Discipline").

Early empathy is, in any case, a long way from mature empathy, and inductions can contribute to developmental advances in empathy by suggesting the child put himself in the victim's place, or by explaining less obvious distress feelings in a victim such as disappointment in his or her own performance. More important, even highly empathic children can get emotionally involved when pursuing their goals or when their desires conflict with others. They therefore require inductions, like anyone else, and, indeed, they are the ones that may benefit most from inductions. In other words, even mature empathy does not, by itself, make children aware of the harmful consequences of their actions for others, nor does it make them moral. What it does do is make them receptive to environments that can make them aware of the consequences of their actions, and thus contribute to their moral development. In this chapter I suggested that inductions are a necessary part of such environments and theorized about how inductions capitalize on children's empathic proclivities and foster moral development.

Guilt feeling is something else. Parents are likely to use inductions before children are capable of true guilt feeling. Guilt has many prerequisites besides awareness of another's distress: a sense of control over one's actions, awareness of the consequences of one's actions, the ability to attribute causality and tell the difference between intentions and accidents. Most of these are cognitive and emotion-regulation skills that can serve egoistic as well as prosocial ends. As the child acquires these skills, they can be recruited in discipline encounters and integrated with empathic distress and self-blame attributions to produce the prosocial cognitive, motivational package that I call empathy-based guilt feeling. This integration is more likely to occur in response to inductions than other known socialization methods. Once children begin to acquire a guilt capability, I assume this becomes an added inducement for parents to use inductions. And eventually, as the theory states, inductions become unnecessary, except perhaps in new or ambiguous situations.

To conclusively test these ideas and find out once and for all what the relations are between induction, empathy, and guilt would seem to require longitudinal research involving the use of structural equation modeling or some such method. The children studied should be less than 2 years of age when observations and testing begin, as that is when parents start using inductions with any frequency and this would make it possible to ascertain the contribution of induction to empathy and especially guilt. DeVeer (1991) used LISREL to study the effects of induction on guilt over 2-year intervals, at three age levels, but her youngest subjects were 5 years old. Induction correlated positively with guilt at each of the three age levels (5 to 6 years, 7 to 8 years, 8 to 10 years), in keeping with the previous research, but there was no evidence of a causal relation, that is, the cross-lagged correlations were not significant. DeVeer suggests, and I agree, that the lack of a causal relation may be due to the subjects' being too old, that is, by the time children are 5 or 6 years of age the mutual influence between induction, empathy, and guilt may have been established and this could mask induction's earlier contribution to the children's guilt. To tease out a causal influence requires younger subjects.

I hope my main point here is clear. No one can deny the influence of children on the parent's choice of discipline methods, but this does not negate parent discipline's importance for children's moral development. Recognizing bidirectionality raises new issues but by itself provides no answers. It makes teasing out parental influence processes more difficult, which is not a reason to stop studying them but to study them in new ways.

# PART III

# Virtual Transgression

# CHAPTER 7

# Relationship Guilt and Other Virtual Guilts

Once children have Transgression → Guilt scripts and the awareness of harming others makes them feel guilty, they may feel guilty any time they *think* they committed a transgression, even when they did not. I call this virtual guilt, and the presumed harmful act, virtual transgression. In virtual transgressions one has not caused another's distress, at least not knowingly, but blames oneself for it anyway. This is not a new concept: One of the definitions of guilt in *Webster's Ninth New Collegiate Dictionary* (1985) is "feelings of culpability especially for imagined offenses" (p. 542).

The developmentally earliest instances of virtual transgressions were reported by Zahn-Waxler et al., (1979). Children 15 to 20 months old who encountered their mother looking sad or sobbing for no apparent reason, would look sad themselves, approach and try to comfort the mother. This suggests they felt empathic distress (but also perhaps some anxiety, as this was their mother, their source of security). More important for present purposes, about a third of the infants seemed to blame themselves for the mother's distress, saying something like "I sorry, Mommy, did I do anything wrong?" or spanking themselves. There is no evidence they actually felt guilty: They could have simply imitated the behavior of others in similar situations. But there is evidence their behavior reflects at least a rudimentary form of self-blame: In laboratory assessments 5 years later, infants who showed this guiltlike behavior produced more guilt themes than the infants who did not (Cummings, Hollenbeck, Iannotti, Radke-Yarrow, & Zahn-Waxler, 1986).

Four factors may have combined to enable children that young to blame themselves: (a) They were among the most highly empathic children in the sample, hence particularly sensitive to changes in the mother's mood; (b) their primitive causal schemas, based on the temporal and geographical proximity of events, led them to assume "I was nearby, so I did it"; (c) their sense of agency, of having an impact on others, which is powerful but limited to a fuzzy awareness of causing or not causing things to happen, led them to think "I could have done it"; (d) their memory for previous instances when they clearly did cause the mother's distress led them to think "I did it before, so maybe I did it now."

This combination of factors could produce self-blame when the cause of the mothers distress is unclear: "She's sad, I'm nearby, I could have made her sad, and I have in the past. So I must have done it." If so, this self-blame could be an early precursor of a type of empathy-based guilt that I think is inherent in all close relationships: "relationship guilt." We now turn to more mature forms of relationship guilt.

## RELATIONSHIP GUILT

Close relationships are necessary for a full emotional life but one pays a price. Baumeister et al., (1995) asked adults to describe the most recent instance in which they felt guilty; the largest response category was neglecting a relationship partner and another was failure to live up to an interpersonal obligation. This is probably due to the fact that close relationships provide endless opportunities for hurting one's partner, "from mundane unintended slights, thoughtless remarks, or forgotten appointments to more serious betrayals of confidence, bald-faced lies, and crushing infidelities" (Tangney & Fischer, 1995, p. 134) – that is, endless opportunities for experiencing transgression guilt.

But close relationships also provide endless opportunities for blaming oneself when innocent. The reason is that relationship partners tend to become so dependent on each other that their feelings and moods depend heavily on the other's feelings and moods, as well as on the other's actions. More importantly, each partner knows the other is similarly dependent on him or her. Indeed, owing to countless interactions over time, each partner is likely to become acutely aware of new and unpredictable ways of unintentionally distressing the other. In short, each partner develops a keen sensitivity to the potential impact of his or her words and deeds on the other.

It may therefore seem entirely reasonable when one's partner is sad or unhappy and the cause is unclear, not only to feel empathic distress but also to blame oneself and feel guilty for the partner's unhappy state. One would not feel guilty if certain of one's innocence but it is hard to be certain without keeping accurate mental records of previous interactions in which one did or did not hurt the other. Such emotional bookkeeping is rare in close relationships. Adding to uncertainty are the many ways of harming others that are unique to close relationships and involve a partner's changing, sometimes unpredictable moods and expectations, which one may violate at times without realizing it. Included are neglecting an obligation, not being attentive enough, and actions like those quoted from Tangney and Fischer above. **Feeling guilty over a partner's distress when the cause is unclear may therefore be endemic to close relationships. I call it "relationship guilt" because it is generated more by the relationship than by a particular act**, and I count it as a type of virtual transgression because it is not based on an actual transgression but an imagined one.

Relationship guilt need not operate alone; it often functions to intensify transgression guilt when one actually did something that harmed a relationship partner. The long quote I gave in chapter 6, describing a young man who stayed out late and did not call his mother, is a case in point. The son felt guilty over not calling his mother (transgression guilt), but the intensity of that guilt was magnified by relationship guilt over "disappointing" his mother ("I hope to God I never make her feel like that again").

Here are two less dramatic examples of relationship guilt reported by college students. One student reported feeling "really down one day. My boyfriend was near crying and asked 'What did I do?' I said it's not your fault. He asked again. I said no, it's not your fault. He said 'Then why are you so down?' I said I don't know but it's not your fault. He said 'I must have done something.' " Another student said: "My boyfriend seemed worried and I knew right away I must have done something. I asked what was the matter. He didn't know. Then I knew it must have been because he spent too much money on my birthday present."

Some aspects of close relationships that cause relationship guilt are present in mother–infant relationships and may explain why the infants discussed earlier blamed themselves when their mothers were distressed for no apparent reason. Infants cry and mothers come immediately. They get injured or ill, or hurt the mother (get a hand tangled in her hair and pull) – and she responds with vocal, facial, or bodily expressions of pain or sorrow. Infants crawl, walk, or talk for the first time, and mothers express delight. These responses by mothers to children's needs and actions, in addition to mothers' explicit statements of how important their children are to them, may create omnipotence feelings in children toward their mothers. As a result, long before developing a "theory of mind" that enables children to *infer* the impact of their actions on others, infants can connect their actions to immediate changes in mothers' moods by simple association. In this context, as in adult relationships, it is reasonable for infants, especially empathic infants, to view their mother's sad expression or sobbing without a clear cause to be due to something they did.

This early self-blame in infants may be a precursor of self-blame in adult relationships, but the differences should be clear. Adult relationships involve peers and are multifaceted, unlike the single-dimensioned nurturer–nurturee mother–infant relationship. Self-blame in adult relationships is not due to the partners' incompletely developed causal schemas, but to their learning from experience about the subtle ways of hurting each other that may not be apparent until long afterward, about how one's words and deeds can be misinterpreted by the partner, and about one's limited memory for past encounters that might explain the partner's distress. *Self-blame in adult relationships thus results from a complex web of interactions in which the partners are certain of their importance to the other but uncertain of the cause of the other's emotional state at a given time.* Each partner is therefore vulnerable to self-blame when the other is distressed without a clear cause, just as infants are, though for different reasons.

When a person commits suicide, his partner may feel guilty ("I should have known he was depressed"; "If only I had [or had not] . . ."). This relates to the general human tendency, shown also in guilt over inaction (chapter 4), to imagine something one could have done to prevent a harmful event, and then to switch from "I could have" to "I should have" and feel guilty. It is easy to imagine after the fact what one might have done – something virtually impossible to know ahead of time – so one really did nothing wrong. Yet people may disregard the impossibility of knowing ahead of time, blame themselves, and feel guilty. The "I could have" part is often true; it is the switch to "I should have" that is not logical and leads to guilt, yet people do it all the time, which makes this an excellent example of a virtual transgression.

This feeling of "I should have" is of course not confined to suicides. In close relationships, one may feel guilty over not doing something to prevent one's partner from having a serious accident, a heart attack, a stroke. Here is a dramatic example, which also shows the powerful effect of combining relationship guilt (over not giving enough attention to one's partner) and transgression guilt (over fighting and arguing with the partner):

> I felt guilty when my mother died . . . like it was all my fault. Like if I would have paid more attention to her and helped her, that she wouldn't be dead right now. . . . She was an alcoholic. And I knew it and instead of helping her and trying to understand her, I'd fight with her. [She died] of a stroke. I also blame that on myself because we had an argument before she went to the hospital. . . . [After she died] I started thinking over and over of all the things I could have done to keep her from doing what she did. . . . I didn't sit down and try to talk to her . . . I should have been more open . . . I didn't push my own problems aside . . . so I could help her. . . . [There were things I could have done. Things I did that didn't work out. I should have tried harder.] (Lindsay-Hartz, De Rivera, & Mascolo, 1995, p. 277)

Relationship guilt is intensified in certain dysfunctional relationships, such as those described by Baumeister et al. (1995), in which one partner tends to exaggerate his or her suffering precisely for the purpose of increasing the other's guilt. On the other hand, relationship guilt can be avoided by constantly guarding against upsetting one's partner, although this destroys spontaneity and can lead partners to hide their concerns about their own health (and be overly sensitive to signs of the other's illness because one assumes the other is doing the same thing). A better way is to express relationship guilt when one feels it, and rely on corrective feedback from one's partner to reduce uncertainty over whether one actually harmed the other. Honesty in these cases should reduce relationship guilt over time although it has its limitations, as when it might reveal an irreconcilable difference or unpleasant truth that threatens the relationship.

A final point: Relationship guilt, like other empathy-based guilt, can make a prosocial contribution. It makes one less likely to hurt, disappoint, neglect, or alienate one's partner and motivates one to pay attention, express positive feelings, and in general alter one's behavior in ways that strengthen the relationship. Because people occasionally do harm their partners, these expressions of concern may also help overcome any implications of one's harmful actions that one does not care. Expressing relationship guilt and getting corrective feedback probably characterize good relationships and help reduce relationship guilt over time: Each partner knows the other is not motivated to hurt him or her and assumes the other feels the same way.

## RESPONSIBILITY GUILT

Being responsible for others goes with age and maturity, but here again one often pays the price of feeling guilty. Parents are responsible for their children, and parents whose children have a fatal disease often blame themselves and feel guilty; they are convinced despite all evidence to the contrary that they could have done something to prevent their children's diseases (Chodoff, Friedman, & Hamburg, 1964).

In certain jobs where one is responsible for others' lives, guilt can be especially acute when things go wrong. This quote from a police sergeant, a subject in a study by Lindsay-Hartz et al. (1995, p. 290), who had watched two of his men standing next to him get shot by a sniper whom no one knew was in the vicinity, describes the self-recriminating thoughts a person in charge can have when disaster strikes through no fault of his own.

> I was the one making decisions here [to lead his men down the street].... It was my responsibility.... He got hit and I didn't...I brought him to that door.... Maybe if I was slower or faster ... if I had been on the right side instead of the left side.... Did I do something wrong? Was there any other way I could have handled it?...I was responsible.... Maybe we could have hit the door a second earlier.

One does not have to be in a responsible position to feel responsibility guilt.

> On Christmas break my best friend returned from college. She stayed with me and my parents. One night I went to a play with my parents. That night she stayed with her ex and got pregnant. She had all sorts of problems after that. It sounds crazy but I can't get it out of my mind that I should have been with her and it never would have happened. (undergraduate student)

One can feel responsibility guilt over accidently harming someone even if one tried to avoid the accident, logic says one was not to blame, and witnesses say it was the victim's fault. I suggested earlier that a person might drive well below the speed limit, yet feel extremely guilty over hitting a child who darts between parked cars into the road. In one of my story-completion guilt items the central figure, a seventh grader, is sledding on a hill with a friend. The posted rules say clearly that the children should climb up the side of the hill, not the middle, to avoid being hit by the sledders coming down. The central figure reminds his friend to climb up the side of the hill. Later, when the central figure is sledding down the hill, he swerves to avoid a log, sees his friend climbing up the middle right in front of him, tries to avoid hitting his friend but it is too late. The friend is badly injured and rushed to the hospital.

Everyone says it was his friend's fault, not his. And he knew he had cautioned his friend. Still, in most of the story endings the child felt guilty: "If I had stopped him from going up the hill he wouldn't be in the hospital right now"; "His parents kept telling him it was not his fault but he knew it was"; "He knows he shouldn't feel bad because he warned his friend but he feels terrible"; "I should have checked the hill first, then I would know about the log."

I suggest that what happens in responsibility guilt is similar to what happens in guilt over inaction (chapter 4): One empathizes with the victim's pain, reviews the situation in one's mind, realizes that one could have acted differently and prevented the accident, shifts from *I could have* to *I should have*, blames oneself and feels guilty.

## DEVELOPMENTAL GUILT

If close relationships are the context for virtual transgressions featuring relationship and to some extent responsibility guilt, an individualistic, competitive society like ours can make growing up and pursuing normal personal goals and interests the context for virtual transgressions involving "developmental guilt." Thus, a person may come to believe that by leaving home, achieving more than his peers, or benefiting from privileges others lack, one is responsible for harming others.

### Separation Guilt

Separation from parents is part of growing up in Western cultures. But clinicians often describe patients who are excited about leaving home and going to college but feel empathic distress and guilt whenever they think about it, as though by becoming autonomous and having a separate life they will destroy their parents or cause them serious pain (Modell, 1963). In extreme cases, any personal success, or even interest in the opposite sex, can make one feel guilty because it signifies one's readiness to separate from the parents.

Parents may contribute to their children's separation guilt by sending mixed messages: They want their children to grow up and achieve high goals and are thrilled by their children's accomplishments, but they also communicate how important the child is to them and how unhappy they would be if he or she leaves. A friend's separation guilt drove him to turn down a top university for a local college (which he regretted for the rest of his life). His mother's saying she would not stand in his way, though she would be unhappy if he left, did not help. Children may of course sense parents' anxiety over their leaving even when parents are less explicit about their anxiety than my friend's mother was.

All parents probably have mixed feelings about their child's leaving home, and all children may therefore have some separation guilt. A certain amount of separation guilt (and some anxiety over the unknown) – and learning to handle it – may be as much a part of growing up as actually making the move and leaving home. Separation guilt gets dysfunctional when it prevents one from making the move. I would expect "only" children of single parents to be especially vulnerable to separation guilt because if they leave, the parent will have no one.

## Guilt Over Achievement

A talented child draws a picture that attracts adult attention and wins praise and hugs. His peers look on dejectedly. When teachers start grading children on their performance relative to others rather than their own previous performance, high performers soon realize their achievements make others feel inadequate. Adolescents may feel guilty if they are the first in their family or peer group to go to college, because they think it lowers the others' self-esteem: "I diminish them in their own eyes, if not mine." It could of course give the others vicarious pride ("one of us made it"), but that seems unlikely in societies that value individual over collective achievement. The issue is "social comparison," which, Festinger and others taught us long ago, is necessary to evaluate performance in the absence of objective standards. But social comparison also tells children that their success may lower their peers' self-esteem; and if they empathize with their peers, they may feel guilty about their own achievement.

Since growing up with high self-esteem in America requires achieving, which after the fourth or fifth grade is measured relative to others, to feel that one has achieved requires doing better than others, which may lower their self-esteem. This suggests that all achievers may be vulnerable to achievement guilt. The sense of achievement may thus have a bittersweet quality, although there is no evidence that achievement guilt is powerful enough to interfere with performance. Perhaps most empathic achievers are sensitive to the effect of their success on their peers' self-esteem and feel guilty about it, but this does not prevent them from achieving and feeling good about it. There is no research on achievement guilt but one reason for the "fear of success" found in the 1970s research was that it "makes others feel like failures."

### Guilt Over Affluence

Older children and adolescents are sensitive to lifestyle differences based on affluence, and being more affluent than others is a potential source of guilt (Hoffman, 1989). Guilt over affluence, or "class" guilt, is reflected in some of the responses given by the 1960s civil-rights activists interviewed by Keniston (1968). They seem to have transformed their empathic distress for society's disadvantaged into "guilt over affluence" when they became aware of the difference between their advantaged life and the meager existence of others.

Keniston notes that these social activists were highly empathic and sympathetic individuals who experienced a shock when they "really" understood that the benefits they had experienced had not been extended to others and became aware of the vast discrepancy between their own good life and the misery that many others experienced all their lives. The point is illustrated in this quote from one of Keniston's interviewees who was discussing some poor Mexican children he had known years earlier:

I was the one that lived in a place where there were fans and no flies, and they lived with flies. And I was clearly destined for something, and they were destined for nothing. . . . Well, I sort of made a pact with these people that when I got to be powerful I might change some things. And I think I pursued that pact pretty consistently for a long time. (p. 50)

These activist youths appear to have concluded that their privileged position, especially their education, made it possible for them to do something to alleviate the condition of the less fortunate, and that doing nothing would therefore make them personally responsible for perpetuating the conditions they deplore – a type of guilt over inaction that served as a motivation for prosocial activism. This prosocial motivational potential of guilt over affluence is illustrated in the above quote about Mexican children.[1]

The statements and actions of 1960s activists suggest two necessary conditions for guilt over affluence: (a) direct exposure to the less fortunate whose lives can then be vividly imagined, as was afforded the 1960s Peace Corps and Vista volunteers, or vicarious exposure through books, television, travel, and social sciences; and (b) cultural nonjustification for vast discrepancies in wealth, which preceded the 1960s and began with the scientific evidence against racial superior-

---

1. Not only radicals feel this way. David Hilfiker, a physician who left his medical practice in rural Minnesota and moved with his wife and three children to inner-city Washington to work with the poor, is quoted in *Newsweek* as saying he remains convinced that "we who had grown up with education and opportunities had not so much deserved our affluence as inherited it and that the poor were – by virtue of their oppression – deserving" (Aug. 22, 1994, p. 60). And I have a news clipping (but not its source) that says Francis Tarkenton, one of the premier quarterbacks in National Football League history, made a large contribution to the Minneapolis Association for Retarded Children. He said: "The game has been good to me financially. Sometimes I feel a little awkward when I meet and talk with people who need. I mean I look at my own life and say, 'It's exciting and good and prosperous.' Then I remember all the noble words about trying to ease the hardships of others. All of us try to help some time or other. But I think a person always has to ask himself, 'Do I share enough of myself?' . . . I consider it a privilege to give in this way. I wish it could have been much more."

ity, and the diminished hold of religions that view one's well-being as a sign of grace. Guilt over affluence seems less prevalent now, perhaps because of diminished opportunities for direct exposure (except to the homeless), the newly embraced cultural value on material success and accumulation of wealth, and the perception that the affluence discrepancy has been sharply reduced by affirmative action. It thus appears that although guilt over affluence is an advanced form of guilt developmentally, building on empathy's final stage (chapter 3), it is likely confined historically to certain times and places.

The activists' statements and actions suggest that guilt over affluence can be a more potent motive than transgression guilt: It may require continued activity to alleviate human suffering rather than a discrete act of restitution. And, as with bystander guilt, if one does nothing one continues to feel guilty; blames victims; cognitively restructures to justify inaction, deny or justify one's affluence: "They have their pleasures and enjoy the way they live"; "I worked hard for what I have" (less applicable if one's wealth is from parents or lucky investments).

*Guilt by association.* Guilt over affluence may include an element of "guilt by association" when a person views his own social class as culpable. A congressional intern clearly expressed both guilt over affluence and guilt by association, when he was asked why many middle-class youth were "turned off by the very system that gave them so many advantages and opportunities":

> They feel guilty because while they are enjoying this highest standard of living, American Indians are starving and black ghettoes are overrun by rats. . . . This goes on while they eat steak every day. Their sense of moral indignation can't stand this; and they realize that the blame rests on the shoulders of their class. (*New Republic,* Nov. 28, 1970 p. 11)

Guilt over affluence and association is heightened if one feels that one benefits from the victim's misery, that one's affluence and lifestyle actually *require* hard work and sacrifice by others. This was true of some 1960s activists who felt that their parents, some of whom were bankers or executives, exploited others on their behalf. George

Orwell (1958) made the point years earlier when he said: "Watching coal-miners working brings home to you . . . that . . . all of us really owe the comparative decency of our lives to poor drudges underground, blackened to the eyes, with their throats full of coal dust, driving their shovels forward" (pp. 34–35).

Another dimension, perhaps a higher stage of empathy-based guilt over affluence, was expressed even longer ago by James Agee (1941). Agee, an unusually empathic journalist and author, reported feeling intensely guilty when observing people "whose poverty puts them in undignified and embarrassing positions, and knowing one can't fully identify with them because one can return to his former life when he chooses" (p. 417).

Guilt over affluence, or "class guilt," can be felt by older adults,[2] but I class it with developmental guilt because I believe it is more likely to be found in adolescents and young adults (at least it was in the 1960s), and when it is, it can be a significant part of their prosocial moral development, as suggested by the above examples.[3] In a study of German college students, guilt over affluence was associated with acceptance of responsibility for society's ills, and it was found to be a better predictor of prosocial political behavior than sympathetic distress (Montada and Schneider, 1989).

## SURVIVOR GUILT

It is known that people who experience the traumatic death or injury of someone else while they remain unharmed often feel guilt

2. A colleague touring in Spain was robbed by a hotel employee and reported it. When she found out that the culprit was fired on the spot, she felt terribly guilty over "causing him to lose his job. I should have been more careful and not left my purse in such an obvious place."
3. But what happened to them later? Some succeeded in business and finance. Others, according to a mid-1970s survey by the *New York Times*, worked as inner-city teachers, social workers, or consumer advocates, or went into "poverty law" or "poverty medicine." But many of the latter group found they could not accomplish much and left for better paying, more personally satisfying work, feeling guilty for doing so little for the poor and for leaving Starr (1974). See also Franz and McClelland (1994).

over surviving. The guilt is compounded by conflicting emotions of joy at surviving and sorrow for the dead. Add to this the hidden relief that the worst happened to someone else, and one can have a painful case of guilt. Guilt may be the survivor's answer to the question "Why me – why was I saved and not somebody else?" In any case, people feel guilty when they survive natural disasters (earthquakes, floods, fires), man-made catastrophes (Hiroshima, the Holocaust), fellow soldiers dying in battle, terrorist bombings, plane or car accidents, suicide or death of family members, and downsizing the workforce (though here survivor guilt is tempered by fear that one may be next).

Less well-known is the guilt a person may feel over surviving a disadvantaged background. This quote from an African American student at Harvard in the activist 1970s combines survivor and affluence (as well as achievement) guilt and also illustrates their motive power. He said that he and others like him

> have had to wrestle with the keen sense of guilt they feel being here while their families still struggle in black ghettoes. . . . The one sure way of easing guilt was (by demanding) "relevance" from Harvard, which means, in effect, instruction that can be directed toward improving the quality of life for blacks as a whole in this country . . . (and) via building takeovers, strikes, and other kinds of demonstration. (Monroe, 1973, p. 46)

Reactions to the Oklahoma City bombing by people many miles away were interesting in this connection. I expected compassion but not necessarily guilt. Discussing the bombing in my New York University class, one student said: "It made me feel guilty about worrying about grades and getting into the best grad school. Especially the kids. I couldn't stop imagining their mothers waiting to know if they're OK." Another student said: "My own worries stopped, they felt silly, seemed trivial. I felt so sorry for them. I had to do something. I gave money to the Red Cross – first time in my life. I don't have much but had to do something." Other students said they felt personally implicated: "It could have happened here but for no *jus-*

*tifiable* reason it happened there." This sounds like survivor guilt by people who were nowhere near the tragedy.

It is not entirely clear why people feel guilty over surviving. It may be the unfairness of it and the lack of justification. "It may be an unconscious perception of organic social balance that makes one feel that his surviving was made possible by others' deaths: if they had not died, he would have had to, and if he had not survived, someone else would have" (Lifton, 1968, p. 56). Another explanation can be derived from the hypothesis that survivor guilt within a family is due to everyone's having "an unconscious bookkeeping system that accounts for the available 'good' within a family so that the current fate of other family members will determine how much good one possesses" (Modell, 1984, p. 76). Thus, if an individual feels that he has done better than other family members, then he may feel guilty over having gotten more than his fair share *and having taken the excess portion from others* in the process.

Such an unconscious bookkeeping system may extend beyond the family. If so, it could explain guilt over affluence as well as survivor guilt. It might account for New York University students' feeling guilty over the fate of Oklahoma City bombing victims. It might also account for the finding by Schmitt, Bauerle, and Donke (1989) that adults feel guilty over the misfortunes of people in other countries, although it may be true, as Lifton (1968) claims, that survivor guilt is most focused and intense in relation to family members, relatives, and intimates.

## GUILT OVER RELATIVE ADVANTAGE

Guilt over affluence is one type of guilt over relative advantage but there are others, as illustrated by this statement by a German who rescued Jews from the Nazis: "It was unfair that I was safe simply because I was born a Protestant. That was the main reason [I helped Jews]. . . . It was a very humble thing because I was in a privileged situation compared with other people who didn't deserve their situation at all" (Oliner & Oliner, 1988, p. 166). What this person

is saying, what this statement has in common with guilt over affluence and survivor guilt, and what may transform empathic distress
into guilt feeling, is that one cannot justify and therefore does not
deserve the advantage one has over the victim; that one's advantage,
surviving or being affluent while others starve or die, violates the
principle of fairness, justice, or reciprocity (see discussion of reciprocity in chapter 9). One has an empathic feeling of injustice (chapter 4)
that is transformed into guilt feeling, because one is the beneficiary
of the injustice.[4]

### ARE HUMANS GUILT MACHINES?

Virtual transgressions are all existential in the sense that they
derive from normal existential aspects of life – from the mutual
support and other positive aspects of close relationships, from famil-
ial love and mutual dependency in the home, from achievement and
self-fulfillment. Virtual transgressions are also not totally "virtual";
most of them have a germ of truth. One might have indeed been the
cause of one's relationship partner's distress; as the person in a
responsible position one might indeed be expected to anticipate
events and act more effectively; one's parents probably will be unhappy about one's leaving home; one's peers may indeed feel inadequate because of one's achievements; given the scarcity of resources
one's affluence might indeed contribute, albeit indirectly, to another's having very little. And yet, these cannot be classed with
actual transgressions, despite the overlap, because one intended no
harm, nor can one be said to have violated any moral principles, at
least not in the Western sense.

The existence of virtual guilt confirms my belief that humans are
"guilt machines," which is fortunate given the evidence that guilt
functions as a prosocial motive. To end this topic on a cross-cultural
note, though my examples of virtual guilt have mostly been Ameri-

---

4. This is not true of achievement guilt, where one presumably earned one's
   advantage but feels guilty over making others feel inadequate by comparison.

can, Americans do not have a monopoly on it. Here are two examples from Japan, a country that combines both modern and traditional ways and has sometimes been thought of as a shame rather than guilt culture. The first is to me an astonishing case of empathy-based guilt by association with one's ancestors. I quote from the *New York Times*:

> The money the Japanese government allocates to take care of the Ear Mound in Kyoto (memorial to hundreds of thousands of ears and noses of Koreans killed in the Japanese invasion of Korea in 1597) is insufficient and so several Japanese and Korean volunteers cut the grass and clean up the mound as well. "As a Japanese, I feel badly for what we did to the Korean people and so I try to do something to make up for it," said Shiro Shimizu, 85, a volunteer who lives next to the Ear Mound. (*New York Times*, Sept. 14, 1997, p. A3)

The second is a well-known example of survivor guilt: the Hiroshima atom bomb survivors, as described by Lifton (1968). Despite being seriously maimed and disfigured, the survivor typically felt guilt "for selfishly remaining alive" while others died. He could not

> inwardly, simply conclude that it was logical and right for him, and not others, to survive. Rather he was bound by an unconscious perception of organic social balance that made him feel that his surviving was made possible by others' deaths: If they had not died, he would have had to: if he had not survived, someone else would have. (p. 56)

Lifton points up the importance of relative advantage:

> The survivors felt guilt toward the dead; ordinary Japanese felt guilt toward survivors; the rest of the world felt guilt toward the Japanese. Proceeding outward from the core of the death immersion, each group internalizes the suffering of that one step closer than itself to the core, which it contrasts with its own relative good fortune. (p. 499)

Lifton also notes that many survivors felt additional guilt because they could not help others. Their need to help was intense, and some were able to do it by praying for the souls of the dead: "In the midst of the disaster I tried to read Buddhist scriptures continuously for about a week. . . . In Buddhism we say that the souls wander about in anxiety, and if we read the scriptures to them, they become easy and settle down" (p. 375).

## FOUR GUILT-AROUSING PROCESSES

Cutting across the varieties of empathy-based guilt, including transgression guilt and all the virtual guilts, are four guilt-arousing processes – processes by which empathic distress and self-blame combine to produce guilt feeling.

1. Arousal and integration of empathic distress with self-blame, driven by external intervention. This is the main guilt-arousal process in development of transgression guilt in children, as described in chapter 6. The key intervention is inductive discipline, which both arouses empathic distress and makes the child aware of the harmful consequences of his or her action or contemplated action for others. This awareness transforms the empathic distress into guilt feeling.

2. Spontaneous arousal and integration of empathic distress with self-blame when one has harmed someone. This spontaneous empathy-based transgression guilt is the result of (a) inductions creating the seeds of their own dispensability and becoming unnecessary over time (as described in chapter 6); and (b) advances in cognitive development that enable children spontaneously to feel guilt over the harmful consequences of their action and of their inaction, and to feel anticipatory guilt over the harmful consequences of their contemplated action.

3. Spontaneous arousal and integration of empathic distress with self-blame, resulting from previous interactions with significant others and ambiguities in the immediate situation. This is the main process in relationship guilt, although there is an enormous difference in complexity between infants' guilt over distressing their mothers and guilt in adult relationships.

4. Once empathy-based transgression guilt becomes independent of the discipline encounters that gave rise to it, and once it is established as part of the child's own repertoire, it may add a feeling-of-

being-a-transgressor component to the guilt he or she experiences over inaction in bystander encounters. This is because any guilt feeling, including guilt over inaction, may activate the Transgression → Guilt script, which, among other things, makes one feel like a transgressor. The same process may lie behind relationship guilt, guilt over separation, guilt over achievement, guilt over affluence, and survivor guilt. In other words, *empathy-based transgression guilt may be the prototype for all empathy-based guilt, real or imagined.*

# PART IV

# Is Empathy Enough?

# CHAPTER 8

# Empathy's Limitations: Over-Arousal and Bias

Having pointed up empathic motivation's positive contributions to prosocial moral action, I now turn to empathic motivation's limitations, expanding on the limitations I noted some time ago (Hoffman, 1984b, 1987). The limitations are due mainly to empathy's dependence on the intensity and salience of distress cues and the relationship between the victim and the observer. The first limitation is this: We generally expect the intensity of empathic arousal to increase with the salience and intensity of the victim's distress: the more intense and salient the cues of distress, the more intense the observer's empathic distress. But, if the signs of distress are too intense and salient, the observer's empathic distress may become aversive enough to be transformed into a feeling of personal distress. I call this "empathic over-arousal."

The second limitation is empathy's vulnerability to two types of bias: "familiarity bias" and "here-and-now bias." The research (chapter 2) shows that most people empathize with and help others in distress, including strangers (the victims in most of the research were strangers), but there is also evidence that most people empathize to a greater degree (their threshold for empathic distress is lower) with victims who are family members, members of their primary group, close friends, and people whose personal needs and concerns are similar to their own. And, because most empathy-arousing processes (at least the primitive, less cognitive ones) depend on immediate situational and personal cues, people are vulnerable to empathic bias in favor of victims who are present in the immediate situation. Thus a cry of pain may arouse more empathic distress than a facial grimace; a friend's or relative's cry, more than a stranger's; the distress of someone who is present, more than that of someone who is absent. I now discuss these limitations in detail.

## EMPATHIC OVER-AROUSAL

Observers will empathize with another's distress when they are in a relatively comfortable state themselves; otherwise they might be too focused on their own needs to be open and responsive to cues signifying another's distress. If an observer is anxious about failure or loss of approval, or if he or she is very uncomfortable physically (noisy surroundings), this can reduce the tendency to empathize with someone in distress (research reviewed by Hoffman, 1978). Since empathic distress itself can be intense and highly aversive, it can at times divert the attention of observers away from the victim to their own very real distress. This **"empathic over-arousal" can be defined as an involuntary process that occurs when an observer's empathic distress becomes so painful and intolerable that it is transformed into an intense feeling of personal distress, which may move the person out of the empathic mode entirely** (Hoffman, 1978). At the other extreme, empathic distress can be too weak to motivate prosocial action. Empathic distress can thus run the gamut from being too weak to being too strong, depending on the salience and intensity of the distress cues. It is within these extremes that empathic distress (and presumably sympathetic distress, empathic anger, guilt, and empathic feeling of injustice) can be expected to motivate prosocial moral action.

Empathic over-arousal is a limitation that may, paradoxically, result partly from empathy's biggest strength – its many modes of arousal. In chapter 2, I noted the advantages of multiple modes and discussed the contribution of each mode (mimicry's sensitivity to victims' facial expressions; conditioning and association's sensitivity to situational cues). The advantage is that multiple modes help assure empathic responses to victims regardless of the cues available. The disadvantage, I now suggest, is that the combined effects of several arousal modes can make a suffering victim the stimulus for empathic distress so painful to some observers that they become empathically over-aroused, with the negative consequences just mentioned.

But multiple modes operating simultaneously are not necessary for empathic over-arousal. One mode can do it all by itself when the conditions are right: self-focused role-taking in particular. Through self-focused role-taking, any distress cue can produce empathic over-arousal in an observer if it evokes highly painful events in the observer's past and the pain and anxiety associated with those events – and the result can be empathic distress in the observer that can at times exceed the intensity of the victim's actual distress.

There is little research on the topic. In discussing the partial transformation of empathic into sympathetic distress (chapter 3), I mentioned the first finding in the literature that could be construed as empathic over-arousal: the observation by Stotland, Matthews, Sherman, Hansso, and Richardson (1979) that nurses in training experienced a conflict between feelings of sympathetic distress, which included an intense desire to help their severely ill patients, and their own empathic distress, which made it difficult at times for them to stay in the same room with those patients. In a study by Strayer (1993), 5- to 13-year-old children were shown videotaped vignettes of individuals in highly distressing situations (a child unjustly punished by his parent; a disabled child learning to climb stairs with a cane; a child separated from her family by immigration authorities). Strayer found that the more intense the victim's distress, the more intense was the observer's distress and the more focused was the observer's attention on the victim. But these correlations broke down when the intensity of the observers' empathic distress become greater than that of the victims' distress. At that point, the observers' focus shifted from the victim toward themselves, illustrating "egoistic drift" (chapter 2). In other words, the observers' empathic distress increased along with the victims actual distress until the observers' empathic distress exceeded the victims' actual distress, at which point empathic over-arousal "kicked in."

*Compassion fatigue.* A challenge confronting nurses, social workers, and other health-care professionals that has deepened in recent years stems from new treatments that have extended the lives of terminally ill patients, giving professionals a longer time to form bonds; and the rise of AIDS has greatly increased the number of sick and dying young adults and children. As a result, many health-care workers who interact daily with terminally ill AIDS or cancer patients, as well as people who counsel victims or "clean up" after natural and man-made disasters, are apt to experience empathic over-arousal repeatedly over long periods of time. This makes them subject to a chronic condition called "vicarious traumatization" or "compassion fatigue" to a greater extent than before, and they have to deal with it.

One way to deal with it is to turn off emotionally. "That is the only way to minimize the pain, and it's tempting to do that," said a specialist in bereavement, who formed a support group for health-care workers, as reported by Pederzane (1998). "When we know we can work through our own grief, then we're not so afraid to get involved." At one group meeting a social worker said she was having a particularly hard time because an 8-year-old was very near death. "I can't cry," she said. "I don't sleep. If I don't sleep I won't have the strength to deal with it and every one else who is counting on me. I feel angry. Angry at the illness, angry at God. I have a problem with anger and if you feel anger at God then you're in trouble" (p. B2 ).

Figley (1995) reports that psychotherapists who work with patients who have suffered traumas are often hard-pressed to balance objectivity with empathy. Those who cannot achieve an acceptable balance may become so hardened that they cannot be there emotionally for the patient, or so horrified and outraged – vicariously traumatized – by their patients' vivid, sometimes graphic descriptions of their brutal victimizations, that they are too paralyzed to help. The patients' specific traumatic images may be carried with the therapist and at times appear to him unbidden, as clear as his own internal images. The cumulative effect of story after story, client after client, day after day, Figley suggests, can become a chronic condition.

Figley describes his own research in which he interviewed Vietnam veterans who discussed their traumatic experiences and the impact of these experiences on their interpersonal relationships after they returned from the war. He reports that the interviews left an indelible impression on him and at times incapacitated him. He had nightmares and was obsessed by the traumatic experiences described. His overall impression was one of anger and frustration about how the men and women were traumatized. It is a noteworthy tribute to empathic distress's potential as a prosocial motive, that the only way Figley could cope with his compassion fatigue was to engage in a prosocial act: He established a consortium on veterans' studies. Similarly, the bereavement support groups described earlier were not just formed to ease the health-care specialists' compassion fatigue but to enable them to redouble their efforts on behalf of their patients. And, Stotland's empathic nurses returned to their terminally ill patients once they discovered they could actually help them.

What these cases illustrate is the *potential power of empathic over-arousal as a prosocial moral motive.* They differ dramatically from the instances of empathic over-arousal mentioned earlier in which people's attention turned from victims toward themselves. Why the difference? I think that Figley was empathically committed to his Vietnam veteran subjects and could not turn away. The health-care specialists and Stotland's nurses were empathically committed to their patients. I would expect the same of parents and spouses. In short, in relationships in which empathy, love, or role-demands makes one feel compelled to help, empathic over-arousal may *intensify* rather than destroy one's focus on helping the victim. This suggests an affirmative answer to the question raised by Neuberg, Cialdini, Brown, Luce, Sagarin, and Lewis (1997): Does empathy lead to more than superficial helping?

*Underlying processes and coping mechanisms.* Little is known about the psychological processes involved in empathic over-arousal, that is, the processes underlying the shift from empathic distress to personal distress. The quotations from Figley suggest a process: Victims describe their traumatic experience in terms of vivid, sometimes graphic images; the empathic observer imagines the traumatic experience, and empathic distress is aroused in the observer, probably through mediated association and role-taking. *These imagined images may be as clear and vivid to the observer as the images the observer has of his or her own experience.* Indeed, they may be more vivid than his or her own, as when they cause nightmares in observers who would otherwise not have nightmares. The result is that the observer feels empathically over-aroused, and, furthermore, the cumulative effect of frequent repetitions of this process, when the observer cannot leave the situation, may produce chronic empathic over-arousal – "vicarious traumatization" (Pearlman & Saakvitne, 1995).

Figley's report suggests another thing that certain observers do when they are compelled to remain in the situation: They "harden" themselves or create psychological distance between themselves and the victim. The way they do this, I think, is to employ certain perceptual and cognitive strategies to reduce the intensity of their personal distress. To give you an idea of how these strategies can work, I quote from an experimental study done years ago by Bandura and Rosenthal (1966). The subjects, college students, were given a dose of epinephrine before observing someone receiving electric shocks. Epinephrine increases emotional arousal and should therefore heighten observers' empathic distress. One subject was particularly articulate about what went through his mind as he observed the victim:

> After the first three or four shocks, I thought about the amount of pain for the other guy. Then I began to think, to minimize my own discomfort. I recall looking at my watch, looking out the window, and checking things about the room. I recall that the victim received a shock when I was thinking about the seminar, and that I didn't seem to notice the discomfort as much in this instance. (p. 60)

The subject's comments illustrate at once the involuntary tendency to empathize with someone in distress, the personally aversive quality that empathic distress can have, and the use of cognitive strategies to eliminate the aversive state or reduce it to a tolerable level. These strategies, which may be called "defensive" because the motivation to use them is to reduce one's discomfort, may be involved when a person transforms empathic into personal distress, although they may often be employed unconsciously rather than consciously and deliberately as they were by Bandura and Rosenthal's subject. In any case, these are not prosocial strategies that will benefit a clinician's patient – unless they are a temporary defense in the service of enabling the clinician to continue to function effectively in the long run.

Apart from "strategies," empathic over-arousal may be diminished passively, through habituation, when a person is exposed to another's distress repeatedly over time; and the cumulative effect may be that the person's empathic distress diminishes to the point of indifference to the victim's suffering.

*Individual differences.* Individual differences in empathic over-arousal may be due to differences in empathic tendency, the ability to help, and the ability to regulate one's emotions.

1. Being exposed to victims in extremely painful or distressing situations may be especially stressful for highly empathic people, who should therefore be especially vulnerable to empathic over-arousal. There is evidence for this. In a study by Kameya (1976), kindergartners were presented with several stories involving children who were ill, deprived, in pain, or combinations of these. The subjects took turns playing each of the story children's roles and then discussed the feelings of the story children. The subjects' general empathic tendency, measured independently, was found to correlate *negatively* with one of the helping indices: The high-empathy subjects who played the distressed children's roles helped less than did the low-empathy subjects who played the distressed children's roles. Evidently, the empathic distress evoked in the high-empathy subjects by the role-playing was too intense and aversive for them to maintain their other-oriented helping orientation. Similarly, in Stotland et al.'s (1979) observation, it was the highly empathic nursing students who became emotionally "exhausted" when they first began working in hospital wards and felt compelled to avoid their terminally ill patients. And finally, Figley (1995) reports that the clinicians most vulnerable to vicarious traumatization are those who are most caring and empathic.

2. Aside from being highly empathic, Stotland's student nurses displayed another factor that contributed to empathic over-arousal:

All felt unable to help the terminally ill patients. After six months on the job, these student nurses realized they could make a difference in the patients' lives and that was enough to bring an end to their empathic over-arousal and avoidance of terminally ill patients (Williams, 1989). In other words, having the ability to help victims can reduce one's vulnerability to empathic over-arousal.

3. Being able to regulate one's own emotions and handle one's own anxieties constructively can also reduce one's vulnerability to empathic over-arousal. There is some evidence for this: Children whose parents handled the children's anxiety by teaching them coping strategies were less prone to empathic over-arousal than children whose parents did not teach them coping strategies; and children who have a low empathy threshold and find it difficult to regulate their emotions in general are more prone to empathic over-arousal than other children and less likely to help others (Eisenberg, Fabes, Schaller, Carlo, and Miller, 1991; Fabes, Eisenberg, Karbon, Troyer, & Switzer, 1994).

*Hypotheses about empathic over-arousal.* Putting all the findings and observations together, the following hypotheses seem in order. (a) The intensity of observers' empathic distress and their motivation to help increases with the intensity of the victim's distress. (b) At some point, as the observer approaches his or her threshold of distress tolerance and becomes empathically over-aroused, the observer may think of leaving the situation and if that option is available, as with a stranger, the observer may leave or turn off emotionally by consciously or unconsciously using perceptual and cognitive strategies to gain distance from the victim. (c) But when a person is in a relationship and committed to help another (owing to some combination of empathic distress, love, and role expectations), empathic over-arousal may intensify both the person's focus on the victim and his or her motivation to help. The person may feel compelled to maintain contact with the victim and struggle to achieve a balance between feeling empathically distressed and distancing (temporary distancing in the service of helping?). The person will likely feel both empathic distress and sympathetic distress, side by side or in sequence, as in the distinction between the two that I made earlier (chapter 3).

Empathic over-arousal is thus a limitation in bystander situations involving strangers, but it may provide an added incentive to help in relationships with people to whom one is committed. If a person continues to help in these relationships, especially if the person is highly empathic to begin with, he or she is apt to help the victim, though at the cost of being vulnerable to vicarious traumatization. Vicarious traumatization can thus be an occupational hazard associated with being an empathic clinician with certain patients.[1] It may be one of those cases in which an empathic person truly makes a personal sacrifice for another.

## Other Empathic Self-Destructing Mechanisms

I consider empathic over-arousal an example of empathy's self-destructing capabilities. I discussed another self-destructing mechanism in chapter 2: *"egoistic drift,"* in which self-focused role-taking can trigger a process in which one gets caught up in ruminating about one's own experiences and concerns and drifts out of the empathic mode. We can now see that egoistic drift is part of empathic over-arousal initiated by self-focused role-taking. The hypothesized sequence is this: One imagines oneself in the victim's situation; this leads to empathic distress plus associations to similar painful events in one's past that evoke personal distress; ruminating about those events and experiencing the pain associated with them pulls one's attention away from the victim. Personal distress thus replaces empathic distress.

Another self-destructing mechanism, one applicable to direct af-

---

1. Since all patients are in pain, empathic therapists are always vulnerable to compassion fatigue. It adds to their involvement with patients and can make it hard for them to have anything left for their own families (Edwards, 1995). If it is an occupational hazard, therapists need to learn how to deal with the problem of balance between too much and too little empathy.

fect as well as empathic affect, is *habituation*: If a person is exposed to another's distress repeatedly over time, habituation may occur, as noted above, and the cumulative effect may be that the observer's empathic distress diminishes to the point of the person's becoming indifferent to the victim's suffering. This may explain the growing indifference of many city dwellers to the suffering of homeless people. It may also explain a less well-known phenomenon: the diminished effectiveness of "social reform photography." People have long been moved to prosocial action (give money, travel long distances to help) by photographs showing the sad lives of others, especially children, who are poor, victims of floods and earthquakes, refugees (Rwanda, Bangladesh). It now appears that "our hearts may have grown indifferent under a barrage of such images" (Goldberg, 1995).

### FAMILIARITY BIAS

Evolution theorists agree that humans evolved in small groups and that although altruism was necessary for survival within groups, the scarcity of resources often pitted one group against another. It should therefore not be surprising that a person is more likely to empathize with and help those who are members of his or her family, ethnic or racial group – his or her in-group, in short. And when we consider that members of one's in-group are similar to each other and to oneself and share feelings of closeness and affection, it should not be surprising that a person is also more likely to empathize with friends than with strangers and with people who are similar to oneself than with people who are different.

The one thing that family, in-group members, close friends, and people similar to oneself all have in common is familiarity: They are in close personal touch with each other and have similar life experiences. Hence the all-embracing term "familiarity bias" seems appropriate. Indeed, there is evidence for a "pure" familiarity bias: People who are repeatedly exposed to a stimulus – any stimulus, even an inanimate one – develop a preference for that stimulus (Zajonc, 1968; Harrison, 1977).

## In-Group Bias

There is surprisingly little evidence for in-group empathic bias but there is some. In a study of empathy in children across race, Klein (1971) made slide sequences depicting Black or White girls in happy, sad, and fearful situations that were then relevant to White and African American cultures. The subjects, all girls, verbalized more empathy in response to slides depicting children of the same race. Regarding transgression guilt, it is well-known that perpetrators of violent crimes distance themselves from their victims by derogating them, sometimes regarding them as subhuman. This is especially likely when the victim belongs to a group that can be clearly separated from the culprit's; and culprits feel less guilt over committing the same crime against a victim of another group (Katz, Glass, & Cohen, 1973; Lifton, 1968; Meindl & Lerner, 1984). And, finally, while the survivor guilt of Hiroshima atom bomb victims was not confined to family members, relatives, and intimates, it was most focused and intense in relation to these individuals (Lifton, 1968).

## Friendship Bias

Costin and Jones (1992) found an empathic bias that favored friends in 4- to 5-year-olds. The subjects watched eight puppet scenarios in which a target child was in some kind of difficulty (climbed too high on a tree and felt he couldn't get down; another child threatening to push him off the jungle gym). In each scenario a picture of either a close friend of the subject or an acquaintance was affixed to the back of the puppet's head to encourage the subject to think about the puppet as that person. The subjects expressed more empathic distress toward the "friend" than toward the "acquaintance." And when asked to "pretend that you are in the story. What will happen next?" they were more likely to say they would help when the target child was the friend.

### Similarity Bias

Feshbach and Roe (1968) found that 6- to 7-year-old girls verbalized more empathy in response to slide sequences depicting girls in happy, sad, and fearful situations than to slides of boys in the same situations; boys gave more empathic responses to slides involving boys. The findings surprised me a little; according to sex-role stereotypes, males are more likely to help females than to help males. Indeed, I have been told that male youth gangs view helping a male outside the group as a sign of softness, but helping a female is acceptable. A gang member said, "I would definitely help an old lady because if that was my mom, I'd want someone to kick that guy's ass." Perhaps the stereotype is confined to adolescent and adult males. In any case, the Feshbach and Roe finding suggests that, other things being equal, one is more empathic toward one's own gender.

The Klein study of racial bias mentioned earlier can be viewed as a study of similarity bias. In addition, Klein investigated an abstract, cognitively mediated type of similarity between observer and model, which stressed common preferences, attitudes, and interests rather than skin color. The subjects' empathy scores were not affected by this type of similarity, perhaps because abstract similarities of this kind are beyond the reach of young children. Empathy scores were affected, however, in three similar attempts to induce a perception of personality similarity in college students (Gruen & Mendelsohn, 1986; Houston, 1990; Krebs, 1975). I will describe the first and last of these in detail.

In the study by Krebs, the subjects, who had previously been given personality tests, were told that they had been paired with another student on the basis of a computer analysis of their test responses. Half the subjects were told that the other student's personality profile was similar to theirs and half were told the other's profile was different. The subjects who believed the other student was similar showed more pronounced physiological responses when the other appeared to be experiencing pleasure or pain. They also reported that they identified more with the other and felt worse (had more empathic distress) while the other was waiting to receive an electric shock.

In Houston's research, the subjects first listed up to ten personality traits that described themselves as they were (actual self) and as they would like to be (ideal self). Self-discrepancy scores were obtained, based on the difference between actual-self and ideal-self descriptions. Next, the subjects read a purported transcript of another student's interview in which he related his chronic difficulties in meeting new people because of shyness, his strong desire to change, and a recent incident in which his shyness caused him extreme distress. He communicated his distress in that incident by a detailed description of his gestures, voice (low), facial reactions (eyes downcast), and his feelings. He said he felt highly dejected because of a discrepancy between his actual self (shy) and ideal self (social competence). Subjects who read the interviews experienced more empathic distress if their own self-discrepancy score reflected a chronic shyness problem, and when asked if they thought the student's high level of anxiety was justified by the personal problem he described, they were more likely to answer yes. In short, subjects concerned about shyness were more likely to empathize with others who were concerned about shyness.

## HERE-AND-NOW BIAS

I assume that empathy is naturally biased in favor of victims in the immediate situation because the automatic, involuntary, and salient empathy-arousing processes (conditioning, association, mimicry) require situational and personal cues that are at their peak when a victim is present. This bias is also in keeping with the point made earlier that natural selection favored empathy toward family and in-group members over strangers, as family and in-group members are more likely to be present. When I first suggested empathy's susceptibility to a here-and-now bias (Hoffman, 1984, 1987), it was pure conjecture. Now there is evidence for it. Two experiments by Batson, Klein, Highberger, and Shaw (1995), both employing college students as subjects, illustrate it well. In one study, the subjects had to assign a desirable or undesirable task to two other students designated as workers. They were told that "flipping a coin is the fairest way to assign workers to the tasks but the decision is entirely up to you. You can assign the workers anyway you wish. They will not know how they were assigned, only to which task they were assigned. And your anonymity is assured" (p. 1044). Before assigning the tasks, the experimental group read a "personal note" from one of the two workers that described a recent life event and were instructed to "try to *imagine how this student feels* about what is described . . . how it has affected his or her life and how he or she feels as a result" (p. 1044).

The main finding was that two-thirds of these subjects assigned the desirable task to the worker whose note they had read and the undesirable task to the other worker. This contrasts with two control groups: one that read the note but was instructed to "take an objective, detached perspective and not get caught up in the writer's feelings," and another that was not given a note. The subjects in both control groups assigned the tasks randomly (flipped a coin). In other words, the experimental group was more likely to empathize and help the "victim" who was at the focus of their attention, and in that sense "present," than victims who were absent or with whom they were instructed not to empathize. And they did this despite being told that the fairest thing to do was to assign the tasks randomly.

In the second experiment the subjects were told about a 10-year-old girl with a fatal muscle-paralyzing disease; there was no cure but a new drug could improve her quality of life; the drug was expensive and her family could not afford it; she had been placed on a waiting list. The subjects then listened to a taped radio interview of the child discussing her disability and saying at the end how great it would be if she got the medicine. The subjects were then told that children were ranked on the list according to the date they applied, how serious their need was, and their life expectancy; children often remained on the list for months and some died before being helped. They were told that in return for their assistance they could, if they wished, help the child they had heard by moving her from the waiting list into the group that would receive the drug immediately. They were also reminded that if they did this, children who were higher on the list due to earlier application, greater need, or shorter life-expectancy would have to wait longer. "On the other hand, moving this child up will make a very significant difference in the quality of life for the time this child has left . . . the child and her family know nothing about this and will be informed *only* if you decide to move the child" (Batson et al., 1995, p. 1047).

As in the first experiment, the subjects in the experimental group were instructed to "imagine how the child who is interviewed feels about what has happened and how it has affected this child's life. Try to feel the full impact of what this child has been through and how she feels as a result." Control subjects were instructed to "take an objective, detached perspective and not get caught up in how the child who is interviewed feels" (p. 1047). The findings were that three-quarters of the experimental subjects, compared to half the controls, empathized with the interviewed child and moved her into the immediate-help group. In other words, as in the first experiment, the subjects were more likely to empathize with and help the victim who was at the focus of their attention than victims who were absent or with whom they were told not to empathize, despite being reminded that other, more needy children would lose out as a result.

A third study done in the same laboratory produced similar results. This study was designed to show that a person's empathy for a member of his group could operate to the disadvantage of the group as a whole (Batson, Batson, Todd, Brummeth, Shaw, & Aldeguer, 1995). To test this prediction, college students were told they were part of four-person groups (actually fictitious) and then faced with a dilemma in which they could choose to allocate more or fewer raffle tickets to themselves, their group, or other members of the group as individuals. One member of each group was reported as recently having had a very sad and distressing personal experience. The subjects who experienced high empathy for that person allocated more raffle tickets to him, reducing the amount available to the group.

Examples of here-and-now bias from real life abound. Here are three. The first is a quote from the *New York Times*, which attributed a here-and-now bias to the then-president of the United States: "[The President] would give a hungry child his lunch, but he can't understand that when he voted against the hot lunch program he was taking lunches away from millions of children (Sherrill, 1974). The second example is a different point attributed to that same president's Chairman of Economic Advisers who was discussing the importance of a balanced budget amendment for present and future generations:

> Of course one can look at the question in another way. The Old and New Testaments both call on us to love our neighbors as ourselves. If "neighbor" can be interpreted temporally as well as spatially, we can say that the generations to come are our neighbors and we are instructed to show as much concern for future generations as for our own (Stein, 1994).

The chairman's comments do not reflect a here-and-now bias but they clearly imply that such a bias exists and that the country would be better off without it, at least as regards the question of a balanced budget.

My third example of what might be called "media-enhanced here-and-now bias" is more dramatic. It seems to me that a here-and-now bias goes far toward explaining, at least in part, the tendency to forget about victims who have long been out of the picture and to empathize with certain *culprits* who are now the focus of attention and, for one reason or another, appear to be victims themselves. The 1997 trial of the young British "nanny" is a case in point. When the 8-month-old child in her care died, there was widespread sympathy for the parents and condemnation of the young woman, who apparently shook the child to death.

With her trial and conviction, the empathic tide shifted in her favor: She became the victim and the recipient of widespread empathic distress especially from her homeland, partly because of the severe sentence. My point is not her guilt or innocence or the empathic reaction of the British. It is that the compassion for this young woman who became the focus of attention and, by virtue of television, *the victim of the moment,* largely replaced the compassion for the dead baby and his parents who were the original, true victims. (Indeed, many people ended up "blaming the victim" – the parents for expecting too much of the girl or being too cheap to hire a professional nanny, or the mother for working instead of being home with her babies.)[2]

## IMPLICATIONS FOR EMPATHIC MORALITY

What can we make of empathy's limitations? Do they disqualify empathy as a motivational base for prosocial moral action? I think not: Empathic over-arousal and bias *are* problems but probably not fatal ones. Over-arousal is a limitation in bystander situations but, as in compassion fatigue, it can *intensify* one's dedication to help in existing relationships especially those in which one is in the role of helper.

Regarding familiarity bias, the research shows that humans *do* help strangers (in most of the research the victims are strangers); it is a matter of degree. Furthermore, it may be possible to "recruit" familiarity bias in the service of helping strangers, by imagining strangers as part of one's family. This can happen spontaneously, as with the young hero described in chapter 4 who chased down a man who pushed an elderly woman onto the subway tracks "because that could have been my mom, because that could have been a friend of mine." Or it could be encouraged by moral educators (see chapter 13). Familiarity bias can also be reduced when empathy is embedded in moral principles, as will be discussed. And it can be transcended when highly principled people, driven largely by empathic motivation, are compelled to make life-and-death choices, as witness the Germans who rescued Jews in the Holocaust; when asked how many

2. The media-enhanced here-and-now bias is not the total explanation. The court case, especially the severe sentence, activated various deep-seated attitudes (toward mothers who work, toward America by Britain), which interacted with a here-and-now bias and helped transform the girl into an international victim.

of the people they helped were strangers, over 90% said at least one was. Even one is a lot, considering the risk.

As for here-and-now bias, a correction for it, at least with respect to a single victim, is built into my empathy scheme as the fourth stage in which one empathizes with another's condition beyond the immediate situation. Here-and-now bias may have a potentially positive side. Whereas the "nanny" incident and Batson's 10-year-old-fatally-ill-girl research show the power of here-and-now bias to defeat society's notions of justice or fairness (more on this in chapter 11), the power of a salient victim and especially a media-enhanced salient victim to evoke empathy can just as well serve society's prosocial purposes. It depends on the context. Consider the example I gave in chapter 3 of media-produced or enhanced empathic distress for a group (Oklahoma City bombing victims) – the famous picture of a fireman carrying a dead baby, which presumably evoked empathic distress for the baby and his or her parents in millions of people. This empathic distress for the particular victim could well have become generalized and produced or intensified existing empathic distress for the bombing victims as a group. This in turn may have contributed to the many people throughout the country who volunteered to help the bombing victims or donate money.

There are interesting questions here: With all of television's faults, has it, by depicting victims close-up, contributed to an enlarged awareness and empathic feeling toward victims around the world? Or, does exposure to victims repeatedly over time result in habituation and a lowering of people's empathic distress to the point of making them indifferent to another's suffering? Or, as I suggested earlier, does depicting people in one's primary group as victims of another group foster ethnic hatred? Possibly all of the above apply and the net effect of television on "mass empathy" depends on the frequency and context of one's exposure. Only research will tell.

Another, quite different point can be made about empathic bias. Empathy is like attention: Attention is necessary for learning, but if we attended to everything we would not learn anything: learning requires selective attention. Likewise, while empathy may be the "glue" of society, as I claim it is, if we empathized and tried to help everyone in distress – "promiscuous" or "diffuse" empathy (Shweder)[3] – society might quickly come to a halt: When conflicts arise, promiscuous empathy could interfere with justice (so can empathic bias, but more about that later).[4]

Promiscuous or diffuse empathy is unlikely, precisely because of empathic bias and over-arousal. Seen in this light, empathic bias and over-arousal may be empathy's ultimate self-regulating, self-preserving mechanism. In other words, what keeps promiscuous empathy from becoming a significant problem for society are empathic bias and over-arousal and the powerful egoistic motive system that underlies them. Also contributing are the moral and legal responsibilities of guardianship in our society, which, together with the effect of genetics and evolution, make parents' own children more important to them than other children.

If empathy's limitations are not fatal, then they should not pose a significant problem in the moral encounters discussed so far – bystander, transgressor, virtual transgressor – which mostly involve a single victim, at least in small ethnically homogeneous "primary-group" societies. They might pose a problem when there are multiple victims and one must choose which one(s) to help or when helping conflicts with justice (see chapter 11).

The problem could be serious in multicultural societies because familiarity bias, which promotes empathy and positive relationships within groups, could increase antipathy and intensify conflicts between groups. There may be a reality basis for conflict between groups, such as competition for scarce resources (class conflict); and seeing another group as an enemy can lead a person to feel empathically angry and act violently toward that group. *Reducing* empathy in these situations might be necessary for intergroup coexistence. An activist I know recognized this point and said my research is "reac-

---

3. Personal communication.
4. Promiscuous empathy can pose problems for people in authority, who are expected to behave in a principled manner. An example is President Clinton, who at one point was criticized for feeling everyone's pain and seeing their point of view. It is difficult to empathize with everyone and put up a principled fight for a cause.

tionary." Why? Because empathy would reduce workers' hostility to owners.

These issues raise the question of whether empathic morality can live up to moral philosophy's criterion of impartiality.[5] How can it, when empathic bias is the antithesis of impartiality? In short, empathic morality may be ideal in homogeneous groups. But in moral encounters involving multiple moral claimants, conflict between helping and justice, and intergroup conflict, *empathic morality, at least empathic morality alone, may not be enough.*

I have argued (Hoffman, 1987), and will update and expand the argument in the next three chapters, that empathy's limitations are minimized when it is embedded in relevant moral principles. Briefly, the way it works is that the cognitive dimension of a moral principle – including its formal properties as a category and its semantic meaning – helps give structure and stability to empathic affects, which should make empathic affects less vulnerable to bias. The cognitive dimension should also make moral affects less dependent on variations in intensity and salience of distress cues from victims, and thus it should reduce tendencies toward empathic over-arousal (and under-arousal). And, finally, the cognitive dimension should make empathic affects more likely to survive in long-term memory, as in transgression-induction scripts (chapter 6). This is what cognitive representations generally do: They capture stimulus inputs, including affects, give them structure, and stabilize people's responses to them (Fiske, 1982; Hoffman, 1985; Tulving, 1972). The cognitive dimension of moral principles should do the same thing for empathic moral affects.

For empathy to be embedded in a moral principle it must be congruent with that principle, that is, its implications for human behavior must point in the same direction as the principle. The question is whether empathy is congruent with society's major moral principles: caring and justice. I think it is and in the next three chapters I try to show that it is. I suggest how empathy becomes

5. For perspective on this question, see my argument that other types of morality are also biased (Hoffman, 1987).

embedded in a moral principle, how empathy benefits from the embeddedness, and what it gives to the principle (a motive base). And I point to empathy's contributions in moral encounters characterized by conflicting moral claimants and conflict between empathy and justice.

# PART V

# Empathy and Moral Principles

# CHAPTER 9

# Interaction and Bonding of Empathy and Moral Principles

Although empathic morality can explain a lot of prosocial behavior, a comprehensive theory also requires moral principles. I suggested in chapter 8 that moral principles can reduce empathic bias and over-arousal. Another reason for moral principles' importance is that my analysis of bystander and transgressor encounters was incomplete, because bystanders and transgressors not only respond to victims with empathy and guilt but they may also come equipped with moral principles that are reflected in their response. The principles can be activated by the empathy and guilt with which they are associated; but principles can transcend the situation and transform the victim from someone to be pitied into someone who represents a larger category of injustice or lack of human concern. Moral principles can also help a person decide which victim to help when a choice must be made and whether caring or justice should prevail when they conflict (chapter 11).

I here introduce moral principles and discuss whether empathic emotions are congruent with them and can thus be embedded in them. I then introduce reciprocity (mentioned briefly earlier), which underlies many justice principles. Empathy and reciprocity are orthogonal; I suggest how they may combine to produce a powerful justice motive. Finally, I hypothesize that, given empathy's congruence with moral principles, empathy may play an important role in moral judgment and reasoning. Developmental processes linking empathy and moral principles are proposed in chapter 10.

## MORAL PRINCIPLES

Moral principles are grounded in bodies of philosophical and religious thought that are rooted in the histories of many cultures. In societies where people live in a relatively communal fashion, as in traditional societies, developing nations, and in modern Israel kibbutzim, people are more interdependent in their daily existence, and expectations and ties of responsibility for each other are binding. These societies place more emphasis on the welfare of group or nation than the individual and the moral principles highlighted are apt to revolve around caring and responsibility for others to a greater extent than in the contemporary Western world. And, within the (rapidly changing) West, events in history can shape peoples' views of morality, even within a single lifetime. Vietnam, the women's movement, and Watergate shaped a generation, sensitizing many to issues related to principles of justice and fairness (introducing, for example, "guilt over affluence," for the first time on a large scale).

It should therefore not be surprising that there is no universally agreed upon moral principle. There are two that stand out, however, and are often viewed as universal moral principles in Western society: caring and justice.[1] The principles of caring and justice and their connection to empathy are the focus of this chapter.

**1. Caring.** Utilitarian theory holds that a moral act or decision is one that maximizes the extent to which goals are achieved over all who are affected. One version, perhaps the best known (see Kymlicka, 1990, for others), is maximization of happiness or well-being for all ("the greatest good for the greatest number"). This version of Utilitarianism has become for some, at the face-to-face level, the principle of considering the welfare of others, or "caring." It includes concern for the well-being of others – their need for food, shelter,

---

1. Other principles are sometimes considered moral that have little if any prosocial implications. One is prudence: A person should do what is best for him in the long run (work hard, defer gratification, invest wisely, be careful). Another is self-fulfillment: One should fulfill one's potential ("Be all that you can be"); it is immoral to squander one's competence.

avoidance of pain, self-respect – and helping those in need or distress.

Caring is highly regarded in America: The day after Jimmy Stewart died (July 2, 1997), the media agreed he was loved by film audiences for decades because he represented kindness and consideration. Every newspaper I saw ran this quote: "I wouldn't give you two cents for all your fancy rules if behind them they didn't have a little bit of plain, ordinary kindness and a little lookin' out for the other fella" from his role as Sen. Jefferson Smith during a filibuster in *Mister Smith Goes to Washington*.

**2. Justice.** The more complex principle of justice, discussed mainly by followers of Kant (1785/1964), pertains broadly to the moral rightness of a person's due, a person's treatment by others and by nonhuman forces. What is just involves a balance between input and outcome in most areas of life; imbalance is unjust. Justice includes fairness when there are competing claims and conflicts of interest among people. Issues of justice and fairness include how society's goods and services should be distributed (according to merit or need), the rights of ownership of property (to use, enjoy, or transfer it) and temporary possession of property. Justice also pertains to how punishment should be allocated (it should fit the crime). And finally, justice requires that people be treated in a manner consistent with their "rights" as human beings. That is, people are **entitled** to certain things (food, shelter, absence of pain) and this entitlement transcends the personal predilection of a bystander: "Rights" is different from "caring." Underlying all of these substantive justice principles are two abstractions: **impartiality** – the principles apply equally to everyone – and **reciprocity** between actions and outcomes.

Advocates of one principle, "caring" or "justice," accept the other as important but subordinate, especially Kantians who argue that judgments based on individual welfare are not justice judgments unless the welfare is seen as a matter of a "right" that the individual has. Otherwise, caring issues are personal (not subject to legitimate social control), involve affective rather than rationally based decisions, pertain to particular victims and are thus not universal, and lack the formal properties of justice obligations. Caring is therefore logically subordinate to justice obligations in situations in which the two conflict. Miller and Bersoff (1992) disagree, pointing out that in India where social duty, not justice, is society's starting point, caring is linked to "rights" and subject to social control and the moral code views responsibility for others as fully principled as justice obligations and often accords it priority over justice obligations. This fits well with Deutsch's (1985) experimental research, which led him to attribute the preoccupation with "merit" to our society's having economic productivity as the primary goal. Deutsch found that when good social relations are the primary goal "equality" is the likely choice, and when personal development or welfare is the primary goal "need" is the choice.[2]

I find it more useful to view the principles as "ideal types" that apply in varying degrees to each situation. The principles may be compatible: One can sympathize with hard-working farmers who lost their farms because of economic forces beyond their control (caring), and also feel that they were treated unfairly because they were not rewarded for their efforts (justice). Or the principles may be incompatible: whether to give tenure to a colleague one sympathizes with because he has a chronically ill child (caring) or deny him tenure because of his weak publication record (justice). Conflicts between caring and justice will be discussed in chapter 11.

Psychologists have long studied justice and caring: Justice is central to Kohlberg's cognitive moral theory; caring is central to people like me who study moral affect and motivation. I suggested some time ago (Hoffman, 1987) that empathy is congruent with caring and most justice principles and it is therefore reasonable to hypothesize that empathy can bond with caring and most justice principles. The result of this bonding are principles that are charged with empathic

2. Deutsch also challenges the common belief that people work more productively under merit incentives than under equality or need. He found that when people are intrinsically motivated and are not alienated from work or from the social context in which they work, equity incentives do not enhance performance.

affect, with resulting benefits to both empathy and the principles. This chapter is taken up with a further analysis of the bonding of empathy and moral principles and with empathy's contribution to moral reasoning and judgment.

## EMPATHY'S CONGRUENCE WITH CARING

The principle of caring, like other moral principles, does not refer to a particular act. It is an abstraction, a moral imperative, a fundamental value, a philosophical ideal. It says that we must **always** consider others. The link between empathic distress and caring is direct and obvious. Indeed, caring seems like a natural extension of empathic distress in specific situations to the general idea that one should always help people in need: "We are our brother's keeper," "We must alleviate suffering," "Treat people as ends, never as means," "Treat others as you would have them treat you."

An observer may feel empathically motivated to help someone in distress, but he may in addition feel obligated to help because he is a caring person who upholds the principle of caring. This activation of a caring principle and the addition of one's "self" (the kind of person one is or wishes to be) should add power to one's situationally induced empathic distress and strengthen one's obligation to act on principle. Empathy and caring principles are thus independent, mutually supportive, hence congruent dispositions to help others.

The link between empathy and caring is reflected in the prosocial moral reasoning that accompanies people's behavior when they encounter someone in distress. In the book *Uncle Tom's Cabin*, an affluent, politically uninvolved housewife's empathic distress for slaves she knew who "have been abused and oppressed all their lives" leads her to oppose a newly passed law against giving food, clothes, or shelter to escaping slaves. Arguing with her husband who supports the law, she states what amounts to a caring principle: "The Bible says we should feed the hungry, clothe the naked, and comfort the desolate," adding that "people don't run away when

225

they're happy, but out of suffering." She becomes so intensely op-posed to that "shameful, wicked, abominable" law that she vows to break it at the earliest opportunity (Kaplan, 1989; Stowe, 1860/1966, p. 45).

Similar to this is Huckleberry Finn's moral conflict between em-pathic feeling for the slave Jim, whom he helped to escape, and both Missouri law and church teaching at the time which strongly op-posed helping slaves escape. In a famous passage, Huck writes a letter exposing Jim's hiding place, but then, after much agonized soul-searching driven by conflicting moral feelings (between sympa-thetic distress and guilt over what will happen to Jim if exposed, and the awful "sin" of keeping Jim's whereabouts secret), he tears the letter up and says to himself, "All right then, I'll *go* to hell" (Twain, 1884/1959, p. 270).

Huck's statement shows a willingness to sacrifice himself, hence the potential power of empathy to motivate prosocial behavior. But the *Uncle Tom's Cabin* episode is more important for present purposes because it shows how empathic distress and empathic anger aroused in relation to particular victims may activate a **general caring prin-ciple** that transcends the particular victims. That is, empathizing with particular victims led to both affirming the caring principle and using the principle as a premise for judging laws that violate it as morally wrong.

### EMPATHY'S CONGRUENCE WITH JUSTICE

The link between empathy and justice is less obvious but it exists, as I hope to show. I noted above that justice is concerned with society's criteria for allocating resources (distributive justice) and punishments (criminal justice). My focus is distributive justice, but first a word about criminal or punitive justice.

It seems likely that the punishment assigned to certain crimes is influenced by the extent to which people empathize with victims and are empathically angry at perpetrators of these crimes, and the extent to which the empathic distress and empathic anger are affected by the age, gender, and ethnicity of victims and perpetrators. People serving on juries are susceptible to empathic appeals by defendants, for example, especially if those making the appeal are similar to themselves (women can more easily identify with a battered wife who killed her husband). Lawyers know this, of course, and select jurors who will empathize with their clients. There is also the "sympathy defense" (don't blame me, I was abused) used famously (and successfully in their first trial) by the Menendez brothers who killed their parents.

Judges are not immune to empathic appeals. "It is my judgment that it is time to bring the judicial part of this extraordinary matter to a compassionate conclusion," said the judge in the 1997 "nanny" case discussed in chapter 8 on overturning the jury's murder verdict. He described the defendant's action empathically as "characterized by confusion, inexperience, frustration, and anger, but not malice in the legal sense." A prominent criminal defense lawyer said the sentence was "surprisingly on the low side, which confirms the one predictable notion about Judge Zobel, that he's compassionate" (*New York Times*, Nov. 11, 1997), p. A1). When defendants are to be sentenced, their family may speak to the court in order to arouse the judge's compassion. Judges' compassion often favors the defendant, who is foregrounded at sentencing time, suggesting that judges are vulnerable to empathy's here-and-now bias, which can transform defendants into victims.

To summarize, empathy can influence punitive justice. Since weighing personal sympathies is not the job of judge or jury, empathic bias may often interfere with punitive justice.

### Distributive Justice

Whereas criminal justice seeks a correlation between punishment and crime, distributive justice seeks a correlation between reward and some measure of deservingness. There are three principles of distributive justice:

**1. Merit.** Merit-based justice calls for allocating resources according to the amount or quality of goods and services an individual contributes: that is, the individual's *productivity, effort, or competence.*

Competence includes talent, training, knowledge, skill, all of which are assumed to contribute to productivity in the long run. Investment in productivity through money or education may also be included here.

**2. Need.** Need or communitarian justice calls for allocating resources according to people's needs regardless of their productivity (the Marxist maxim, "to each according to his needs"). Need can be based on poverty, handicap, or past grievances and discrimination that demand redressing.

**3. Equality.** Justice based on equality assumes each person has the same intrinsic worth in some larger religious or philosophical sense (Bentham's "Each person to count for one and none for more than one"). Everyone should therefore receive the same amount.

Distributive justice in our contemporary Western world dictates that resources be allocated *primarily* according to merit; "need" (social welfare) is also considered, though differently in each country. "Equality" is not taken seriously except in expressions of concern about the gap between rich and poor – and by young children, as we shall see (chapter 10). My aim here is to show that empathy has clear links to "need" and the "effort" version of merit, and more tenuous links to the "competence" and "productivity" versions of merit.

### Empathy and Distributive Justice

As context for empathy's congruence with justice, a few words about reciprocity, which is discussed at length later. Reciprocity is structurally congruent with justice. It underlies all justice concepts except "equality": People who need more, who work harder, or who produce more should get more; punishment should fit the crime. If humans prefer reciprocity over nonreciprocity (most do, I think), then a person who works hard and produces as much as someone else but gets paid less will feel angry, unjustly treated, and motivated to rectify the injustice. He will also, *to the extent that he is empathic,* feel empathic anger, have empathic feelings of injustice, and be motivated to rectify the injustice when someone else is treated unjustly. Thus, **while empathy may not make a structural contribution to**

**justice, it may provide the motive to rectify violations of justice to others.**

Second, empathy may make a direct *substantive* contribution to justice based on "need" and "effort." A bystander may respond empathically to someone who needs food and shelter (chapters 2–4). His empathic distress may also reflect a "caring" principle (we should help those in need), as discussed above. But if he views food and shelter as everyone's "right," then his empathic distress may be transformed in part into a need-based justice response: The victim **deserves** food and shelter. The bystander then not only has empathic feeling for the victim's personal distress but also sees him or her as a victim of injustice whose rights have been violated.

Empathy may link directly to effort-based justice for reasons suggested by my 13-year-old subject's explanation of why stealing is wrong (chapter 2). That is, unrewarded effort may connote the victim's inner states – the victim's motivation to work hard, the victim's future plans based on expected rewards, and the victim's disappointment at being denied the rewards. These are feelings with which observers can readily empathize. Middle-class Americans, among others, have traditionally been socialized to defer gratification and work hard for greater future rewards. They may as a result feel that they deserve to be rewarded for deferring gratification and working hard, and they may view others whose hard work goes unrewarded as victims with whose expectations and disappointments they can readily empathize.

Empathy does not link directly to "productivity" or "competence," which say little about a person's inner states. But there are circuitous links: (a) If one views productivity and competence as requiring hard work, long training, and deprivation, then the empathy-effort link extends to productivity and competence (empathic feeling of injustice for Ph.D.s who cannot find jobs); (b) if one accepts merit-based society's "trickle down" assumption that rewarding productivity and competence motivates people to produce more, and this in turn benefits everyone including the poor, then one might support productivity or competence on empathic grounds.

Empathy thus seems congruent with justice principles – directly congruent with need, and to some extent effort, and circuitously with productivity and competence. It follows that people who empathize with the homeless or hard-working poor will prefer "need" or "effort" over "productivity" or "competence." In a study of adults in what was then West Germany, Montada, Schmitt, and Dalbert (1986) found empathy correlated positively with a preference for need-based justice and negatively with a preference for productivity-based justice. I found the same in an unpublished study of American college students; and when asked to explain their choices, my high-empathy subjects more often said productivity-based distribution harms the disadvantaged. Empathy thus seems to dispose young adults, even in merit-based societies, to prefer need over productivity (at least when making the choice on paper). The same is true of young children, who support need and equality over productivity, and whose support for need is enhanced by empathic arousal (chapter 10).

Need, equality, effort, and productivity are not mutually exclusive. They may occur in different combinations, with one dominant and others playing a constraining role. Such a justice system was suggested long ago by the philosopher Rashdall (1907) who insisted that "equality is the (morally) right rule for distributive justice in the absence of any special reason for inequality" (p. 225). Cited as "special reasons" were need, productivity, and effort. Rawls, as we shall see, claims that rewarding "productivity" is the morally right rule, but only if "trickle down" actually happens and benefits the poor.

To summarize, if one thinks about how society's resources should be distributed one might focus on the implications of different distributive systems for oneself or for others. A self-serving perspective would lead one to prefer principles that coincide with one's own condition: A high producer would choose output, competence, or effort and a low producer would choose need or equality. An empathic perspective, on the other hand, would lead one to take the welfare of others into account: It might transform the task of choosing among abstract principles into an empathy-relevant task that leads one to imagine the consequences of different systems for society's least advantaged people or for people who work hard. One might then, even if a high producer, advocate a system based on need or equality, or one that rewards effort.

More likely, in a merit-oriented society, one's self-serving proclivity will prevail, though tempered by empathy. One might then choose a distribution system based on productivity but regulated to prevent extreme poverty (need) or vast discrepancies in wealth (equality). This type of regulated merit is at the heart of the philosopher John Rawls's (1971) influential theory of justice. Rawls explicitly argued *against* the importance of empathy or sympathy for distributive justice, but I of course disagree with that. I now turn to Rawls's theory of justice and discuss it as a special case that I believe actually highlights empathy's congruence with justice.

*Rawls's theory of justice.* Rawls advocates distributing goods and services on the basis of merit (productivity), but merit alone does not justify unequal distribution, because merit-based inequalities are ultimately due to advantages associated with heredity or class and are therefore undeserved. Merit-based inequalities are justified when there is fair and equal opportunity for all ("fair" means the handicapped get a head start) but, more importantly, only when inequality results in an overall increase in goods and services which are distributed in a way that maximizes the benefits "for everyone, and in particular the least advantaged members of society" (Rawls, 1971, p. 15). This "trickle down" justification of merit-based inequality – Rawls's "difference principle" – exemplifies merit-based justice constrained by "need." It is central to my argument about empathy's links to Rawls's theory.

Rawlsian justice also includes liberty: free speech and assembly, the right to vote and own property, freedom from torture, slavery, and arbitrary arrest. For liberty, only one justice principle applies: equality. Everyone must have the maximum liberty compatible with the liberty of others. Inequality of liberty is *never* justified. Furthermore, liberty has priority over distribution and distribution must not destroy liberty. Empathy's link to "liberty" is obvious: One empathizes with others whose liberties are violated. Examples, already cited, are Germans who rescued Jews from the Nazis and Huckleberry Finn's and the *Uncle Tom's Cabin* housewife's empathic responses to the fugitive slave law. Rawls posits liberty's preeminence but takes it for granted and focuses on the difference principle: **Merit-based distribution of society's resources is acceptable only if the resulting economic inequalities operate to the greatest benefit of society's least advantaged.**

Rawls's method is particularly interesting. To support the "difference principle," he constructs a formal hypothetical model of a group of "free and rational persons concerned to further their own interests" who are engaged in a bargaining game. They give serious consideration to several distributive justice principles, each representing a major position in moral philosophy. They must reach unanimous agreement on which principle will serve as the guide for constructing and evaluating social institutions and practices that will make life worthwhile. The participants must take a *purely rational, egoistic, self-serving perspective.* They must seek to advance their own interests (protect their liberties, widen their opportunities) *without regard for the interest of others.* They must not try to benefit or harm others, only to attain the highest gain for themselves (and their descendants). By making rational self-interest the guiding principle, Rawls seeks to rule out empathy, sympathy, and the "benevolent spectator" of some Utilitarian theories.

Rawls's hypothetical game is played under two constraints. One is that all participants agree in advance to be bound by the chosen principles for the rest of their lives even when they go against their self-interest. The second constraint is Rawls's famous "original position of equality" – the "veil of ignorance." The participants do not know their place, class position, social status, or political clout in the society they are constructing. Nor do they know their race, gender, religion, their natural assets and abilities (intelligence, strength), or even their conception of what a good life is. *They will therefore not be able to assert selfish interests to favor particular kinds of persons.* All they have is the *capacity* for a sense of justice. In this mental state (which resembles the state of nature in "social contract" theory), they are to choose the principles of justice they prefer.

The veil of ignorance interests me because it puts the person in the position of trying to satisfy his or her egoistic needs without the information needed to do so. Lacking this information, the person cannot choose the justice principles of most benefit to the person in his or her present position. On the contrary, in making a choice the person will feel compelled to seriously consider and calculate the possibility of occupying any position in the new society, from the most to the least advantaged, and to deduce which principles will maximize his or her welfare in any position. Rawls assumes that because the choice is momentous and the outcome uncertain, rational self-interest dictates that each person will try to protect himself and his descendants against an extremely uncomfortable, unpleasant life. The person can only do this by choosing the principle whose worst outcome for the person, his or her children, and their children's children, is better than the worst outcome of alternative principles. The principles that emerge logically from the original position, according to Rawls, would grant to each person an equal claim to "personal rights and liberties" and would tolerate inequalities based on merit only if "they are to be to the greatest benefit of the least advantaged members of society" (Rawls, 1971, p. 75) – in short, the difference principle.

To summarize, the veil of ignorance is an analytic device to ensure that in their reasoning the participants do not take account of their particular fortunes, talents, or abilities. It forces them to adopt an abstract, more general point of view rather than advocate a society that would reward themselves for talents and abilities they happen to possess. Through this reasoning, the individual, operating from the original position, would, in order to assure economic justice and basic liberties for himself and his descendants, end up constructing a just society that incorporates the difference principle (and the priority of liberty). Rawls claims these principles are superior to others precisely because they are more compatible with the original position. **One chooses them on the basis of rational self-interest but one's reasoning makes one assume every possible position in society. One's choice is therefore the most rational and self-evidently just principle for anyone in any position.**

What intrigues me is that Rawls's analysis starts with individuals taking a rational self-interested perspective and ends up with their constructing a moral society that takes the welfare of others into account, especially the "least advantaged." This to me translates into society's most vulnerable, that is, society's victims, which is where empathy comes in.

Rawls's theory has been criticized, though not, it seems to me, fundamentally,[3] and the original position remains without peer as a formal device for generating justice principles that meet philosophers' criteria of impartiality and self-evident fairness. Its genius lies in the reasonable assumption that anyone who makes a serious effort to imagine himself in each and every position, because he wants to maximize his own outcome without knowing which position he will occupy, will try to construct a society with the best outcome for people in all positions including the most vulnerable. In seeking the best outcome for oneself, one duly considers every position from the same unbiased perspective. Because the original position considers all perspectives, it is the fairest way to design a just society. The impartiality and self-evident fairness, plus the challenge of Rawls's

3. Rawls is criticized for assuming that institutions are reciprocal arrangements that are mutually advantageous to cooperating equal partners, thus ignoring class conflict, and for being unrealistic about human nature in assuming that competent people will find risk-taking aversive and be unwilling to gamble on "winning big" (Wellbank, Snook, & Mason, 1982; Wolff, 1977). These and other critics seem to miss the point that Rawls did not make a statement about social structure, human nature, or how people would actually behave in the original position. He set up a device in which the situation's *logic* dictates a fair, bias-free principle for distributing society's resources. I imagine that a computer might give the same answer if programmed to consider all positions in society, to work out the permutations for generations of descendants for each position, and to come up with the best available justice principles for everyone. It is interesting to speculate whether an omniscient "benevolent spectator," who empathized with occupants of all positions in society and their descendants, would come up with the same answer. In any case, Rawls came to view his theory not as universal but as providing justice principles for modern democratic society (Rawls, 1985).

explicit denial of a role for empathy, is why I give the theory so much attention.

*Rawlsian justice and moral behavior.* I accept the self-evident fairness of Rawls's difference principle but the question remains, why should people, especially high producers, abide by the difference principle in real life when they are *not constrained by the veil of ignorance, and are aware of their position in life*? Rawls does not deal with this question but seems to assume that the principle's self-evident fairness is convincing enough for people to abide by it.

To me, it is too cognitive, rational, and idealistic of Rawls to expect an abstract, intuitively appealing idea *by itself* to be motive enough to keep high producers from acting in terms of self-interest and ignoring the needs of others. There must be something else: a motive to help the vulnerable that is powerful enough to operate as a constraint against self-interest. The evidence for empathy's being that motive is in chapter 2. The difference principle's self-evident fairness might do the trick, if linked to empathy. I think this link exists, because the vulnerable are precisely the people highlighted by the difference principle. That is why the difference principle seems to me to be made to order for empathy, despite Rawls' contrary assertion. My empathy analysis follows.

*Empathy and Rawls's difference principle.* The research shows that people respond empathically to victims (chapter 2). This includes people who fit Rawls's definition of society's least advantaged: Economically deprived through no fault of their own, they work hard for little reward. People might also feel empathic anger and find society's institutions unjust for treating these people badly; and affluent people might feel guilty over benefiting from these institutions (chapter 7). These empathy-based affects could provide the motive for abiding by Rawls's difference principle in real life – sharing some of one's gains with society's least advantaged – outside the constraints of the veil of ignorance.

**This suggests that empathy and the veil of ignorance, seemingly so different, are functionally equivalent regarding matters of justice: They both constrain self-interest, though in different contexts.**

**235**

The veil of ignorance constrains self-interest when one is mentally constructing a morally fair society, by guiding one's self-interested reasoning in a direction that takes the most vulnerable into account. Empathy constrains self-interest in real-life contexts when one's interests and the most vulnerable's needs conflict, by creating a motive to help the most vulnerable. In other words, the veil of ignorance is necessary to derive the abstract, self-evidently fair difference principle. But only empathy can provide the internal motive basis for acting in accord with the principle and promoting institutions that embody it (services, taxes) – thus also, incidentally, reducing the need for external, coercive measures to accomplish these ends.[4]

*Empathy in the original position.* It is not necessary for my argument, but it seems plausible that empathy might operate in the original position if we think of it not as a game or mind experiment but as real people following Rawl's instructions. A real person might try to imagine living in various positions in the new society. When he or she imagines living in the lowliest position, images of people in that position – society's victims – might be primed and come to mind from past experience, books, or films (*The Grapes of Wrath*). These images could evoke empathic distress, which then supplements self-interest as the motive for choosing the difference principle: One chooses the principle because it not only benefits oneself but also treats the vulnerable with care and justice.[5]

If so, then a participant's examining justice principles and choos-

---

4. There are other motives for affluent people to share some of their wealth (to provide incentives for the less affluent to do society's unpleasant but necessary work; to reduce crime; to avoid class conflict), but these are unreliable because some affluent individuals might hoard their resources and rely on others to do the sharing. Empathic motivation is intrinsic; it should therefore, alone or in combination with other motives, help assure at least a modicum of sharing by most of the affluent.
5. This process in which the priming of victim images produces empathic distress, which in turn contributes to a moral principle, has much in common with the process I described earlier in which choosing abstract principles can be transformed into an empathy-relevant task by imagining the consequences for others.

ing the difference principle while feeling empathic distress can contribute to prosocial moral development. That is, thinking about the principle and feeling empathic distress concurrently may create a bond between the principle and empathic distress, which is likely since they both point to considering society's victims. The difference principle then becomes charged with empathic affect. Though generated in the original position, it might operate in life, not only because it is self-evidently fair but also because of its associated empathic affect.

To summarize, the veil of ignorance is needed to derive the abstract, self-evidently fair difference principle. But empathy, due to its congruence with justice principles and its possible role in the original position, may give people the internal motivation to abide by the principle. Empathy may thus be a blessing in disguise for Rawls, despite his attempt to discard it, because it connects his theory to the world. It also gives his theory an underpinning in psychology – and possibly biology, given the possibility that empathy survived natural selection and is part of human nature (Hoffman, 1981).

*An illustration.* In the "Bishops' Pastoral Letter on Catholic Social Teaching and the U.S. Economy" (1984, 1985), an analysis of America's economy is transformed into an empathy-relevant task by imagining the economy's effects on the poor. Included are many statements describing in eloquent detail and empathic tone the plight of the poor ("feelings of despair," "vulnerability," "daily assaults on their dignity"). It concludes that gross inequalities are morally unjustifiable, particularly when millions lack the basic necessities of life, and it characterizes the levels of unemployment and poverty at the time as morally unacceptable. The statement thus starts with empathy and compassion for the poor and then attributes their suffering to the prevailing distribution system. It affirms need as a basic principle of justice and sees need as violated by the system, which is insensitive to people's needs, creates many victims, and is therefore morally wrong.

The statement ends up supporting merit-based justice, tempered by need. It claims the concentration of privilege in contemporary

Western society results more from institutions that distribute power and wealth unequally than from differences in talent or lack of desire to work. And, it contends that the basic moral criterion for economic decisions, policies, and institutions is that they must serve all the people, *especially the poor*. The statement bears a remarkable resemblance to Rawls's "difference principle" and supports empathy's congruence with distributive justice principles.

To conclude, empathy can be linked to caring and distributive justice, as well as punitive justice; it can also be linked to justice issues concerning human rights because denying people's rights makes them victims. This lends credulity to my hypothesis (chapter 8) that empathy can be embedded in or bonded with moral principles and can benefit from this bonding because the principle's cognitive dimension (semantic meaning, categorical property) reduces empathy's vulnerability to over-arousal and bias. The principle, on the other hand, may benefit from the bonding by acquiring empathic affect's motive property. What follows are hypotheses about the affective–cognitive interaction processes that are involved, after which I discuss empathy's relation to reciprocity and its effect on moral judgment and reasoning. Developmental processes linking empathy and moral principles are discussed in chapter 10.

## CONSEQUENCES OF EMPATHY'S BONDING WITH MORAL PRINCIPLES

This is how moral principles may stabilize the empathic affect aroused in situations involving victims. When one encounters another in distress, two things happen: Empathic distress is aroused; and one's empathically charged moral principles, along with their cognitive and affective components, are activated. A principle's cognitive component helps one to "decenter" from the salient features of the victim's situation, assess the long-term significance of the victim's plight, and thus respond with more appropriate (the highest level of) empathic distress.

My hypothesis is that a moral principle's empathic affect (principle-driven empathic distress) helps stabilize the empathic affect aroused directly by the victim (situation-driven empathic distress), as follows. If the victim-driven empathic distress is intense, a less intense principle-driven empathic distress will lessen the observer's overall empathic distress. If the victim-driven empathic distress is weak, a more intense principle-driven empathic distress will intensify the observer's overall empathic distress. **In other words, when a moral principle charged with empathic affect is activated, this has the stabilizing effect of heightening or lowering the intensity of the observer's empathic affect. The empathic response by observers is thus less dependent on variations in intensity and salience of distress cues from victims, and empathic over-arousal (or under-arousal) is less likely.**

What do moral principles gain from the bond with empathy? My hypothesis is that abstract moral principles, learned in "cool" didactic contexts (lectures, sermons), lack motive force. Empathy's contribution to moral principles is to transform them into prosocial hot cognitions – cognitive representations charged with empathic affect, thus giving them motive force. How is this accomplished? I suggest that people in a moral conflict may weigh the impact of alternative courses of action on others. This evokes images of others' being harmed by one's actions; these images arouse empathic distress and anticipatory guilt; the images and empathic affects activate one's moral principles. The concurrence of empathy and principle creates a bond between them, which gives the principle an affective charge.

An example is Coles's southern schoolboy's empathic response to the Black youth (chapter 4). I suggest the boy had previously been exposed to the principle of justice, which was stored in memory and activated in the situation by his empathic response to the obvious violation of justice and the Black victim's admirable response – activated *because of empathy's congruence with justice.* This concurrence of empathy and violation of principle produced empathic feelings of injustice in the boy and a bonding of empathic affect and justice principle that gave the principle motive force.[6] This may explain the

---

6. An alternative path to empathic feelings of injustice is that one's own experiences as victim (of theft, undeserved aggression, verbal abuse) may

boy's subsequently going beyond situational empathy and adopting the principled stance of advocating "an end to the whole lousy business of segregation."

To summarize, I hypothesize that when principles are coupled with empathic affect they acquire an affective charge, along with the affect's motive property. They are then stored in memory as prosocial, affectively charged representations or "hot" cognitions, which can be activated on witnessing a violation. A simple three-fold prediction from this hypothesis is that empathy relates to prosocial action; upholding a prosocial moral principle relates to prosocial action; and empathy plus principle relates to prosocial action to a greater degree than either alone. This hypothesis has not been tested but if we can accept other-oriented prosocial moral reasoning (reasoning in terms of another's needs or based on taking another's perspective) as an approximation or precursor of "caring" principles, then the research done by Eisenberg and her associates supports the hypothesis – at three age levels: preschool, middle childhood, adolescence (Eisenberg, Carlo, Murphy, & Van Court, 1995; Miller, Eisenberg, Fabes, & Shell, 1996). That is, empathy, other-oriented prosocial moral reasoning, and especially the combination of the two correlate positively with prosocial behavior at all three age levels.

More interesting than the additive effect of empathy and moral principle is the information-processing question: Are the principle's empathic and cognitive components activated simultaneously or does one come first? I predict empathic affect comes first when victims' distress is salient, as in Coles's example. In cognitively focused contexts (playing Rawls's mind game, answering Kohlberg-style questions), cognition comes first and it can prime images of victims, which in turn arouse empathy, as may have occurred in my seventh-grade subject's response to the abstract question of why is it wrong to steal (chapter 4). Moral principles charged with empathic affect should be enduring, for two reasons: Semantically integrated cate-

combine to form a concept of unfair victimization, which one then applies to other victims of unfairness through empathy. This seems unlikely in the case under discussion, given the boy's popularity.

240

gorical knowledge (principle) is stored in long-term memory (Tulving, 1972); and affect (empathy) is a powerful retrieval cue (Bower, 1981). These principles should not only persist in memory but should also be available for activation in future moral encounters even in the absence of situationally induced empathy.

To date, there is only modest indirect evidence for these processes. Arsenio and Ford (1985) found that young children had negative feelings when told stories in which a child was inconsiderate of a peer; their later recall of the stories was aided by experimentally induced negative affect. This suggests that when caring violations are coupled with negative affect, they are stored in memory and are available for activation when one experiences negative affect. It seems reasonable to expect the same of *categories* of violations – caring principles: When a caring principle is coupled with empathic affect it is stored in memory and available for activation when one experiences empathic affect.

Eventually, experiencing empathic affect may not be necessary. Batson, Turk, Shaw, and Klein (1995) found that when adults place a positive value on people in need and this is coupled with empathic affect, valuing the welfare of others becomes a stable disposition. It remains and leads to prosocial action even after the empathic affect has declined. This should also be true of caring (and perhaps justice) principles: When coupled with empathic affect a principle may subsequently lead to prosocial action even in the absence of empathic affect, fitting my hypothesis that empathy can give moral principles a motive base.

## RECIPROCITY

Reciprocity pertains to the perception of balance or harmony (Feather, 1995; Heider, 1958), which in the moral domain translates into fairness or justice: earning what one deserves, being rewarded for good deeds and punished for bad; punishments fitting the crime (eye for an eye); treating others as one would be treated by them. Damon (1977) suggests humans naturally prefer reciprocity and that is why children are receptive to inductions that point up the unfairness of certain of their actions. There is no evidence that reciprocity is a prosocial motive, although I noted (chapter 4) how it can transform empathic distress, which is a prosocial motive, into an empathic feeling of injustice.

It seems reasonable that a preference for reciprocity survived natural selection. Trivers's (1971) theory of the evolution of reciprocal altruism (helping people in danger), which is an important part of my argument for the evolution of empathy (Hoffman, 1981), might also be an argument for the evolution of reciprocity. That is, it follows from what is known about early human life that species survival required rewarding individuals for performing well (as hunters, for example). Expecting a match between productivity and reward may thus be a part of human nature. People expect to be rewarded for productivity and feel it is unjust when they are not.

Whether reciprocity is the product of evolution or culture, it appears that American adults (not children, as we shall see) prefer it. They want outcomes to be proportional to inputs, and deviations either way can be distressing. Receiving fewer benefits than one deserves produces anger, resentment, feeling cheated. Receiving more is less distressing but can produce guilt, especially when one receives a larger reward than someone who performed equally well (Austin, 1980; Baumeister et al., 1994). As Schroeder, Penner, Dovidio, and Piliavin (1995, p. 214) observed, "Recipients who think they've received more than they deserve may feel over-benefitted, and this can evoke feelings of guilt and the expectation they may be punished for this."

## Empathy and Reciprocity

How do empathy and reciprocity interact? Developmentally, empathy appears in infancy (chapters 2 and 3). But not until 8 to 10 years of age do children show signs of reciprocity and assign rewards based on merit. Before then, they assign rewards based on self-interest, "equality" (sharing), and "need" (chapter 10); they may say "that's not fair," but they do so mainly when they feel short-changed themselves. The reason empathy appears earlier may be its primitive arousal modes, whereas reciprocity has heavy cognitive demands, such as the ability to focus on multiple aspects of a situation which is necessary for one to see violations of reciprocity. This suggests that young children's receptivity to inductions pointing up the unfairness of their acts, noted by Damon, is more likely due to empathic distress and guilt (chapter 6) than reciprocity. In older children reciprocity may play an important role, for example, in organizing these empathic affects into feelings of injustice. For similar reasons, people of all ages may feel empathic distress in bystander situations before recognizing that the other may be a victim of reciprocity violations.

To generalize the point, I suggest the motivation to comfort a victim comes from empathic emotion; the empathic emotion may be intensified and given shape by reciprocity and transformed into a relatively powerful motive not only to comfort but also to rectify injustice. Thus *a cognitive preference for reciprocity may add an injustice component to a person's empathic emotion, while gaining motive strength from being associated with the emotion – not just motive strength, but prosocial motive strength.* Reciprocity may of course have its own motive component (to rectify nonreciprocity). This has not been established but even if it is, *reciprocity is not intrinsically prosocial: It is neutral, encompassing non-prosocial "eye-for-an-eye" as well as "hard-work-should-be-rewarded" thinking. If reciprocity is a motive it can serve many masters; it becomes prosocial through association with empathy.*[7]

Thus the reciprocity concept, like substantive justice principles, can be charged with empathic emotion and become a prosocial "hot cognition." It can then be activated in situations in which one observes nonreciprocity, even when one hears or reads about it without

7. If reciprocity turns out to have intrinsic motive properties, then I suggest it is the context that determines whether empathy or reciprocity operates. If one encounters a victim, one feels empathic distress, and if he or she is a victim of injustice, reciprocity may also be activated and transform the empathic affect into a feeling of injustice. If, on the other hand, one encounters someone who gets more than he or she deserves, reciprocity is activated but not empathic distress – unless one imagines a victim (for example, the person who got less than he deserved in the same situation).

a victim's being present. That is, though the developmental process is "bottom-up" – from empathy to reciprocity – once a "hot" reciprocity concept is formed, it can, like substantive justice principles, be activated "top-down."

*Empathy, reciprocity, and moral principles.* The interpretation I gave of Coles's southern schoolboy's changed behavior toward a Black youth suggests the following general process sequence: (a) One empathizes with victims' distress; (b) one's empathic distress is transformed by an obvious contrast between what victims deserve (or their rights; their character) and how they are treated – that is, by clear violations of reciprocity – into empathic feelings of injustice; (c) empathic feelings of injustice may prime relevant moral principles and charge them with empathic affect. In Coles's example the principle is equal rights. We can similarly imagine empathizing with another's distress at being cheated: Our empathic distress is transformed by the contrast between what the cheated person deserves and how he or she is treated, into an empathic feeling of injustice. This in turn primes the principle that one deserves what one earns and cheating is unfair, thus charging the principle with empathic affect (if it isn't already charged).

Other empathy-charged principles (concerning verbal abuse, betrayal, stealing, etc.) may similarly be acquired. Several principles may combine to form an abstract though empathy-charged principle against unfair victimization. A principle's motivational component may be strengthened further by one's own personal experiences as victim (of cheating, robbery, abuse, betrayal): Having experienced unfair victimization makes one readier to empathize with others who are unfairly victimized. The result of all this is that witnessing unfair victimization evokes empathic feelings of injustice that activate relevant moral principles (and evoke anticipatory guilt when one is tempted to engage in victimizing actions).

*Reciprocity and empathic bias.* So far empathy and reciprocity are congruent. But reciprocity, unlike empathy, is supposed to be neutral and free of bias: People should be appropriately punished for crimes and rewarded for output regardless of who they are. This would happen if crimes and productive output could be defined, measured objectively, and connected appropriately to punishments and rewards. This is the main purpose of laws. But as noted, judges, juries, and others involved in punitive justice, are vulnerable to empathic bias; and so are the people involved in distributive justice (employers, teachers). Nevertheless, insofar as the rules of reciprocity have intuitive appeal, insofar as society's laws and customs are designed to fit these rules, and insofar as administrators of justice try to abide by them, they may operate to minimize empathic bias. Reciprocity may thus not only add a justice component to empathy but may also act as a constraint on empathic bias. In short, empathy supplies the prosocial motive force; reciprocity, usually in the form of justice principles, shapes and controls it.

In conclusion, empathy is a prosocial motive that operates against people's powerful egoistic motives. Though fragile, it sometimes prevails over egoism in bystander and simple transgressor situations (chapter 2). It is limited, however, and not enough by itself to satisfy the demands of justice, especially in caring versus justice encounters (chapter 11), because of its over-arousal and especially its bias tendencies. These limitations can be minimized when empathy is combined with reciprocity and embedded in moral principles, making empathy a more powerful counterweight to egoism in these encounters.

## Implications for Bystander and Transgression Models

It follows that a comprehensive bystander model and a comprehensive transgression model must include not only the empathic distress and guilt aroused, but also the moral principles that may be activated. The principles may be activated directly or primed by the empathic distress and guilt. In didactic contexts the sequence may be reversed: The principles capture the observer's attention first and produce victim images that evoke empathic distress and guilt.

## Empathy and Moral Judgment

The idea that empathy influences moral judgment is not new; David Hume suggested it over two centuries ago (1751/1957).

Hume's argument was that we obviously applaud acts that further our own well-being and condemn acts that may harm us. If we empathize with others we should therefore applaud or condemn acts that help or harm others; and, unless we are abnormally callous, we will feel indignant (empathic anger) when someone willfully inflicts suffering on others. Hume argued further that empathy provides the ultimate validating criterion for a moral judgment's correctness. Because most people respond empathically to events in similar ways, talk to each other about these events, and respond empathically to each other's descriptions of relevant acts and their consequences, empathy provides the common informational input needed by impartial observers to achieve a reliable consensus on moral judgments.

This view was criticized by Rawls (1971) who argued that empathy lacks the situational sensitivity necessary for a rational consensus; and, as I noted, Rawls's scheme was designed to exclude empathic emotion. My own empathy scheme (chapter 3) is less vulnerable to this criticism because mature empathy involves processing a network of situational cues and information about the other's life condition that bear on the severity and consequences of different actions for different people. An informed, rational consensus based on empathy should therefore be possible – at least in homogeneous ethnic societies. But there is the rub: In view of empathy's vulnerability to over-arousal and familiarity and here-and-now bias, I would not want to follow Hume and rely on collective empathic responses to validate moral judgments.

Still, given empathy's prosocial motive qualities and its congruence with caring and most justice principles, empathy should be able to make positive contributions to prosocial moral reasoning and judgment. Cases in point are the woman in *Uncle Tom's Cabin* who progressed from empathy with her slaves' distress, to espousing a principle of caring, to using the principle as the basis for judging laws that violate it as morally wrong; the U.S. Bishops' Pastoral Letter which moved from empathy with the poor, to a justice principle that included need, to using the principle as the basis for judging the distributive justice system as morally wrong; and Coles's schoolboy who moved from empathy with a particular victim, to judging the institution of racial segregation, which he had previously accepted, as morally wrong.

In moral judgment and decision-making research, subjects are asked how a person in a moral dilemma should act and why, or they are asked to identify the moral issue. It is different in life. Some occupations (judges, business executives) require making judgments and deciding on the rewards and punishments that others should receive, but most people's moral encounters do not begin with such a cognitive task. People encounter someone in distress and feel a conflict between the wish to help and the wish to continue what they were doing; they feel outraged by someone's unjust treatment of another (Coles's schoolboy); they discover that their own action harmed or may harm someone; they are tempted, or under external pressure, to act in a way that violates another's reasonable expectations (break a promise, violate a trust); they feel conflict between the urge to help and the law (the housewife in *Uncle Tom's Cabin*).

It impresses me that most moral dilemmas involve victims or potential victims (and beneficiaries) of one's own actions. It seems reasonable that thinking about what to do in these situations will often activate images or thoughts about people being helped or harmed by one's actions. One may do the same thing when judging the actions of others. Empathy may thus be aroused in judging one's own and other's actions and making moral decisions. And if my previous argument for links between empathy and moral principles is correct, then this empathy may prime one's moral principles, which, along with the "raw" situationally induced empathy, contribute to the moral reasoning process, more or less as in the examples I cited.

In sum, I am arguing that most moral dilemmas in life arouse empathy because they involve victims, seen or unseen, present or future. Empathy activates moral principles and, either directly or through these principles, influences moral judgment and reasoning. This can even happen in didactic contexts when people construct a victim. I adapted this Kohlberg moral dilemma for my research: Al broke into a store and stole $500; Joe lied and told a known benefactor in town that he needed $500 for an operation; both men skipped town with the money. Who did worse, Al or Joe? Why was that worse? (Hoffman, 1970). Most of the answers given by fifth- and seventh-graders and their parents were based on law and order, the Ten Commandments, and the likelihood of getting caught. But although the question mentioned no victims, over a quarter of the subjects made it a question involving a victim with whom they empathized. Examples: Joe was worse because he misused the man's faith and pity, made the man feel betrayed by someone he trusted, made him lose faith in people and become bitter, or because people who really needed help could no longer get it; Al was worse because the store owner worked hard for the money, saved for his family, and needed the money.

It is noteworthy that switching the question from "Who did worse" to "Which would make you feel worse if you did it?" resulted in doubling the frequency of empathic responses. Also, although most empathic responses involved Joe's being worse, when asked "what kind of person" the benefactor was, the subjects who gave empathic responses were as likely as those who did not to criticize him for being foolish or naive. In other words, they empathized and felt it was wrong to deceive him, even though they were critical of him. These are more convincingly *moral* judgments because they transcend simply empathizing with a generous person.

### Empathy, Distributive Justice, and Society

Virtually all domestic reforms entail some cost or sacrifice or at least diminished privileges on the part of some people in society for the sake of making things more equitable for others. These costs are better when accepted than imposed, which is difficult in a society as atomized into its racial, ethnic, class, and regional components as ours seems to be becoming, where personal and group interests are compelling and people may not see why they should bail out troubled communities half a country away. Many seem to reject the idea of a national responsibility for the well-being of others. This is why empathic morality is important, and why empathic moral education that promotes crossing boundaries and empathizing beyond one's group is also important (see chapter 13).

# CHAPTER 10

# Development of Empathy-Based Justice Principles

Empathic emotions, which begin developing in infancy and continue through childhood and beyond (chapters 2–6), are clearly congruent with "caring" and with the "need" version of justice, as just discussed. Besides being congruent, "need" may be linked to empathy by the inductions parents use when children make fun of economically deprived or homeless people ("Don't laugh at him, he can't help it the way he is, he has no home"). Before speculating about socialization's contribution to the links between empathy and "effort" and between empathy and "productivity," which, as discussed in chapter 9, are less obvious than empathy's link to "need," a summary of the research on children's distributive justice concepts, apart from empathy, is in order.

## "Stages" in Justice Development

The research on what children of different ages view as fair, beginning with Damon's (1977) pioneering work, has yielded a fairly clear consensus about children's notions of fairness, as reflected in their reasoning about distributive justice. In this research, children are typically asked to allocate rewards for work done, to recipients who differ in productivity and other respects. This research reveals a developmental trend from allocating rewards on the basis of self-interest (and irrelevant factors such as age) in preschoolers; to a strong preference for equal division of rewards at about age 5 or 6; to an increasing emphasis on reward in proportion to productivity or productivity integrated with need (poverty) among older children

(Damon, 1977; Hook & Cook, 1979). Older children can also juggle competing claims and devise compromise solutions in which each claim is given some recognition.

Sigelman and Waitzman (1991) criticize this generalization. They suggest it may result from the research focus on reward-for-work situations, which are more likely than other contexts to produce a developmental trend from equality to productivity-based distribution. To correct this problem, they studied age differences in distributive justice decisions by kindergartners, fourth, and eighth graders in three contexts: a reward-for-work situation intended to activate a productivity-based justice norm, a voting situation that would make the norm of "equality" salient, and a charity situation in which the principle of "need" might be expected to influence decisions. They predicted that with age children would become aware not only of norms supporting reward in proportion to productivity in work contexts, but also of democratic ideals of equality in political contexts, and social responsibility norms when needs are salient.

The findings fit these expectations. Five-year-olds preferred to distribute resources equally in all contexts and did not modify their distributions to fit the different situational demands. By contrast, both 9- and 13-year-olds varied their allocations as a function of context, favoring a productivity rule in the reward-for-work situation, an equality rule in the voting situation, and a combination of equality and need in the charity situation. The authors conclude that "the hallmark of mature distributive justice reasoning may not be the application of a performance rule in preference to an equality rule, or even an attempt to integrate claims of merit and need, but rather an ability to choose and apply the principle of justice most appropriate to the demands of the situation at hand" (p. 1369).

This makes good sense from a cognitive-developmental perspective: Older children *should* be able to take context into account.[1] In life, however, it may not always be that simple: Not only young

---

1. It also fits with Rawls's distinction between distributive justice and liberty: People may be rewarded for increased output if it serves the needs of the least advantaged; liberty must always be equally available to everyone.

children but also adults may be uncertain about which type of justice applies in a situation; they may experience conflict between types of justice and even between justice and caring, as discussed in chapter 11. My earlier suggestion against reifying moral principles, and in favor of viewing principles as "ideal types" that are applicable in varying degrees to all situations (chapter 9), seems relevant here.

Another contextual variable that has been studied is the effect of the relationship on children's distributive justice reasoning (McGillicuddy-De Lisi, Watkins, & Vinchur, 1994). Kindergarten, third-grade, and sixth-grade children were told two stories about a group of children who made artwork that was subsequently sold at a craft fair. The characters in one story were described as friends, while the characters in the other story were described as strangers. One character in each story was presented as the oldest in the group, one as the most productive, and one as the poorest. Children were asked to allocate $9.00 to the three characters. Kindergartners' allocations did not vary with relationship (just as Sigelman and Waitzman's kindergartners' allocations did not vary with context).

The most interesting finding was that sixth graders, but not younger children, allocated more money to productive strangers than to needy strangers, more to needy friends than to needy strangers, and *the same amount to productive strangers and needy friends*. That is, older children applied the productivity criterion to strangers, whereas they treated friends well whether they were productive or needy. This fits the findings for adults: Austin (1980) reported that strangers based reward allocations on productivity, but college roommates who worked on a task together overlooked productivity differences and distributed rewards equally; Clark and Reis (1988) found that adults in close relationships allocated on the basis of equality or need rather than keeping track of individual outputs.

Little research has been done on the effect of empathy on children's distributive justice. Damon's (1988) review concluded that by 4 years most children have a firm sense of obligation to share with others **(but not necessarily that they should be as generous to others as to themselves)**. They also have a sense of sharing as obligatory in social relationships and as a question of right and wrong. The relevance to empathy is that when 4-year-olds were asked the reason for sharing, the most common rationale given was empathic: It makes the other kid happy; when I don't share, my friend gets sad and feels like crying. (The most frequent nonempathic reasons were pragmatic: to avoid a fight).

Damon suggests that empathic reasoning derives from the child's well-developed capacity to respond empathically, plus the reasons (inductions) parents give to justify their demands to share ("Ginny will feel sad if you don't give her some"). He also found that when asked to explain why stealing is wrong, about half the 4- to 8-year-olds and 80% of the 9-year-olds gave empathic reasons (harm done to the victim) rather than fear of punishment.

In a study of older children who made bracelets to get candy bars and then discussed how to allocate the rewards, the high producers who expressed empathic concern for low producers voted to divide the rewards equally or according to need rather than output (Damon, 1977). In a study by Wender (1986), second graders watched films of a pair of twins who differed in the number of books they carried from one room to another and then rewarded the twins from a small supply of chewing gum. Most of the children divided the gum equally, regardless of output, and those in an experimental group previously exposed to an empathy-arousing film were more likely to divide the gum according to need.

The upshot of this research is that American children support need-based and equality-based distribution and downplay productivity. And their support for "need" is enhanced by empathic arousal. Damon's study is especially interesting because the empathic high producers actually voted against their self-interest.

## DEVELOPMENTAL PROCESSES IN EMPATHY-BASED JUSTICE

There is no research on the developmental processes underlying children's progression from self-interest to empathy-based internalization of justice/fairness principles, that is, on the developmental processes that contribute to the confluence of empathy and justice/ fairness. I suggest there are at least five such processes: (a) personal experiences as bystander or victim; (b) socialization at home, mainly by parental inductions; (c) socialization beyond the home: in peer interactions, in school, by the media; (d) abstraction and organization of justice principles from the preceding; (e) commitment and the possible role of triggering events.

### Personal Experience As Bystander and Victim

I have in chapters 4 and 9 discussed this process. Children as bystanders can empathize with another's sadness at being cheated out of his or her rewards for hard work, and their empathic distress may interact with their natural preference for reciprocity to produce an empathic feeling of injustice. This empathic feeling of injustice reinforces the link between empathy and the principle of "effort." The link between empathy and effort can also be reinforced by the child's own experiences of being cheated. Indeed, as suggested in chapter 9, all the child's experiences as victim – of theft, undeserved aggression, verbal abuse, unfair treatment of any kind – can combine to form a concept of unfair victimization, which can then be extended, through empathy, to others who are unfairly victimized. Personal experiences as victim can thus contribute to empathic feelings of injustice.

### Justice Socialization at Home

Two-year-olds may spontaneously comfort an upset peer by offering to share a cookie or toy, but they act differently when embroiled in conflict over a toy they both want. Three- and four-year-olds often engage in disputes over possessions at home and preschool (8 to 10 disputes per hour according to Hay, 1984, and Shantz, 1987). In these disputes, children's competing claims must be weighed and reasons given for determining who gets the resource, but as suggested in chapter 5, young children cannot do this. Their self-serving behavior in relation to desired objects reflects the salience of their own claims and needs, and unless an adult is present, the child's own viewpoint captures most of his attention. Adults who are present may intervene with inductions that point up the other's viewpoints and wishes and encourage the child to consider them (chapter 6).

Smetana (1989) found that parents' interventions in disputes over possessions are attuned to children's concerns and often enunciate principles of justice. It appears the immediate beneficiary of these interventions is usually the *other* child: Ross et al. (1990) observed mothers of 20- and 30-month-old children playing at home with the same peer over a 4-month period. In conflicts over the use of a toy, the mothers usually intervened and *were nine times as likely to side with the peer and encourage their own child to take turns or share*, which usually meant giving the peer a turn with the toy their child was playing with.

Here are some sharing inductions used by parents of preschoolers in my research, many of which integrate empathy-arousal with sharing or taking turns: She won't have any toys and will feel sad if you take them all. He is going to cry and he is just a little baby; he doesn't know what he is doing and he wants to play with it; let him play with it. Let her play with it because she doesn't have one like it at home and she really wants to play with it. Couldn't you let him have it for a few minutes just so he can look inside; I don't think he'll do it any harm. Why don't you let Penny ride the trike and you play on the swing and then Penny will play on the swing and you can ride the trike; take turns; that will make Penny very happy. Preschool teachers use similar inductions, except that the "other" may be the group: Give some back because it's not fair to the others who don't have any.

Ross et al. suggest the adults may be as motivated to maintain harmony as to instill a value on sharing. But whatever the motive, sharing inductions introduce children to both the principle of "equality" and the general idea, pertinent to all justice principles, that one cannot keep everything to oneself.

Parents also teach children it is good to work hard, do one's best, a person deserves to enjoy the fruits of his or her labor – in short, the justice principle of "effort." They may use inductions that fuse the empathy aroused with the child's violation of "effort": Two 4-year-olds argue over whose block tower is nicer; one kicks over the other's tower and the other starts to cry; the kicker's mother says "Bobby is crying because he worked hard on his tower and it is only fair that he has a chance to play with it; you knocked it down, now go help him build a new one." Another 4-year-old takes credit for building a tower; his mother says "That's not fair, that's cheating; he did most of the work and you say you built it and should get the candy, but he deserves more candy."

These examples show how some of the empathy-charged transgression scripts described in chapter 6 involve children's acting "unfairly" (not sharing or taking turns, cheating). I assume children progressively integrate these scripts into broader, increasingly abstract justice/fairness concepts like "need," "equality," and "effort." These scripts may be increasingly abstract but they are still for the most part rudimentary. It remains for socialization and other experiences beyond the home – peer interactions, school and media influences – to solidify justice/fairness principles and connect them to the individual's prosocial motive system.

## *Justice Socialization Beyond the Home*

To sum up so far, it is natural empathy-development processes, abetted by parents who model empathy and helping and use inductive discipline that involves sharing and taking turns, that create children who are empathic, consider others, and have rudimentary justice concepts. These children are ready to move ahead and refine their justice concepts through constructive peer interactions, learning in school, and exposure to the media.

*Peer interaction.* As noted in chapter 5, Piaget and others view adults as preventing children's moral internalization because they have the power to impose their will on children without their consent. Parents have that power, of course, but they are not compelled to use it, as I pointed out in chapter 6. Instead they often use inductions, which can integrate empathy arousal with sharing, producing a bond between them. In keeping with my hypothesis that a moral principle gains motive properties when combined with empathy (chapter 9), the bonding of empathy with sharing may be an early rudimentary form of empathy-based justice principle that has motive force. It can motivate children to use their perspective-taking ability to take another child's claim seriously and be willing to negotiate, rather than simply manipulate the other for their own ends – that is, to use perspective-taking in conflict situations for prosocial ends rather than, or in addition to, self-serving ends.

To sum up the point, inductions help children gain control of their own desires and understand and feel a certain amount of empathy for the other child's claims. **Inductions thus make children more receptive to the kind of negotiation, compromise, and successful conflict resolution that can only occur between equals. Inductions thus extend children's empathic capability into the realm of conflict: Children can now have empathic feeling toward others even in the context of conflict.**

I am suggesting, finally, that Piaget and others may be right about the unique benefits of peer interactions, especially for developing justice notions revolving around possession, ownership, and, perhaps to a lesser extent, merit. But, ironically, in view of these writers' negative view of parents as abusing their power over children, it may only be the parents, that is, nonabusing, inductive parents, in a sort of "coaching" role (Hoffman, 1988), who can set the stage and get children ready for the unique benefits of peer interaction. Peer interaction may otherwise have no unique benefits.

*School.* The socialization for "effort," begun at home and continued to some extent in peer interactions, expands in school, owing to the focus on academic performance and its assessment. Grading in many elementary schools is at first based on self-improvement. Children get stars and approval from teachers (and parents) and feel proud of themselves when their performance improves. This is their first systematic introduction to "effort" – hard work deserves reward – because improvement requires mostly effort. Social comparison is there too (not everyone gets a star), but it is a minor factor because children's performance levels are not *directly* compared. Children do expect rewards when they work hard and improve, however, and feel unjustly treated when their efforts are not rewarded; they are likely to assume that other children feel the same way and may therefore have empathic feelings of injustice when a classmate's or friend's efforts to improve are not rewarded.

In the fourth or fifth grade or thereabouts, the basis for adult approval often shifts abruptly from self-improvement to direct comparison with peers. Children are encouraged to work hard and do better than their peers and expect to be rewarded when they do better. They feel unfairly treated if they are not rewarded (parent says "you can still do better"), and they may have empathic feelings of injustice when this happens to a friend or classmate. An empathic child who gets high grades and notices his peers' distress when they do poorly may also feel achievement guilt (chapter 7).

The shift from self-improvement to social comparison is significant developmentally. Before the shift, caring and achievement apply in different contexts (caring when one observes another in distress; achievement when one first crawls, walks, talks, improves in school) and are thus compatible. But after the shift, caring and achievement may apply in the same context and conflict with each other, as when friends compare their grades (each wants to do better than the other, feels bad when he does not do as well as the other, and may have mixed feelings when he does better than the other).[2] This conflict is repeated throughout life: competition for top colleges, graduate schools, jobs. To summarize the point, the principles of "equality" and "need," associated with caring early in life, are largely left behind; the shift to social comparison adds competitiveness to peer relationships and prepares children cognitively and emotionally for the merit-based justice orientation that will dominate their adult lives (in the Western world) especially in the domain of work.

I mentioned earlier that "equality" as a distributive justice princi-

2. The same thing may happen in sports. I remember poignant moments when the best baseball or basketball players would pick teams and choose who they wanted on their side. One empathic leader always made sure to include a weaker player whose anxiety over being left out was never verbalized but always obvious.

ple is not taken seriously in our adult world, which stresses "merit." Not surprisingly, adults find it easier than children to think of situations in which they would *not* share, and they place a higher value on property rights, which conflict with sharing (Furby, 1978). There is also evidence that parents may actually support their children's cheating if necessary to get good grades (Burton, 1972). These findings show, among other things, how moral socialization in school can feed back and affect parents' socialization goals.

That children are socialized initially to share but are later taught to value merit suggests a discontinuity in justice socialization: Children must begin to unlearn "equality" in favor of "merit." We can only guess the long-term effects of the discontinuity between "equality," intense motivation to compete, and achievement guilt, until research provides more definitive answers.

*Media.* Development of moral principles, especially in adolescence and adulthood, is likely affected by books, newspapers, films, and TV. Victims of floods, earthquakes, tornados, massacres, terrorism, and wars are often presented sympathetically and (in TV) close up. Reading an account of the U.S. Bishops' statement described earlier, in which images of victims accompany abstract discussion of distributive justice, could add an empathy-charged, need-based component to one's distributive justice principles or fortify an existing principle acquired in childhood. Exposure to books and films like *The Grapes of Wrath* and *Les Miserables* (which puts stealing a loaf of bread in a larger sympathetic, moral context) might do the same thing.

These narratives can be important justice socializers because they enable readers to empathically identify with another's entire life (hard work, expectations, disappointment) and respond, where appropriate, with empathic feelings of injustice. They provide especially effective settings for concurrences of empathic affect and abstract justice principles that can transform the principles into "hot" cognitions and give them prosocial motive power. One can thus internalize complex justice principles with little or no external pressure because they fit with one's empathic leanings.

## *Abstraction and Organization of Justice Principles*

With language and cognitive development, children can, on their own and in conversations with others, begin to make moral inferences in light of the interpretations, explanations, and emotional reactions of adults, the arguments, negotiation attempts, and efforts at compromise of peers, together with their own cognitive and emotional reactions to morally relevant events. The child does not construct a moral code anew, as some cognitive-developmental writers claim, but is active nonetheless in reconstructing and understanding moral rules on the basis of information obtained from adults, peers, the media, and his or her own experience.

There may be a division of labor, at least in early childhood, between inductions which communicate rules of fairness and carry the force of authority, children's ability to cognitively decenter and their preference for reciprocity, and peer interactions that highlight the equality of disputants. This division of labor, implied in my earlier discussion of peer effects, is as follows: (a) Peers advancing their own claims **compel** the child to realize that the child's desires are not the only thing that must be taken into account; (b) decentering and reciprocity **enable** the child to grasp and understand the basis of another's claims; (c) inductions, acting on the child's natural empathic proclivity, **make the child receptive** to those claims. The empathy-based fairness concepts that result are shaped further by the values expressed by parents, teachers, religion, and the media. The result is that children who have these experiences become well versed in rudimentary forms of our society's caring and justice principles.

These processes are relatively haphazard until adolescence, when children are more "formally" introduced to moral principles in the sense of knowing they exist as guides to behavior. It is then, **if ever,** that the individual's active role in constructing a moral code, evident throughout childhood, takes center stage. The raw materials for this construction continue to be the products of socialization at home, with peers, and in school, including empathy-charged justice/fairness scripts generated in discipline encounters by inductions bearing on sharing and effort. These scripts are enhanced by the individual's direct, personal and media-enhanced, emotionally salient experiences as bystander and victim of injustice. The individual thinks and reasons about these raw materials and on his or her own or in debates with peers, analyzes, interprets, compares and contrasts, accepts or rejects them. In this way one constructs one's own set of general, relatively abstract though emotionally charged moral principles.

### Commitment

When one has internalized and committed oneself to a caring or justice principle, realizes that one has choice and control, and takes responsibility for one's actions, one has reached a new developmental level. From then on, considering others, refraining from harming them, and acting fairly not only reflect one's empathic concern but may also be an expression of the moral principle one has internalized and a kind of affirmation of oneself. One feels it is one's *duty* or *responsibility* to consider others and be fair in one's dealings with others. One may feel that he is not the kind of person who would knowingly harm another or act unfairly, and that he would find it hard to live with himself if he seriously harmed someone.

Commitment to "caring" or treating others in a just manner may add a dimension to anticipatory guilt. One not only feels anticipatory guilt at the thought of harming or treating another unfairly, but also guilt over violating one's principle-based self-image. The combination may make a more powerful prosocial motive than empathy-based guilt alone. If a person wants something badly and getting it requires harming someone or being unjust, and if anticipatory empathy-based guilt over one's harmful or unjust act is not strong enough to make one resist the temptation, the concern over violating one's moral self-image might tip the scale in favor of resisting.

*Triggering events and moral transformation.* Haste and Locke (1983) describe "triggering events." These are sudden unexpected occurrences that create a powerful emotional response which triggers a reexamination of one's life choices and can lead to a new moral

261

perspective and sense of social responsibility. Triggering events include witnessing extreme injustice, as happened in the events I have cited: the social activist whose close contact with poor Mexicans triggered guilt over his relative advantage and made him resolve to dedicate his life to the disadvantaged; the Germans who, confronted with Jews who were to be killed, decided to risk their lives to rescue them; Coles's White schoolboy whose empathic feeling of injustice on a particular occasion was instrumental in changing his mind and making him see racism in a new light; George Orwell, whose close contact with miners triggered guilt over affluence that led him to support socialism and distributive justice based on need and equality; Huckleberry Finn, and the woman in *Uncle Tom's Cabin*, who were each moved by a personal event involving slaves to change their mind and see laws against helping slaves escape as morally repugnant enough to warrant breaking them; the story-completion responses in my guilt research where the story child's guilt led to a resolution to become a more considerate person in the future. Historical circumstances play a big role, but not every one becomes a moral hero when faced with these circumstances (Colby & Damon, 1992). One requirement may be having strong empathic feelings of injustice. In any case, triggering events that produce moral transformations are likely to be rare though important.

# CHAPTER 11

# Multiple-Claimant and Caring-Versus-Justice Dilemmas

In complex moral encounters, bystanders must choose which victim to help. I deal first with moral dilemmas within the caring domain and then dilemmas involving conflict between caring and justice. A third type, conflict between caring and duty or responsibility, is often a sub-variant of one of these.

## MULTIPLE CLAIMANT DILEMMAS

Multiple claimant dilemmas in the caring domain that come to mind are people drowning or caught in a burning building; the bystander cannot help them all and must make a choice. There are other highly visible and controversial dilemmas: A doctor deciding whether to perform an abortion on a pregnant teenager – the moral claimants are the teenager, her parents who are concerned about her future, and, depending on its age, the fetus; a lawyer deciding whether to defend an accused murderer he or she believes is guilty – the moral claimants are the defendant who the law says has a right to a legal defense, the victim's family, and potential victims if the defendant goes free.

Another example is Kohlberg's hypothetical World War II air-raid warden who had to choose between remaining at his post or leaving to help his family when he heard his family's part of town was on fire. And the similar but very real dilemma faced by a nurse who was helping a victim of the Oklahoma City bombing when she heard the second bomb blast. She left the victim and rushed home to help her own family. She later said "I felt it was my family or her." She felt terribly guilty over leaving the victim, despite having helped many others before leaving the bombing scene.

In some of these multiple claimant dilemmas the actor is an innocent bystander: a passerby deciding whom to save in a burning building; a German deciding which Jew to save from the Nazis. In others, a person's social role makes him or her responsible for acting on behalf of one of the claimants: The nurse's role demanded that she stay with the bomb victims (which is why she felt guilty afterward); the air-raid warden's role demanded that he remain at his post. In some dilemmas a person's role demands that he or she help but it is not entirely clear which claimant has priority. The person may nevertheless feel duty-bound to act on behalf of one of the claimants: a doctor who feels duty-bound to perform a late-term abortion on a woman whose life may be in danger; a lawyer who feels duty-bound to defend an accused murderer despite the evidence of the accused person's guilt and the potential risk to others.

Some multiple claimant dilemmas are not obvious as a dilemma because there is only one claimant at the focus of one's attention and mental effort is required to realize there are other claimants. Consider a professor who is asked to write a recommendation for one of his students who is applying for an important job. The student is good but not outstanding. If the professor has some friendship with the student and knows other things about the student (such as that there is a sick child in the student's family), the professor might write a strong letter of support without giving it further thought. But things get complicated if the professor also empathizes with other moral claimants: the colleague who needs an especially outstanding applicant; the other unknown candidates who need the job. The familiarity and here-and-now biases discussed in chapter 8 may reinforce each other and prevail, in which case the professor might go ahead and write an unqualified highly favorable letter.[1]

1. In discussing my use of this example, Vitz (1990) notes that this is the kind of narrative reasoning, based on empathic understanding of others who will be affected by one's decision, that characterizes much of a person's moral life. He suggests that the images and cognition that are part of the empathy-inspired narrative function to generate more empathy, which in

Or take another, more complex dilemma in which a professor is considering whether to sponsor a favorite graduate student's research proposal that requires deception (Noddings, 1984). He might empathize with the student's pride in a well-written proposal, fear of months of work being wasted if the proposal is rejected, and eagerness to start the research. This empathy may be powerful enough to motivate the professor to sponsor the proposal. So far no moral dilemma, but there is one if the professor is against deception on principle. If the principle is activated, along with thoughts about people, especially someone he cares about, being seriously harmed by the deception, this might arouse enough anticipatory empathic distress and guilt to trump the professor's empathy for the student. He might not only reject his student's proposal, he might feel motivated to propose guidelines for controlling all deception research. On the other hand, he might empathize with potential victims of such guidelines: researchers whose careers would be harmed; people who might ultimately benefit from the research. Owing to this multiple empathizing, he might reject his student's proposal but refrain from making rules that bind others. Whatever the outcome, the example shows how one's initial empathic response, which may be biased toward the familiar and here-and-now, can be reduced by empathizing with other potential victims or beneficiaries of one's contemplated actions.

Multiple claimant dilemmas pose difficulties for the actor because he or she is not simply a bystander who is empathically aroused and helps a victim. He may feel like a transgressor because he allowed the other, neglected claimants to continue suffering (guilt, or anticipatory guilt, over not helping). Multiple claimant dilemmas are thus hybrids that have elements of the bystander (chapters 2–4) and virtual transgression (chapter 7) models.

All of the above multiple claimant dilemmas fall into the "caring" domain, that is, dilemmas in which a person's motive is either em-

turn may trigger additional cognition, and so on. Thus a self-constructed internal moral narrative is an interactive sequence of empathy and cognition. I agree.

pathy or a caring principle linked to empathy. The moral issue for ethics is which claimant *should* the person help. The issue for science is who *will* he or she help. Evolutionary biology's answer is simple: The person will help the claimant with whom he or she shares the most genes (Hamilton, 1971).

Psychology's answer is more complex, though in the end it may not be fundamentally different, as we shall see. Psychology's answer is that when there is only one claimant, the person empathizes with virtually anyone in distress (chapter 2). When there are multiple claimants, one may empathize with them all but is more likely to empathize with and help victims one knows and cares about, victims who are similar to oneself and share one's values, and victims who are present and visible (except for absent victims who are kin, like Kohlberg's air-raid warden and the Oklahoma City nurse).

In sum, evolutionary biology says that if we must choose, we will choose to help others to the extent that they share our genes; psychology says we will help others to the extent that we care about them, like them, and interact with them, that is, people who are members of our primary group. But members of our primary group happen to be more likely than others to share our genes. **Empathic bias may thus be psychology's functional equivalent of sharing others' genes: They both lead to helping one's primary group.** Indeed, empathic bias, like empathy itself, may derive ultimately from natural selection (Hoffman, 1981). In any case, it points up a limitation of empathic morality in multiple claimant situations.

Psychology's answer is also to do experimental research. Two of the experiments by Batson and his colleagues described earlier in connection with empathy's here-and-now bias (chapter 8) are also relevant here: one in which college subjects assigned a desirable task to a "worker" whose note, describing a very distressing personal experience, they had read and assigned an undesirable task to another worker; and one in which the subject's empathy for a member of the subject's group led him or her to allocate more resources (raffle tickets) to that person as an individual, reducing the amount available to the group as a whole.

Another thing psychology can do that evolutionary biology cannot is suggest answers to the question of how to reduce empathic bias. The answers require conscious deliberate effort to use our knowledge to reduce empathic bias through moral education (see chapter 13). There is also my earlier suggestion that empathic bias may be reduced when empathic affect is embedded within abstract moral principles. Here is an example in which highly principled people, when compelled to make life-and-death choices, were able to transcend empathic bias. It concerns Germans who rescued Jews from the Nazis. Although the Jews they rescued were generally known to them, over 90% of the rescuers interviewed by Oliner and Oliner (1988) said they helped at least one Jew who was a total stranger. That is a lot when you consider the great personal risk. Furthermore, according to Oliner and Oliner, the rescuers'

> universalist view of their ethical obligations sometimes put them in a tragic situation in which they needed to make a painful choice: which life to save. Some struggled to find a guiding criterion. Should it be the doctor, the judge, or the poor uneducated person whose life promised little more than survival? The child, the aged, or the frail? This "playing God" with people's lives left its mark: choice itself violated the principle of universal responsibility, and guilt feelings continued to plague some of them for years when they reflected on the choices they made. (Oliner & Oliner, 1988, p. 170)

Oliner and Oliner's remarks suggest that the principle of caring can help people transcend empathic bias, though at a cost. They point up the agony of choosing among moral claimants in extreme situations and the intense guilt that principled people who risk their lives for others may nevertheless feel regarding the victims they did not help. And they also show that having principles can "get one into trouble": Without principles, they would not have been so vulnerable to guilt; they might not have taken risks in the first place (see discussion of commitment in chapter 10).

## CARING VERSUS JUSTICE

If caring and justice are valued in our society and children are socialized to internalize them both, and if I am right about empathy's developmental links to caring and most justice principles (chapter 9, 10), then it follows that most mature, morally internalized individuals have empathy-charged caring and justice principles in their motive system. They should therefore be sensitive to both the caring and justice perspectives, capable of experiencing conflict between caring and justice, and vulnerable to empathic distress, anticipatory guilt, and empathic feeling of injustice, depending on which principle they act on and which one they neglect.

An example of a caring-versus-justice conflict occurred when a student nearly convinced me that her "life would be wrecked" if I did not give her a higher grade. My conflict of course was between empathic distress (and anticipatory guilt) for the student and the unfairness to other students of giving her a higher grade than she deserved. Similar conflicts may be experienced by students who, after taking an exam, are asked by friends for the questions so they can perform well on the exam.[2] Two quite different examples of caring-versus-justice conflict are Kohlberg's dilemma based on *Les Miserables,* in which a man steals a drug to save his wife's life; and the experiment described in chapter 8 in which college students who empathized with a girl suffering from a fatal disease had to decide whether to move her up the waiting list for a new drug, at the expense of children who were legitimately higher on the list.

When I analyzed empathy's links to distributive justice principles (chapter 9), I concluded that the "productivity" and "competence" versions of distributive justice were further from "caring" than the "need" and "effort" versions. Productivity and competence are therefore more likely to conflict with caring. Consider the letter-of-recommendation example, discussed above as a straight caring dilemma: The writer could empathize with each moral claimant (student, colleagues, unknown applicants), imagine the claimant's disappointment and distress that would result from one or another type of letter, and perhaps also feel a certain amount of anticipatory guilt in each case. He might then decide to write a letter that made

2. This conflict includes an obvious egoistic (competitive) component as well.

him feel the least empathic distress or guilt overall, or he might simply decide that his student came first and let it go at that. These are all "caring" considerations.

But there are justice issues too. The academic system places high value on merit (scholarly productivity and competence), and the integrity of the system depends on recommenders' candid assessments of job applicants, which the professor's colleagues expect from him. This type of caring-versus-justice dilemma becomes acute when a professor believes that a student may not be the most qualified applicant. If the professor writes a candid letter that reveals the student's weakness, in keeping with "justice," he or she violates "caring" and may feel empathic distress and guilt over betraying the student. If empathy for the student prevails and the professor emphasizes the student's strengths and downplays the student's weaknesses, then he or she violates "justice" and may feel guilty over that. The professor could also think about other candidates for the job and imagine that one of them is the professor's own child and is more qualified than his or her student. That might reduce the empathic bias for the particular student. But I am getting ahead of myself: Teaching people to empathize with the "other" is a method of moral education that will come up in chapter 13.

Similar issues are involved in professors' recommending colleagues for tenure, promotion, and salary increases, or in executives pondering whether to retain an ineffective employee for whom they feel compassion or hire a more competent person. An esteemed faculty member died and his wife, a part-time adjunct instructor with much-below-average teacher ratings, wanted to keep her job. "Caring" and "need" seemed to dictate allowing her to keep the job, and some faculty took this position. But others argued that allowing a poor teacher to stay on would be morally wrong because it goes against the students' best interests ("caring") or because the university should hire the best teachers available and there are many more competent ones to choose from ("justice"). This takes us back to the point about different justice principles applying in different contexts (chapter 10). The academic system is a work context and merit

should theoretically be the sole criterion for hiring, tenure, and promotion decisions; but merit often conflicts with caring and need,
which are difficult for many to ignore.

To summarize, empathy contributes to multiple claimant dilemmas within the caring domain because of the human proclivity to
empathize with victims. Faced with multiple victims and forced to
make a choice, a person may help one victim but feel guilty over
allowing another to suffer. Empathic bias plays a role in this choice,
and I noted this as one of empathy's limitations. It may be argued
that empathic bias is as natural in humans as empathy is, and bias
in favor of one's in-group when one is deciding who to help is not
such a bad thing (Blum, 1987). I agree with that, but empathic bias
*can* become a bad thing when people feel compelled to attack others
in defense of their own group (empathic anger). How to reduce this
"empathy-based violence," bred of empathic anger, is a moral education problem (touched on in chapter 13).

Empathy can contribute to both sides of caring–justice dilemmas
because of empathy's congruence with both, though it is less likely
to contribute to the justice side when productivity is the issue, as is
usually the case in our society. People who value productivity may
feel that it is the "obvious" principle to follow in caring–justice
dilemmas, and the same goes for people who value caring. The
problem is that both caring and justice are powerful, legitimate principles in our society and *both* are valid. The faculty who supported
retaining the widowed part-time instructor were passionate about
the matter and found it hard to believe that their colleagues could be
so callous as to want to add to this woman's grief. The other faculty
were equally passionate and found it hard to believe that their colleagues could not see that only one moral issue was relevant: competence. To them, retaining her would be immoral.

# PART VI

# Culture

# CHAPTER 12

# The Universality and Culture Issue

Since the Holocaust, cultural relativism is dead. We no longer have the luxury of assuming every culture's values or guiding principles will pass the moral test and that each is as good as any other. This does not mean there is only one principle that can pass the moral test. There may be several – one principle that passes the moral test better in one context, one that does better in another context, and in yet other contexts two or more perfectly sound moral principles that may conflict. For these reasons I applaud Kohlberg's and his followers' rejecting relativism and advocating a universal principle of justice. Justice surely meets any moral criterion, although I also place a high value on caring, which at times conflicts with justice (chapter 11) and I have a problem with Kohlberg and his followers: I have always found them rather vague on what justice means.[1] When you get down to actual human behavior, justice can mean many things – punitive justice, retributive justice, distributive justice, meritocratic justice, egalitarian justice, justice based on need. Empathy appears to be congruent with all or most of these justice principles, as well as with caring (chapter 9). This suggests empathy may lay claim to being a universal prosocial moral motive, at least in societies that place high value on caring and justice.

1. An exception is Damon (1988), who has done extensive developmental research on merit and other distributive justice concepts (see chapter 10).

### Empathy's Biological Substrate

Another argument for empathy's universality is one I made some time ago (Hoffman, 1981). The argument is based on evolutionary theory, contemporary behavioral research showing that empathic distress motivates helping behavior (see chapter 2), and evidence for a physiological basis of empathic emotion. The physiological basis cited is the brain's limbic system, an ancient structure that is the seat of emotional experience, and its intricate connections to the prefrontal neocortex, the most recently evolved and distinctively human part of the brain (Brothers, 1989; MacLean, 1973, 1985; Panksepp, 1986). It now appears, more specifically, that the neural basis of empathic distress may be the amygdala and its connections to the orbitofrontal cortex (Blair, 1999). My conclusion was and still is that it must have been empathy, as a *disposition* toward altruism, rather than altruism, that passed the test of natural selection and is part of human nature (Hoffman, 1981). It follows that empathy is a potential prosocial motive in all humans. Other support for empathy's biological basis is the evidence for a hereditary component, that is, the correlation between scores on empathic concern in response to another's (simulated) distress, in home and laboratory settings, at 14 months and 20 months of age, was greater for identical than for fraternal twins (Plomin et al., 1993; Zahn-Waxler et al., 1992).

Putting together the evidence for empathy's biological substrate and its congruence with caring and justice principles, it seems reasonable to conclude that although empathy's prosocial motive property has only been studied in the United States, empathy must be considered a prime candidate for being a universal motive base for prosocial moral behavior when humans observe others in distress. What about the other tenets of my empathic morality theory – the five modes of empathic arousal, inductive discipline's contribution to transgression guilt and moral internalization, and, above all, the hypothesis that empathy develops apace with the child's development of a sense of others as distinct from the self? Are the underlying processes universal or culture bound? There is only one way to approach this question, in the absence of cross-cultural research, and that is to dig in and analyze the key concepts to see which, if any, are plausibly universal. I begin with empathy development and then proceed to the modes of empathic arousal and the role of induction.

## Empathy Development and the Sense of Self

Some cultural psychologists (e.g., Markus & Kitayama, 1991; Miller & Bersoff, 1992) suggest that the development of a separate, distinct, independent sense of self is not universal but encouraged in the United States and other Western individualistic societies. According to these writers, the cultural goals of independence, self-sufficiency, and individual accomplishment require construing oneself as an individual whose behavior is organized and made meaningful by reference to one's own internal repertoire of thoughts, feelings, and actions. As a result, the Western self is more fully developed than the self in more "collectivist" non-Western societies, which can be found all over the world, including Japan, emerging nations like China, India, Indonesia, and Korea, as well as traditional homogeneous societies that place higher value on harmony, tradition, social interdependence, caring, responsibility for the welfare of others, and community obligations over individual rights.

Following the argument, the notions of interdependence, harmony, and caring in these societies require that there be a fundamental connectedness of human beings to each other and a maintaining of this interdependence among individuals. Furthermore, this cultural goal of interdependence produces a *sense of self and others that is merged rather than separate and distinct.* The idea of a merged self in these societies is not only derived from their cultural goal of interdependence but is also supported by observations of certain practices that appear to reflect a less developed individual self. These practices include the apparent willingness of people in these societies' lower rungs to show deference to the elite, respect the elite's privileges, and at times merge their goals with the elite's (gain pleasure from their pleasure). If these writers are correct and self–other differentiation is a culturally determined, primarily Western construction, then my entire empathy development scheme, which is based on the synthesis of empathic arousal and the development of a separate, distinct sense of self, becomes a cultural artifact of the West and certainly not universal.

I think these writers are wrong, for several reasons. First, it seems obvious and fundamental that the human brain and its associated cognitive structures guarantee at the very least that all humans are aware of the continuous kinesthetic sensations from their own bodies. This continuing kinesthetic awareness not only provides infants with an early sense of separation of self from other (Stern, 1985, chapter 3) but also continues past infancy to ensure a certain minimum of separation of self from others throughout a person's life. Second, the brain and cognitive development guarantee that humans from early childhood are aware of their inner feelings, thoughts, and, especially important for present purposes, their needs and desires. Third, the brain and cognitive development guarantee that humans can mentally represent as well as kinesthetically sense their own actions. Fourth, the brain and cognitive development guarantee the individual's ability to represent other people (object permanence) and their actions. Ekman's finding that facial expressions connote the same basic emotions across cultures suggests that if 3- or 4-year-old Americans can infer others' feelings from facial expressions (chapter 3), so can children from "collectivist" cultures.

It should therefore be impossible for an adult with a normal brain to feel that his or her self is merged with others. (This is a limitation of empathic distress as a prosocial motive: One can feel intense empathic distress but one knows that one is not the other.) Furthermore, individuals have needs and desires; and an individual's needs and desires inevitably conflict with the needs and desires of other individuals. Culture can minimize the frequency of such conflicts (there are likely fewer in cooperative than in competitive cultures) and thus affect the number of disputes, fights, arguments, but it seems unlikely that culture can eliminate conflict. In any case, it seems to me that there is nothing more powerful than fights, arguments, and involvement in negotiations over disputes, to sharpen one's self-awareness – indeed, to make it virtually impossible *not* to be aware of the separation of self and other.

Plausibility thus seems to be on the side of a universal sense of self rather than a collective, merged self. So does empirical evidence, scant though it is. The most relevant psychological research bears on gender identity, which is an obviously important dimension of the self: The development of gender identity in other, less individualistic cultures (Belize, Kenya, Nepal, Samoa) shows the same progression (identity, stability, constancy) – though the ages of attainment may differ – as that found in the American middle class (Munroe, Shimmin, & Munroe, 1984).

Other evidence is given by Turiel (1998) who points out, first, that the elite members of non-Western, more "collectivist" societies have a strong sense of autonomy, personal entitlement, and a highly developed sense of self, as evidenced by actions clearly designed by them to maintain their privileges. More important, these societies' less privileged members also conceive of the self as autonomous and independent; and self-interest and personal goals **are** significant in their lives. The people in the lower classes and castes view their selves realistically, however, as part of a social network in which their independence and personal jurisdiction are subordinated to others and to the requirements of their role. A person, in other words, can be aware of the pragmatics of power (one may be punished for disobeying); one can view the elites' privileges as unfair, and yet subordinate oneself to them not because one lacks a sense of self but because the power structure allows no choice. Turiel quotes Spiro's (1993) observation, based on his review of the anthropological research, that there is a lot of "differentiation, individuation, and autonomy in the putative non-Western self . . . and dependence and interdependence in the putative Western self." And more directly to the point is Spiro's conclusion that "cultural ideologies and public symbols do not necessarily translate into individual's conceptions or experience of self and others" (see Turiel, 1998, p. 916).

It follows that there may indeed be less aggrandizement and celebration of the individual, more interdependence, helping, and empathizing than autonomy, and a greater value on community obligations than individual rights in "collectivist" societies than in the West. The differences may not be as great as advertised, however. In any case, a culture's values and practices may determine the context in which the self develops and resides (competition, solidarity), but these values and practices may have nothing to do with whether individuals in the culture have a fully developed sense of self. It seems more likely, in the absence of evidence to the contrary, that everyone has a sense of self – due primarily to brain and cognitive development and the inevitable conflicts between individuals and groups – than that the development of self is problematic and dependent on culture. That is, the self is, in a word, universal.

It also seems plausible, because it fits what is known about cognitive development (see chapter 3), and in the absence of cross-cultural research to the contrary, that the individual self progresses developmentally, as I hypothesized. It develops, that is, from a self/other confusion in infancy, through the stages of a self and others that are physically distinct, a self that has inner states that others do not know and outward characteristics that they do know, and a reflective self that has a life beyond the immediate situation and knows that others do too – in sum, a self that knows others have a self similar to one's own.

## Modes of Empathic Arousal

I begin with the newborn's agitated distress response to the sound of another's cry, a likely rudimentary form of empathic distress that can be considered without further comment as universal and culture-free because it is available to newborns. Second, the three primitive modes – mimicry, conditioned empathic distress, and empathic distress by direct association – are also likely universal empathy-arousing processes. The reasons I say this (see chapter 2) are: (a) given the likelihood that mimicry's two steps (imitation and feedback) are central-nervous-system determined and Ekman's finding of universals in the relation between emotion and facial expression, it follows that anyone in any culture who attends to a victim's facial expression of distress will feel empathic distress; and (b) conditioned empathic distress and empathic distress by direct association are likely to be universal because they, too, have an autonomic, central nervous system base. Furthermore, all humans are structurally similar, are products of a common evolutionary history, and have certain distress experiences in common (pain, fear, loss, separation). People the world over should therefore at some point in their development be capable of feeling empathic distress when they witness someone in distress, due to conditioning or direct association with their own, inevitably similar distress experiences.

Mimicry, conditioning, and direct association must therefore be universal empathy-arousing processes, although cultures vary in how often these processes operate, owing to likely cultural variations in the extent to which different types of distress are experienced. Cultures may also vary in the extent to which observers attend to victims of one or another type of distress, or engage in distracting thoughts that draw attention away from victims. This possibility could affect mimicry in particular and make it subject to cultural variation, as mimicry is totally dependent on the observer's attention to the victim.[2]

Third, language-mediated association ought to be a universal empathy-arousing process for the same reasons as conditioning and direct association, and also because all cultures presumably have language. It seems likely, though, that languages differ in how effectively they can express feelings, including feelings of distress, and so the frequency of language-mediated empathic distress may be expected to vary across cultures. Fourth, role-taking is a more cognitively demanding empathy-arousing process. While it can be automatic, as discussed in chapter 2, it is likely to have a heavy voluntary component and may therefore be dependent on culture. Self-focused role-taking, for example, might be a more prevalent response to distressed others in individualist societies.

It seems reasonable to conclude that the modes of empathic arousal are all universal, that is, regardless of culture, humans are *capable* of being empathically aroused by any of them. Empathic arousal by the primitive modes should be automatic and involuntary

---

2. Given empathy's familiarity bias (chapter 8), distractions are more likely to occur when victims are outside the observer's primary group.

in most cultures. The more cognitively demanding and to some extent voluntary modes, language-mediated association and role-taking, may also be universal though subject to cultural influence. This discussion points up the importance (mentioned in chapter 2) of there being so many quite different modes of empathic arousal.

People all over the world make causal attributions, although anthropologists have long noted that causality means something different in traditional homogeneous societies than in the West. Anyway, it seems safe to assume that people in the developed and developing parts of the world make causal attributions, including attributions of the causes of another's distress, and, furthermore, that these causal attributions are more or less in accord with reality, as in America. That is, observers feel sympathetic distress when the cause is beyond the victim's control (illness, accident) and empathic anger when someone else is the cause. When the observer is the cause, I assume the observer feels something akin to guilt, although there has always been a question of whether guilt is universal. My general point is that causal attributions, like other cognitive capabilites, are brain related and therefore available to people in all cultures, though not all cultures utilize them fully or in the same way. Clearly this is an area that needs research.

## Induction, Guilt, and Moral Internalization

What about the transgression model – the role of induction in the socialization of empathy-based transgression guilt and guilt's functioning as a prosocial moral motive? Are these universal concepts? Here we are on less firm grounds. Parents everywhere undoubtedly find it necessary to intervene and change children's behavior against their will, but most of the research showing induction's role in transgression guilt and moral internalization was done on White middle-class Americans. Do the findings apply to other populations?

The *frequency* of parents' using induction and power assertion – indeed, the frequency of discipline encounters – can obviously not be generalized. The research has long documented more frequent power assertion and less frequent induction (and other reasoning) in lower socioeconomic groups. In an early correlational study that included a lower-class (White) sample, Hoffman and Saltzstein (1967) found that the mother's use of induction did not correlate with children's guilt and moral internalization in the lower-class sample, although it did in the middle-class sample. The lack of lower-class findings was explained as possibly due to the combined effects of several factors: The lower-class mothers used far fewer (statistically highly significant) inductions; more of the lower-class mothers worked full-time outside the home (few middle-class mothers did in the 1960s); the lower-class families were larger (often including three generations) and confined to less living space, which meant the child interacted with many others besides the mother. As a result, the socialization process was more diffuse (spread out over more people) in the lower class. Consequently, the lower-class mother's discipline may have been less crucial and singular a variable in the child's moral internalization.

Similar factors may underlie the finding by Deater-Deckard, Dodge, Bates, and Pettit (1996) that power-assertive discipline correlates with "externalizing behavior problems" in European Americans but not in African Americans. This correlation, between power assertion and externalizing, is not the same as a correlation between induction and internalizing but it is the closest thing we have to go by, because induction and moral internalization have not been studied in African Americans. The jury is therefore still out on whether induction contributes to moral internalization in middle-class African Americans, as it appears to do in middle-class European Americans. My hypothesis is that it does. That is, the *processes* I hypothesized relating induction to transgression guilt and moral internalization still seem plausible to me and to others who have been testing and by and large supporting them – to be sure in European American middle-class samples (chapter 6). In the absence of cross-cultural research, and without any competing hypotheses with anywhere near as much data support, it seems reasonable to conclude, until the research tells us otherwise, that induction will contribute positively and power assertion negatively to transgression guilt, moral internalization, and prosocial behavior – at least in nuclear-family societies in which discipline encounters are frequent, power assertion and induction are often used, and transgression guilt and moral internalization are meaningful concepts.

I added the last qualification because transgression guilt and moral internalization may make little sense in small, traditional, homogeneous societies in which individuals are under constant surveillance by role models and other authorities throughout life, or in some of the large, ethnically diverse "collectivist" non-Western societies described earlier. It is often the case in societies like these that when a person engages in deviant behavior he is likely to be caught and punished by parents or other powerful figures using power-assertive or love-withholding methods. Inductions may be rare and moral internalization relatively unimportant in such societies. In liberal democracies, however, without "a cop on every corner," and especially in the educated middle classes, induction, guilt, and moral internalization are meaningful concepts, as neatly stated in the quote from George Simmel (chapter 5). Whether these concepts apply beyond middle-class Western society, and how far beyond, is a topic for research.

## Conclusion

To sum up, there seems to be more reason to believe that empathic morality is universal than that it is not. Empathic morality is likely to promote prosocial behavior and discourage aggression in cultures guided by caring and most justice principles. Empathic morality does not operate in a vacuum, however: It can be destroyed by power-assertive childrearing, diminished by cultural valuing of competition over helping others, and overwhelmed by egoistic motives within the individual that are powerful enough to override it. This does not contradict the claim that empathy, through evolution, is part of human nature. We assume individual differences in other biologically based motives along some kind of bell-shaped distribution; the same may be true of empathy. Though empathy potentially exists in everyone, it may be reduced by irritability, fearfulness, and other temperamental factors, and by depressive and autistic tendencies that interfere with mimicry, role-taking, and other empathy-arousing processes. Combining these temperamental factors with nonnurturant, excessively power-assertive life experiences may well produce individuals who cannot empathize (psychopaths?).

Empathic morality is also subject to biases that favor friends, relatives, and people similar to oneself. Because of these biases, empathic morality can lead to a certain amount of injustice, which is understandable and may be a minor problem, as some philosophers suggest (Blum, 1980). Understandable and minor, I would agree, in view of the largely prosocial behavior that empathic morality promotes in small, homogeneous, face-to-face communities. Possibly serious, however, in heterogeneous, multicultural societies, especially those characterized by inter-ethnic rivalry, where empathic morality can foster hostility (empathic anger) and possibly even violence between groups, owing to empathy's bias in favor of one's primary group.

It thus appears that empathic morality, though a universal prosocial moral motive, is fragile (the Holocaust did happen). I can see nothing better on the horizon, however, unless it is empathic morality bonded to reciprocity and certain justice principles that guide and stabilize it, as suggested in chapter 9. I have no reason to believe that the joining of empathic morality with reciprocity and justice is universal. On the contrary, to bring about such joining will, I am sure, require cultural resolve, invention, and research.

In the next chapter I discuss intervention methods for socializing children in empathic morality and reducing violence in male delinquents. I also suggest ways of reducing empathic bias for the purpose of increasing people's motivation to live in harmony with others outside their primary group, that is, fostering prosocial action across ethnic and other cultural divides. It is possible that some of these methods could also be adapted for moral education programs aimed at joining empathic morality with reciprocity and justice.

# Part VII

# Intervention

# CHAPTER 13

# Implications for Socialization and Moral Education

It follows from my argument in chapter 12 that empathy, despite its faults, is a good bet for a universal prosocial morality. An important part of empathic morality is that cognitive development (self–other differentiation, language mediation, role-taking, causal attribution) enables simple empathic distress to be transformed into increasingly sophisticated motives to consider the welfare of others, taking their life condition as well as their immediate feelings into account (chapter 3). These cognitive contributions to empathy are brain-related and therefore available to people in all cultures, though not all cultures utilize them fully or in the same way. Empathy's amenity to cognitive influence is also important for another reason: It gives a potentially significant role to socialization and moral education, which may counteract empathic morality's limitations and magnify its capabilities.

## Socialization of Empathic Morality

I described in chapter 6 how empathic distress and empathy-based guilt can, through inductions by parents, create emotionally charged scripts linking a child's harmful actions to empathic distress and empathy-based guilt and how these scripts become functionally autonomous and independent of the inductions that spawned them. Induction appears to be the discipline of choice for many educated middle-class Americans, although in a 1995 Harris poll, 80% of the 1,250 adults surveyed said they had spanked their children (see chapter 6, footnote 1). The poll unfortunately did not ask parents how frequently they spanked, define spanking, or give social class data, but it should put to rest the idea that American parents know that spanking is bad and no longer need advice about discipline.

Parents who do not use induction because of ignorance, impatience, or other reasons can be taught (in parent-education programs) to inhibit their power-assertive or love-withholding tendencies in many situations in order to gain the long-term benefits of induction. Several other suggestions for socialization and moral education follow from the first four chapters of this book.

1. I would expect people to be more likely to empathize with someone else's emotion if they have had direct experience with that emotion, as this would facilitate the operation of at least three empathy-arousing mechanisms: direct association, mediated association, and role-taking (mimicry theoretically does not require direct experience with the emotion). It follows that socialization that allows children to experience a variety of emotions rather than protecting them from these emotions (hothouse flower) will increase the likelihood of children's being able to empathize with different emotions: It will expand their empathic range.

A possible exception is that emotions associated with a highly traumatic experience may be so painful that they produce empathic over-arousal and shift one's attention from the victim to oneself or motivate one to withdraw from the situation. This may relate to my unpublished finding that college students who score high on the Beck Depression Inventory show more empathy with another's sadness than low scorers, although *clinically* depressed people appear to be self-preoccupied and low on empathy.

2. I would expect on the basis of the research mentioned in chapter 6 that giving children a lot of affection would contribute to their feeling good about themselves, which should in turn help make them open to the needs of others rather than self-absorbed, emotionally needy children. I would also expect that exposing children to models who act prosocially would contribute to children's prosocial behavior. It is important especially for younger children that prosocial models occasionally express their empathic and sympathetic feelings openly and verbalize their attributions of the cause of the vic-

tim's distress, for example, in responding to homeless people. This should contribute to children's responding empathically rather than making counterempathic attributions such as blaming the victim.

3. The fundamental contributions of induction to prosocial moral development are given in chapter 6. I will not summarize them here but I would like to point up another contribution that can be derived from empathy's being largely involuntary. That is, if one pays attention to the victim one should respond automatically with empathic distress. Since paying attention is to an extent under voluntary control, it follows that socialization experiences that direct the child's attention to the inner states of others should contribute to empathy development. In situations in which a child harms another, discipline techniques that call attention to the victim's pain or injury or encourage the child to imagine him/herself in the victim's place (inductions) should thus help put the feelings of others into the child's consciousness and enhance the child's empathic potential.

4. Parents do not need to be told that inductions only work when the child stops what he is doing and pays attention. They know or quickly learn that they must often apply a certain amount of power-assertive pressure: enough to get the child to attend, without arousing too much fear or anger that could disrupt the child's processing the induction. The appropriate amount of power-assertion is often nothing more than holding the child firmly, looking at the child, and insisting that he or she listen, though at times it has to be much more forceful than that.

5. The blend of frequent inductions, occasional power assertions, a nurturant tone, and being a prosocial model may also work well in preschool and elementary school contexts, provided discipline encounters are not too frequent and emotionally disruptive. Teachers are often tempted to use power assertion because it can achieve quick compliance and induction may seem a luxury they cannot afford. Because there are many onlooking children in the "audience," however, teachers can get a lot of mileage ("ripple effect") from an occasional induction that is well worded and timed and in keeping with the children's developmental level. The children are bystanders who make causal attributions and can experience the empathic af-

fects typically aroused in bystanders (chapters 2, 3). The occasions on which a teacher disciplines a child for picking on someone else can add up to a significant socialization experience for the entire class, and the teacher's appropriate use of induction can help make sure this happens.

6. Children engage in pretend-play all the time. Adults can inject certain role-taking scenarios into children's pretend-playing that give them, vicariously, some of the emotional experience missing from their lives, including for some overprotected children empathic responses to others in distress. This might not only contribute directly to children's empathic responsiveness to victims but also indirectly by increasing their empathic range.

7. Special attention must be given to the problem of observers' making self-serving attributions of responsibility, blaming the victim in particular, which interfere with empathy. Blaming the victim has become a cliché: Everyone knows about it but this awareness is abstract and people are often unaware of blaming the victim themselves (Staub, 1996). Blaming the victim needs to be pointed up whenever it happens.

## Empathy's Role in Treating Delinquents

Gibbs (1996) and Gibbs, Potter, Barriga, and Liau (1996) use some of the above ideas as an important component of a multifaceted treatment program for aggressive delinquent male adolescents. The program is focused on empathy and fairness, which Gibbs believes are the foundation for universal moral education. Here is a problem situation he uses: Gary is in the kitchen of his apartment. Gary's girl friend is angry at him for something he did to hurt her. She yells at him. She pushes him on the shoulder. Thoughts run through Gary's head. Gary does nothing to correct the errors in his thinking. Gary becomes furious. He swears at her. A sharp kitchen knife is nearby. Gary picks up the knife and stabs her, seriously wounding her.

Gibbs asks the juveniles: "What thoughts do you think ran through Gary's head?" Among the most popular answers, Gibbs reports, is something like this: "Who does she think she is? Nobody hits *me*. I wear the pants around here, I do what I want. How dare she *touch* me!" Such thoughts are self-centered and show no empathy for the girl friend, nor do they show fairness in that Gary can do what he wants but the girl friend cannot. They illustrate a general limitation of antisocial male juveniles, that is, they appear to be "fixated at a level of getting their own throbbing needs met, regardless of the effects on others' (Carducci, 1980, p. 157). In the same vein, Samenow (1984), a criminologist, quotes a 14-year-old delinquent: "I was born with the idea that I'd do what I wanted. I always felt that rules and regulations were not for me" (p. 160).

Gibbs, Samenow, and others believe that even the most hardened criminal offenders evidence some genuine empathic feelings for others, however fleeting or superficial, from time to time. Consider this self-report from a 17-year-old concerning his recent break-in: "If I started feeling bad, I'd say to myself 'tough rocks for him. He should have had his house locked better and the alarm on' " (Samenow, 1984, p. 115). This delinquent would seem to be saying in effect that "if I felt empathy-based guilt for causing innocent people to suffer, I would neutralize the empathy by blaming the suffering on the victim." This fits the following quote from an Orange County, California, Juvenile Court judge discussing the danger of guns and immature youth: "They pull the trigger without thinking of the future consequences. It is not until they are in the courtroom and see the faces of the victim's family in tears . . . that they realize the pain they have caused" (*New York Times*, Jan. 11, 1993, p. A20). It also fits my own finding that seventh graders with an external moral orientation (stealing is bad if you get caught) often respond with guilt feeling to story-completion items in which the central figure harms another, but it is only a momentary guilt feeling that is followed quickly by externalizing blame and other forms of guilt reduction (Hoffman, 1970).

Another cognitive distortion the delinquents use is minimizing the extent of their victims' suffering. They also make the self-serving assumption that because they have been victimized in the past it is legitimate for them to victimize others. This is an inverted form of reciprocity which, like an-eye-for-an-eye thinking, illustrates my claim (chapter 9) that reciprocity is a cognitive concept that can serve antisocial as well as prosocial purposes depending on the context and the motive in question.

One of Gibbs's key aims is to provide his delinquent subjects with a "concentrated dosage" of role-taking opportunities to stimulate both caring and justice. The doses are concentrated to enable the delinquents to make up for what they have missed previously. To accomplish this, Gibbs has them take part in discussions of Kohlberg-like sociomoral dilemmas or problem situations, tailored to be relevant to their lives, which serve as stimuli for role-taking experiences. The subjects must justify their problem-solving decisions in the face of challenges from more developmentally advanced peers and from group leaders.

Gibbs describes a technique advocated by Vorrath and Brendtro (1985) called "confronting," which, like induction, directs the recipient's attention to the harm to others that results from his actions and thereby elicits and strengthens empathic responses. This is deemed necessary to counteract the delinquents' egoism and penetrate their cognitive distortions. Confronting also compels the antisocial individual to put himself in another's position and understand the "chain of injuries" stemming from his harmful actions, including effects on absent and indirect victims. I suggest that these confrontings should also include the other's life condition beyond the immediate situation (chapter 3), which the delinquents seem to ignore on their own.

Gibbs also, where possible, borrows from Goldstein and Glick (1987) who give their subjects fine-grained practice in taking the perspective of others in actual social situations (making a complaint, preparing for a stressful conversation, responding to anger, dealing with an accusation, responding to another's feelings and helping) as a way of reducing their subjects' aggressive behavior. For instance, how to verbalize a complaint is broken down into six steps, one of which is to "show that you understand his feelings." One of the steps in dealing with an accusation is to "think about why the person might have accused you."

I am impressed with the variety of these methods. They are a far cry from traditional power-assertive approaches and seem promising. One thing seems to be missing, however. I did not find any theoretical analysis of why the procedures, which seem to produce the desired effects in the participants during the "treatments," should carry over and affect the individual's behavior in real life. I suggest beginning along the lines of my analysis in chapter 6 of the long-term effects of induction. Are there, for example, certain kinds of transgression-guilt scripts acquired by the participants in the treatment sessions that may be activated and motivate prosocial behavior in real life? If delinquents role-played the scenario about Gary and his girl friend described above, or a rape, and, through proper "confrontings" or inductions by peers and group leaders, were made to feel guilty afterward perhaps for the first time in their lives, they might form transgression-guilt scripts. If they do form such scripts, will the scripts be activated when the delinquents are tempted to act in ways that might harm others in real life? And if they are activated in real life, will their motive component be powerful enough to affect the delinquent's behavior? Finally, if the answer to these questions is yes, then we must ask, What environmental supports will be necessary to maintain the constructive changes in the delinquent's behavior?

## Reducing Empathic Bias and Overarousal

Empathic bias and over-arousal may be reduced in the normal course of development when empathy bonds with moral principles: Principles can give structure and stability to empathic affects (chapter 9). It seems likely, however, that normal developmental processes are not enough, and active efforts by parents and moral educators are needed, such as pointing out cross-cultural commonalities, helping children look beyond the situation, and multiple empathizing.

*Cross-cultural commonalities.* Empathy originates in intimate relationships with parents at home and expands to one's extended family and friends. A major task of moral education is to transcend empathy's familiarity bias and extend empathy to other groups, so that children will be more aware of the impact of their actions on others who differ from them in obvious ways. To reduce familiarity bias, moral educators might first need to identify the bias and perhaps explain it as a normal response that had a purpose in early human evolution but is not suited to life in contemporary multicultural societies like ours which require large doses of impartiality and a concept of one's group that includes all of humanity.

To create a concept of oneness with others, moral educators may have to point up the emotional commonalities that exist across groups despite the differences in social structure, culture, and physical appearance. These emotional commonalities include similar fears, anxieties, and life goals. They include similar emotional responses to being applauded, criticized, and treated unfairly, and similar emotional responses to universal life crises and significant events such as attachment, separation, loss, and aging.

To create a sense of oneness may not be as difficult as it seems. In discussing empathic bias (chapter 8), I reviewed the research showing that people empathize with and help others who they are led to believe share their preferences, attitudes, interests, life goals, and chronic concerns. It seems evident that this similarity bias can be turned against itself and "recruited" in the service of creating a panhuman sense of oneness regarding emotional responses to the important life events I just mentioned. This can be done by pointing out the common emotional responses that all people have, as well as the surface differences that mask the commonalities.

The visual media can play a special role here: Given the evidence for universal facial expression of basic emotions, people in the audience may mimic the facial expressions of actors from other cultures and through feedback experience the actors' emotions in various situations, especially if they are encouraged to look at the actors' faces. Films are also effective means of presenting larger life sequences, which can promote viewers' empathic identification with others' lives. Seeing that people in other cultures have similar worries and respond emotionally as we do to important life events, while

294

sitting in the audience and feeling the same emotions, should contribute to a sense of oneness and empathy across cultures.[1]

Brewer (1993) says that pointing out commonalities may not work because people want to be identified with a group that has some distinctiveness; consequently, they might resist the idea of everyone being the same. That should not be a problem, I think: The similarities in emotional responses to separation, loss, aging, and death allow plenty of latitude for differences in everything else. People can have their "optimal distinctiveness," while recognizing that there are certain human conditions and emotions that all groups share. It should be possible, in other words, for people to identify empathically with both their subgroup and humanity as a whole, which would make cohesion within and co-existence between subgroups possible.

The commonalities, in short, need not destroy the integrity of one's group. Besides, people might be responsive to the idea that there is a larger super-ordinate goal – human survival – to which diversity may contribute and for which empathy across groups, a "universal empathy," is necessary. There is no direct evidence that super-ordinate goals contribute to intergroup or universal empathy, but the finding in the 1940s and 1950s that super-ordinate goals can reduce intergroup hostility, together with experimental evidence that cooperation fosters empathy (Lanzetta & Englis, 1989), suggest that super-ordinate goals may indeed contribute to intergroup empathy. And more to the point, there is evidence that identification with a super-ordinate group can promote cohesion and co-existence between subgroups even for people who identify with their subgroup (Hvo, Smith, Tyler, & Lind, 1996).

This does not mean that a universal empathy is enough to bind

---

1. I talk mainly of basic emotions. I do not wish to underplay the difficulty of empathizing with emotions that are complicated and situation-specific. Consider the difficulty of an American middle-class person's empathizing with a poor Mexican or Colombian mother's joy at giving her baby up for adoption by a United States couple. One would have to immerse oneself in the culture and identify with their hopes for their children in order to feel something of the blend of hope and sadness in a situation like that.

together a democratic society threatened by racial, ethnic, class, and religious conflict. What such hetergeneous societies need to keep them from unraveling are good laws, that is, laws that are just and impartial and can therefore be acceptable to all. Justice-based laws are designed to squeeze out bias, empathic bias included. But the universal empathy I am talking about is different precisely because it is largely unbiased. Indeed, it could make an important contribution by helping to motivate people to abide by just laws and promote institutions that embody them (see discussion in chapter 9, "Empathy and Rawls's difference principle").

*Looking beyond the situation.* Regarding bias, moral educators can teach children a simple rule of thumb, which is to look beyond the immediate situation and ask questions like these: How will my action affect the other person not only now but also in the future? Are there other people, present or absent, who might be affected? If children learn to ask these questions, at least occasionally, this could enhance children's awareness of potential victims and beneficiaries of their actions who are not present and thus children's ability to empathize with them.

I once used a story-completion item about a seventh grader who cheats and wins an underwater swimming race at a school picnic: He only swims part way and back and no one notices because the water is muddy and churned up. He wins the prize and is congratulated by his friends and classmates. The subjects are asked to complete the story with the story child's thoughts and feelings and what happens afterward. Most endings reflected a here-and-now bias and focused on the central figure's dilemma (he feels guilty and confesses, throws the prize away, loses next year's race, lives happily ever after, and so on). A few endings showed concern for the true, "absent" winner (I thought about the boy who deserved the prize; it's not fair; Art went up to the real winner, handed him the prize, and said here you take it, you deserve it).

More of the story endings showed this concern for the absent "victim" when subjects were instructed to complete the story with the story child's *or anyone else's* thoughts and feelings and what happens afterward, and still more when they were instructed to think about others who were affected by the cheating and include that in the story ending. A study using all these instructions could be carried out and then followed by a discussion about why so few subjects thought about the true winner on their own without the prompts. Such discussion might be an effective lead-in to the here-and-now bias issue. Batson's experiments described in chapter 8 could be discussed in a similar way.

*Multiple empathizing.* To increase the motivational power of empathy with absent victims, children could be encouraged to imagine how they would feel in the absent victim's place. To enhance their empathy with a stranger or someone from another ethnic group, they could be shown scenes of someone from that group in an emotionally significant situation and be asked to imagine how they would feel in the same situation.

But even more important, children could be encouraged to imagine how someone close to them, someone they care a lot about, would feel in the stranger's or absent victim's place. This is a way of turning empathy's familiarity and here-and-now biases against themselves and recruiting them in the service of prosocial motive development. Empathy's familiarity bias makes one less likely to empathize with a stranger; what better way to counter that tendency than to transform the stranger into a person one is close to. Remember the truck driver I described in chapter 2 and 8 who intervened to help save an elderly woman from a mugger because "she could have been my mom." It seems to me that some kind of short course in which children were systematically trained in the art of multiple empathizing might reduce the effects of familiarity and here-and-now bias.

I want to repeat something I said earlier: There is nothing inherently wrong with bias in favor of family and friends. It is natural to empathize with people with whom one has grown up, shared important life experiences, and known a long time; logic need not replace feeling and personal preference in close relationships. In-group empathic bias is normal and acceptable as long as it allows people to help strangers as well. The research shows that it does: At least in America, bystanders are prone to help strangers, though to a lesser degree than family and friends (chapters 2, 8).

What I am proposing is *using empathic bias not as the seed of its own destruction but as the seed of its own moderation,* as a way of reducing the gap between empathy toward kin and empathy toward strangers. A more important goal is to reduce the tendency of some people to make *negative* causal attributions to strangers in distress and, still more importantly, to reduce the stereotyping, hostility, and downright hatred toward other groups that derive from traditional ethnic rivalries and other such sources. In short, training in multiple empathizing, which is not a natural thing to do, may capitalize on rather than be defeated by the natural human proclivity to empathize more with kin than strangers. It may help reduce any tendency to blame victims who are not present and counter the other negative effects of empathic bias.[2] All of this of course will be more important as our society becomes increasingly multicultural.

Not just our society. Ignatieff (1999) suggests that empathy ("the human capability of imagining the pain and degradation done to other human beings as if it were our own") provides the basis for a *universal "secular ethics"* – an ethics that demands basic human rights everywhere. He suggests that in order for an empathy-based secular ethics to work, countries must have the "self-correcting mechanisms of a free press and political opposition." I would add laws and institutions that require people to interact in a civil manner, and moral socialization along the lines discussed above that promotes empathizing with the "other" and links empathy to caring and justice principles.

It sounds pretty good – the human capacity for empathy, fostered by empathic moral socialization in the context of a free press, political opposition, and good laws. Will the combination do the trick? Although it may be debatable, human survival requires that it at least be pursued. I'll end on that note.

2. There is evidence that when observers empathize with someone, the "fundamental attribution error" disappears (Regan & Totten, 1975). The empathizer attributes the other's behavior to situational influences rather than character, just as observers usually do when explaining their own behavior. Empathy should therefore reduce any tendency to blame the victim.

# References

Adelman, P. K., & Zajonc, R. (1989). Facial efference and the experience of emotion. *Annual Review of Psychology, 40*, 249–280.

Agee, J. (1941). *Let us now praise famous men: Three tenant families.* Boston: Houghton Mifflin.

Aronfreed, J. (1970). The socialization of altruistic and sympathetic behavior. In J. Macaulay and L. Berkowitz (Eds.), *Altruism and helping behavior.* New York: Academic Press.

Arsenio, W., & Ford, M. (1985). The role of affective information in social-cognitive development: Children's differentiation of moral and conventional events. *Merrill-Palmer Quarterly of Behavior and Development, 31*, 1–18.

Arsenio, W., & Lover, A. (1995). Children's conceptions of sociomoral affect. In M. Killen & D. Hart (Eds.), *Morality in everyday life: Developmental perspectives.* New York: Cambridge.

Astington, J. W., & Gopnik, A. (1991). Theoretical explanations of children's understanding of the mind. *British Journal of Developmental Psychology, 9*, 7–31.

Austin, W. (1980). Friendship and fairness: Effects of type of relationship and task performance on choice of distribution rules. *Personality and Social Psychology Bulletin, 6*, 402–408.

Baillargeon, R. (1987). Object permanence in 3½- and 4½-month-old infants. *Developmental Psychology, 23*, 655–664.

Bandura, A. (1969). A social-learning theory of identificatory processes. In D. A. Goslin (Ed.), *Handbook of socialization theory and research* (pp. 213–262). Chicago: Rand McNally.

Bandura, A. (1977). *Social learning theory.* Englewood Cliffs, NJ: Prentice-Hall.

Bandura, A., & Rosenthal, T. L. (1966). Vicarious classical conditioning as a function of arousal level. *Journal of Personality and Social Psychology, 3*, 54–62.

Bandura, A., & Walters, R. H. (1959). *Adolescent aggression.* New York: Ronald Press.

Batson, C. D., Batson, J. G., Todd, R. M., Brummett, B. H., Shaw, L. L., & Aldeguer, C. M. (1995). Empathy and the collective good: Caring for one of the others in a social dilemma. *Journal of Personality and Social Psychology, 68,* 619–631.

Batson, C. D., Early, S., & Salvarani, G. (1997). Perspective taking: Imagining how another feels versus imagining how you would feel. *Personality and Social Psychology Bulletin, 23,* 751–758.

Batson, C. D., Klein, T. R., Highberger, L., & Shaw, L. L. (1995). Immorality from empathy-induced altruism. *Journal of Personality and Social Psychology, 68,* 1042–1054.

Batson, C. D., & Shaw, L. L. (1991). Evidence for altruism: Toward a pluralism of prosocial motives. *Psychological Inquiry, 2,* 107–122.

Batson, C. D., Sympson, S. C., & Hindman, J. L. (1996). "I've been there, too": Effect on empathy of prior experience with a need. *Personality and Social Psychology Bulletin, 22,* 474–482.

Batson, C. D., Turk, C. L., Shaw, L. L., & Klein, T. R. (1995). Information function of empathic emotion: Learning that we value the other's welfare. *Journal of Personality and Social Psychology, 68,* 300–313.

Batson, C. D., & Weeks, J. L. (1996). Mood effects of unsuccessful helping: Another test of the empathy-altruism hypothesis. *Personality and Social Psychology Bulletin, 22,* 148–157.

Baumeister, R. F., Stillwell, A. M., & Heatherton, T. F., (1994). Guilt: An interpersonal approach. *Psychological Bulletin, 115,* 243–267.

Baumeister, R. F., Stillwell, A. M., & Heatherton, T. F. (1995). Interpersonal aspects of guilt. In J. P. Tangney and K. W. Fischer (Eds.), *Self-conscious emotions: Shame, guilt, embarrassment, and pride* (pp. 255–273). New York: Guilford Press.

Bavelas, J. B., Black, A., Chovil, N., Lemery, C. R., & Mullett, J. (1988). Form and function in motor mimicry: Topographical evidence that the primary function is communication. *Human Communication Research, 14,* 275–299.

Bavelas, J. B., Black, A., Lemery, C. R., & Mullett, J. (1987). Motor mimicry as primitive empathy. In N. Eisenberg & J. Strayer (Eds.), *Empathy and its development* (pp. 317–338). New York: Cambridge University Press.

Berger, S. M., & Hadley, S. W. (1975). Some effects of a model's performance on observer electromyographic activity. *American Journal of Psychology, 88,* 263–276.

Bernal, G., & Berger, S. M. (1976). Vicarious eyelid conditioning. *Journal of Personality and Social Psychology, 34,* 62–68.

Berndt, T. (1979). Effect of induced sadness about self or other on helping behavior in high and low empathy children. *Developmental Psychology, 15,* 329–330.

Bischoff-Kohler, D. (1991). The development of empathy in infants. In M. Lamb & M. Keller (Eds.), *Infant development: Perspectives from German-speaking countries* (pp. 245–273). Hillsdale, NJ: Erlbaum.

Bishops' pastoral letter on Catholic social teaching and the U.S. economy: First draft (1984). *Origins, 14,* Nos. 22, 23. Second draft (1985). *Origins, 15,* No. 17.

Blasi, A. (1983). The self and cognition. In B. Lee & G. G. Noam (Eds.), *Psychosocial theories of the self* (pp. 189–213). New York: Plenum Press.

Blass, E. M., Ganchrow, J. R., & Steiner, J. E. (1984). Classical conditioning in newborn humans 2–48 hours of age. *Infant Behavior and Development, 7,* 223–235.

Blum, L. A. (1980). *Friendship, altruism, and morality.* London: Routledge & Kegan Paul.

Blum, L. A. (1987). In J. Kagan & S. Lamb (Eds.), *The emergence of morality in young children.* Chicago: University of Chicago Press.

Bower, G. H. (1981). Mood and memory. *American Psychologist, 36,* 129–148.

Brehm, J. W. (1972). *Responses to loss of freedom: A theory of psychological reactance.* Morristown, NJ: General Learning.

Bretherton, I., Fritz, J., Zahn-Waxler, C., & Ridgeway, D. (1986). Learning to talk about emotions: A functionalist perspective. *Child Development, 57,* 529–548.

Brewer, M. B. (1993). The role of distinctiveness in social identity and group behavior. In M. Hogg and D. Abrams (Eds.), *Group motivation* (pp. 1–16). London: Harvester Wheatsheaf.

Brody, G. H., & Shaffer, D. R. (1982). Contributions of parents and peers to children's moral socialization. *Developmental Review, 2,* 31–75.

Brothers, L. (1989). A biological perspective on empathy. *American Journal of Psychiatry, 146 (1),* 10–19.

Buder, E. (1991). Vocal synchrony in conversations: Spatial analysis of fundamental voice frequency. Unpublished doctoral dissertation, University of Wisconsin-Madison.

Burton, R. V. (1972). Cheating related to maternal pressure for achievement. Unpublished manuscript, Psychology Department, State University of New York at Buffalo.

Bush, L. K., Barr, C. L., McHugo, G. J., & Lanzetta, J. T. (1989). The effects of facial control and facial mimicry on subjective reactions to comedy routines. *Motivation and emotion,* 31–53.

Camras, L. (1977). Facial expressions used by children in a conflict situation. *Child Development, 48,* 1431–1435.

Carducci, D. J. (1980). Positive peer culture and assertiveness training: Complementary modalities for dealing with disturbed and disturbing adolescents in the classroom. *Behavioral Disorders, 5,* 156–162.

Carlo, G., Eisenberg, N., Troyer, D., Switzer, G., & Speer, A. L. (1991). The altruistic personality: In what contexts is it apparent? *Journal of Personality and Social Psychology, 61,* 450–458.

Chapman, M. (1979). Listening to reason: Children's attentiveness and parental discipline. *Merrill-Palmer Quarterly of Behavior and Development, 25,* 251–263.

Chapman, M., & Zahn-Waxler, C. (1982). Young children's compliance and noncompliance to parental discipline in a natural setting. *International Journal of Behavior Development, 5,* 81–94.

Chapman, M., Zahn-Waxler, C., Cooperman, G., & Iannotti, R. (1987). Empathy and responsibility in the motivation of children's helping. *Developmental Psychology, 23,* 140–145.

Chodoff, P., Friedman, S., & Hamburg, D. (1964). Stress, defenses, and coping behavior: Observations of parents and children with malignant disease. *American Journal of Psychiatry, 120,* 742–749.

Christie, R., & Geis, F. L. (1970). Studies in Machiavellianism. NY: Academic Press.

Clark, M. S., & Reis, H. T. (1988). Interpersonal processes in close relationships. *Annual Review of Psychology, 39,* 609–672.

Colby, A., & Damon, W. (1992). *Some do care: Contemporary lives of moral committment.* New York: Wiley.

Coles, R. (1986). *The moral life of children.* Boston: Atlantic Monthly Press.

Collins, C. (1995, May 11). Spanking is becoming the new don't. *New York Times,* p. C8.

Costin, S. E., & Jones, C. J. (1992). Friendship as a facilitator of emotional responsiveness and prosocial interventions among young children. *Developmental Psychology, 28,* 941–947.

Crockenberg, S. B., & Litman, C. (1990). Autonomy as competence in 2-year-olds: Maternal correlates of defiance, compliance, and self-assertion. *Developmental Psychology, 26,* 961–971.

Cummings, E. M., & Davies, P. T. (1994). *Children and marital conflict: The impact of family dispute and resolution.* New York: Guilford Press.

Cummings, E. M., Hollenbeck, B., Iannotti, R., Radke-Yarrow, M., and Zahn-Waxler, C. (1986). Early organization of altruism and aggression: Developmental patterns and individual differences. In C. Zahn-Waxler, E. M. Cummings, and R. Iannotti (Eds.), *Altruism and aggression: Biological and social origins,* pp. 165–188. New York: Cambridge University Press.

Damon, W. (1977). *The social world of the child,* San Francisco: Jossey-Bass.

Damon, W. (1988). *The moral child.* New York: The Free Press.

Darley, J. M., & Latane, B. (1968). Bystander intervention in emergencies: Diffusion of responsibility. *Journal of Personality and Social Psychology, 8,* 377–383.

Darwin, C. (1862/1965). *The expression of the emotions in man and animals.* Chicago: University of Chicago Press.

Darwin, C. (1877). A biological sketch of an infant. *Mind: Quarterly Review of Psychology and Philosophy, 11,* 286–294.

Davidson, P., & Youniss, J. (1995). Moral development and social construction. In W. M. Kurtines & J. L. Gewirtz (Eds.), *Moral development: An introduction* (pp. 289–310). Boston: Allyn & Bacon.

Davis, C. G., Lehman, D. R., Silver, R. C., Wortman, C. B., & Ellard, J. H. (1996). Self-blame following a traumatic event: The role of perceived avoidability. *Personality and Social Psychology Bulletin, 22,* 557–567.

Davis, M. R. (1983). Measuring individual differences in empathy: Evidence for a multi-dimensional approach. *Journal of Personality and Social Psychology, 44,* 113–126.

Davis, M. R. (1985). Perceptual and affective reverberation components. In A. B. Goldstein and G. Y. Michaels (Eds.), *Empathy: Development, training, and consequences* (pp. 62–108). Hillsdale, NJ: Erlbaum.

Deater-Deckard, K., Dodge, K. A., Bates, J. E., & Pettit, G. S. (1996). Physical discipline among African American and European American mothers: Links to children's externalizing behaviors. *Developmental Psychology, 32,* 1065–1072.

Denham, S. A., & Grout, L. (1992). Mother's emotional expressiveness and coping: Relations with preschoolers' social-emotional competence. *Genetic, Social, and General Psychology Monographs, 118,* 75–101.

DePaulo, B. M., Dull, W. R., Greenberg, J. M., & Swaim, G. W. (1989). Are shy people reluctant to ask for help? *Journal of Personality and Social Psychology, 56,* 834–844.

Deutsch, M. (1985). *Distributive justice: A social psychological perspective.* New Haven: Yale University Press.

DeVeer, A. (1991). Parental disciplinary strategies and the child's moral internalization. Unpublished doctoral dissertation, University of Nijmegen.

Dick, P. K. (1968). *Blade runner.* New York: Ballantine Books.

Dienstbier, R. A. (1978). Attribution, socialization, and moral decision making. In J. H. Harvey, W. Ickes, & R. F. Kidd (Eds.), *New directions in attribution research (Vol. 2,* pp. 182–211). Hillsdale, NJ: Erlbaum.

Dimberg, U. (1990). Facial electromyography and emotional reactions. *Psychophysiology, 27,* 481–494.

Dowdney, L., & Pickles, A. R. (1991). Expression of negative affect within disciplinary encounters: Is there dyadic reciprocity? *Developmental Psychology, 27,* 606–617.

Edwards, R. (1995, September). *APA Monitor,* p. 34.

Eisenberg, N., Carlo, G., Murphy, B., & Van Court, P. (1995). Prosocial development in late adolescence: A longitudinal study. *Child Development, 66,* 1179–1197.

Eisenberg, N., & Fabes, R. A. (1998). Prosocial development. In W. Damon (Ed.), *Handbook of child psychology, Vol. 3: Social, emotional, and personality development* (pp. 701–778). New York: Wiley.

Eisenberg, N., Fabes, R. A., Carlo, G., Troyer, D., Speer, A. L., Karbon, M., & Switzer, G. (1992). The relations of maternal practices and characteristics to children's emotional responsiveness. *Child Development, 63,* 583–602.

Eisenberg, N., Fabes, R. A., Schaller, M., Carlo, G., & Miller, P. A. (1991). Parental characteristics and practices, and children's emotional responding. *Child Development, 62,* 1393–1408.

Eisenberg, N., & Miller, P. (1987). Relation of empathy to prosocial behavior. *Psychological Bulletin, 101,* 91–119.

Eisenberg, N., Murphy, B. C., & Shepard, S. (1997). The development of empathic accuracy. In W. Ickes (Ed.), *Empathic accuracy* (pp. 73–116). New York: Guilford.

Eisenberg-Berg, N., & Neal, C. (1979). Children's moral reasoning about their own prosocial behavior. *Developmental Psychology, 15,* 228–229.

Ekman, P., Friesen, W., O'Sullivan, M., & Chan, A. (1987). Universals and cultural differences in the judgments of facial expressions of emotion. *Journal of Personality and Social Psychology, 53,* 712–717.

Ekman, P., Sorenson, E., & Friesen, W. (1969). Pan-cultural elements in facial displays of emotion. *Science, 164,* 86–88.

Erikson, E. (1968). *Identity, youth, and crisis.* New York: W. W. Norton.

Escalona, S. K. (1945). Feeding disturbances in very young children. *American Journal of Orthopsychiatry, 15,* 76–80.

Fabes, R. A., Eisenberg, E., Karbon, M., Bernzweig, J., Speer, A. L., & Carlo, G. (1994). Socialization of children's vicarious emotional responding and pro-social behavior: Relations with mothers' perceptions of children's emotional reactivity. *Developmental Psychology, 30,* 44–55.

Fabes, R. A., Eisenberg, E., Karbon, M., Troyer, D., & Switzer, G. (1994). The relations of children's emotion regulation to their vicarious emotional responses and comforting behaviors. *Child Development, 65,* 1678–1693.

Feather, N. (1995). Values, valences, and choice: The influence of values on the perceived attractiveness and choice of alternatives. *Journal of Personality and Social Psychology, 68,* 1135–1151.

Feshbach, N. D., & Feshbach, S. (1969). The relationship between empathy and aggression in two age groups. *Developmental Psychology, 1,* 102–107.

Feshbach, N. D., & Roe, K. (1968). Empathy in six- and seven-year olds. *Child Development, 39,* 133–145.

Figley, C. R. (1995). *Coping with secondary traumatic stress disorder in those who treat the traumatized.* New York: Brunner/Mazel.

Finnegan, William. (1994, January 31). Doubt. *The New Yorker,* pp. 48–68.

Fischer, K., Shaver, P., & Cornochan, P. (1990). How emotions develop and how they organize development. *Cognition and Emotion, 4,* 81–127.

Fiske, S. F. (1982). Schema-triggered affect: Applications to social perception. In M. S. Clark & S. T. Fiske (Eds.), *Affect and cognition: The 17th annual Carnegie symposium on cognition* (pp. 55–78). Hillsdale, NJ, Erlbaum.

Franz, C. E., & McClelland, D. C. (1994). Lives of women and men active in the social protests of the 1960s: A longitudinal study. *Journal of Personality and Social Psychology, 66,* 196–205.

Friedman, M. (1985). Toward a re-conceptualization of guilt. *Contemporary Psychoanalysis, 21,* 501–547.

Furby, L. (1978). Sharing: Decisions and moral judgments about letting others use one's possessions. *Psychological Reports, 43,* 595–609.

Gaertner, S. L., & Dovidio, J. F. (1977). The subtlety of White racism, arousal, and helping behavior. *Journal of Personality and Social Psychology, 35,* 691–707.

Geer, J. H., & Jarmecky, L. (1973). The effect of being responsible for reducing another's pain on subjects' pain and arousal. *Journal of Personality and Social Psychology, 26,* 323–337.

Gibbs, J. C. (1987). Social processes in delinquency: The need to facilitate empathy as well as sociomoral reasoning. In W. M. Kurtines & J. C. Gewirtz (Eds.), *Moral development through social interaction* (pp. 301–321). New York: Wiley.

Gibbs, J. C. (1991). Toward an integration of Kohlberg's and Hoffman's moral development theories. *Human Development, 34,* 88–104.

Gibbs, J. C. (1993). Moral-cognitive interventions. In A. P. Goldstein & C. R. Huff (Eds.), *The gang intervention handbook* (pp. 159–185). Champaign, IL: Research Press.

Gibbs, J. C. (1996). Socio-moral group treatment for young offenders. In C. R. Hollin & K. Howells (Eds.), *Clinical approaches to working with young offenders*. New York: Wiley.

Gibbs, J. C., Potter, G. B., Barriga, A. Q., & Liau, A. K. (1996). Developing the helping skills and prosocial motivation of aggressive adolescents in peer-group programs. *Aggression and Violent Behavior, 1,* 283–305.

Gitomer, A., Pellegrino, H., & Bisanz, J. (1983). Developmental changes and invariance in semantic processing. *Journal of Experimental Child Psychology, 35,* 56–80.

Gnepp, J. C. (1989). Children's use of personal information to understand other people's feelings. In C. Saarni & P. L. Harris (Eds.), *Children's understanding of emotion* (pp. 151–177). New York: Cambridge.

Gnepp, J. C., & Gould, M. E. (1985). The development of personalized inferences: Understanding other people's emotional reactions in light of their prior experiences. *Child Development, 56,* 1455–1464.

Goldberg, V. (1995, April 9). Looking at the poor in a gilded frame. *New York Times,* Arts section, p. 1.

Goldstein, A. P., & Glick, B. (1987). Aggressive replacement training: A comprehensive intervention for aggressive youth. Champaign, IL: Research Press.

Graham, S., Doubleday, C., & Guarino, P. A. (1984). The development of relations between perceived controllability and the emotions of pity, anger, and guilt. *Child Development, 55,* 561–565.

Gruen, R., & Mendelsohn, G. (1986). Emotional responses to affective displays in others: The distinction between empathy and sympathy. *Journal of Personality and Social Psychology, 51,* 609–614.

Grusec, J. E., & Kuczynski, L. (1980). Direction of effects in socialization, *16,* 1–9.

Grusec, J. E. & Kuczynski, L. (1997). *Parenting and children's internalization of values: A Handbook of contemporary theory.* New York: John Wiley.

Hamilton, W. D. (1971). Selection of selfish and altruistic behavior in some extreme models. In J. F. Eisenberg & W. F. Sillon (Eds.), *Man and beast: Comparative social behavior.* Washington, DC: Smithsonian Institution Press.

Harris, P. L., Johnson, C. N., Hutton, D., Andrews, G., & Cook, T. (1989). Young children's theory of mind and emotion. *Cognition and Emotion, 3,* 379–400.

Harrison, A. A. (1977). Mere exposure. In L. Berkowitz (Ed.), *Advances in experimental social psychology* (Vol. 10, pp. 40–83).

Hart, C. H., DeWolfe, D. M., Wozniak, P., Burts, D. C. (1992). Maternal and paternal disciplinary styles: Relations with preschoolers' playground behavioral orientations and peer status. *Child Development, 63,* 879–892.

Haste, H., & Locke, D. (1983). *Morality in the making: Action in the social context.* New York: Wiley.

Hatfield, E., Cacioppo, J. T., & Rapson, R. L. (1992). Emotional contagion. In M. S. Clark (Ed.), *Review of personality and social psychology: Vol. 14, Emotional and social behavior* (pp. 151–177). Newbury Park, CA: Sage.

Haviland, J. M., & Lelwica, M. (1987). The induced affect response: 10-week-old infants' responses to three emotion expressions. *Developmental Psychology, 23,* 97–104.

Hay, D. F. (1984). Social conflict in early childhood. *Annals of Child Development, 1,* 1–44.

Hay, D. F., Nash, A., & Pedersen, J. (1981). Responses of six-month-olds to the distress of their peers. *Child Development, 52,* 1071–1075

Heider, F. (1958). *The psychology of interpersonal relationships.* New York: Wiley.

Hoffman, M. L. (1960). Power assertion by the parent and its impact on the child. *Child Development, 31,* 129–143.

Hoffman, M. L. (1963). Parent discipline and the child's consideration for others. *Child Development, 34,* 573–588.

Hoffman, M. L. (1970). Conscience, personality, and socialization techniques. *Human Development, 13,* 90–126.

Hoffman, M. L. (1970a). Moral development. In P. Mussen (Ed.), *Handbook of child psychology* (pp. 261–361). New York: John Wiley.

Hoffman, M. L. (1975a). Moral internalization, parental power, and the nature of parent–child interaction. *Developmental Psychology, 11,* 228–239.

Hoffman, M. L. (1975b). Developmental synthesis of affect and cognition and its implications for altruistic motivation. *Developmental Psychology, 11,* 607–622.

Hoffman, M. L. (1977). Moral internalization: Current theory and research. In L. Berkowitz (Ed.), *Advances in experimental social psychology* (Vol. 10, pp. 86–135). New York: Academic Press

Hoffman, M. L. (1978). Empathy, its development and prosocial implications. In C. B. Keasey (Ed.), *Nebraska Symposium on Motivation, 25,* 169–218.

Hoffman, M. L. (1980). Moral development in adolescence. In J. Adelson (Ed.), *Handbook of adolescent psychology* (pp. 295–343). New York: John Wiley & Sons.

Hoffman, M. L. (1981). Is altruism part of human nature? *Journal of Personality and Social Psychology, 40,* 121–137.

Hoffman, M. L. (1982). Development of prosocial motivation: Empathy and guilt. In N. Eisenberg-Berg, (Ed.), *Development of Prosocial Behavior,* New York: Academic Press, 281–313.

Hoffman, M. L. (1983). Affective and cognitive processes in moral internalization: An information processing approach. In E. T. Higgins, D. Ruble, & W. Hartup (Eds.), *Social cognition and social development: A socio-cultural perspective* (pp. 236–274). New York: Cambridge University Press.

Hoffman, M. L. (1984). Empathy, its limitations, and its role in a comprehensive moral theory. In J. Gewirtz and W. Kurtines (Eds.), *Morality, moral development, and moral behavior* (pp. 283–302). New York: John Wiley.

Hoffman, M. L. (1985). Affect, motivation, and cognition. In E. T. Higgins &

R. M. Sorrentino (Eds.), *Handbook of motivation and cognition: Foundations of social behavior* (pp. 244–280). New York: Guilford.

Hoffman, M. L. (1987). The contribution of empathy to justice and moral judgment. In N. Eisenberg and J. Strayer (Eds.), *Empathy and its development* (pp. 47–80). New York: Cambridge University Press.

Hoffman, M. L. (1988). Moral development. In M. Lamb & M. Bornstein (Eds.), *Developmental psychology: An advanced textbook.* (2nd ed., pp. 497–548). Hillsdale, NJ.: Erlbaum.

Hoffman, M. L. (1989). Empathy and prosocial activism. In N. Eisenberg, J. Reykowski, & E. Staub (Eds.), *Social and moral values: Individual and societal perspectives* (pp. 65–86). Hillsdale, NJ.: Erlbaum.

Hoffman, M. L. (1990). Empathy and justice motivation. *Motivation and Emotion, 4,* 151–172.

Hoffman, M. L. (1991). Toward an integration: Commentary. *Human Development, 34,* 105–110.

Hoffman, M. L., & Saltzstein, H. D. (1967). Parent discipline and the child's moral development. *Journal of Personality and Social Psychology, 5,* 45–57.

Hook, J. G., & Cook, T. D. (1979). Equity theory and the cognitive ability of children. *Psychological Bulletin, 86,* 429–445.

Houston, D. A. (1990). Empathy and the self: Cognitive and emotional influences on the evaluation of negative affect in others. *Journal of Personality and Social Psychology, 59,* 859–871.

Howe, M. L., & Courage, M. L. (1997). The emergence and early development of autobiographical memory. *Psychological Review, 104,* 499–523.

Hudson, J. A., & Nelson, K. (1983). Effects of script structure on children's story recall. *Developmental Psychology, 19,* 625–635.

Hume, D. (1751/1957). *An inquiry concerning the principle of morals.* New York: Liberal Arts Press.

Humphrey, G. (1922). The conditioned reflex and the elementary social reaction. *Journal of Abnormal and Social Psychology, 17,* 113–119.

Huo, Y. J., Smith, H. J., Tyler, T. R., & Lind, E. A. (1996). Superordinate identification, subgroup identification, and justice concerns. *Psychological Science, 7,* 40–45.

Ickes, W. (1997). *Empathic accuracy.* New York: Guilford.

Ignatieff, M. (1999, May 20). Human rights: The midlife crisis. *New York Review of Books,* pp. 58–62.

Izard, C. (1977). *Human emotions.* New York: Plenum Press.

James, W. (1893). *Psychology.* New York: Holt.

Johnson, D. B. (1992). Altruistic behavior and the development of the self in infants. *Merrill-Palmer Quarterly of Behavior and Development, 28,* 379–388.

Jones, E. E., & Nisbett, R. E. (1971). The action and the observer: Divergent perceptions of the causes of behavior. In E. E. Jones et al. (Eds.), *Attribution: Perceiving the causes of behavior.* Morristown, NJ: General Learning Press.

Kahneman, D. (1973). *Attention and effort.* Englewood Cliffs, NJ: Prentice-Hall, 1973.

Kameya, L. I. (1976). The effect of empathy level and role-taking training upon prosocial behavior. Unpublished doctoral dissertation, University of Michigan.

Kant, I. (1785/1964). *Groundwork of the metaphysics of morals* (H. J. Paton, Trans.). New York: Harper & Row.

Kaplan, E. A. (1989). Women, morality, and social change: A historical perspective. In N. Eisenberg, J. Reykowski, & E. Staub (Eds.), *Social and moral values* (pp. 347–361). Hillsdale, NJ: Erlbaum.

Kaplan, L. J. (1977). The basic dialogue and the capacity for empathy. In N. Freedman and S. Grand (Eds), *Communicative structures and psychic structures* (pp. 87–107). New York: Plenum.

Kastenbaum, R., Farber, E., & Sroufe, L. A. (1989). Individual differences in empathy among preschoolers: Relation to attachment history. In N. Eisenberg (Ed.), *Empathy and related emotional responses: New directions for child development research* (No. 44, pp. 51–64). San Francisco: Jossey-Bass.

Katz, I., Glass, D. C., & Cohen, S. (1973). Ambivalence, guilt, and the scapegoating of minority-group victims. *Journal of Experimental Social Psychology, 9*, 423–436.

Keniston, K. (1968). *Young radicals.* New York: Harcourt.

Klein, R. (1971). Some factors influencing empathy in six- and seven-year-old children varying in ethnic background (Doctoral dissertation, University of California, Los Angeles, 1970). *Dissertation Abstracts International, 31,* 3960A. (University Microfilms No. 71–3862).

Kochanska, G. (1995). Children's temperament, mother's discipline, and security of attachment: Multiple pathways to emerging internalization. *Child Development, 66,* 597–615.

Kohlberg, L. (1969). Stage and sequence: The cognitive-developmental approach to socialization. In D. A. Goslin (Ed.), *Handbook of socialization theory and research* (pp. 347–480). Chicago: Rand McNally.

Kohlberg, L. (1984). *The psychology of moral development: Essays on moral development* (Vol. 2). San Francisco: Harper & Row.

Kopp, C. B. (1982). The antecedents of self-regulation. *Developmental Psychology, 18,* 199–214.

Krebs, D. L. (1975). Empathy and altruism. *Journal of Personality and Social Psychology, 32,* 1124–1146.

Krevans, J., & Gibbs, J. C. (1996). Parents' use of inductive discipline: Relations to children's empathy and prosocial behavior. *Child Development, 67,* 3263–3277.

Kuczynski, L. (1983). Reasoning, prohibitions, and motivations for compliance. *Developmental Psychology, 19,* 126–134.

Kuczynski, L., Kochanska, G., Radke-Yarrow, M., & Girnius-Brown, O. (1987). A developmental interpretation of young children's noncompliance. *Developmental Psychology, 23,* 799–806.

Kuczynski, L., Marshall, S., & Schell, K. (1997). Value socialization in a bidirectional context. In J. Grusec & L. Kuczynski (Eds.), *Parenting and children's internalization of values: A handbook of contemporary theory* (pp. 23–50). New York: John Wiley.

Kymlicka, W. (1990). *Contemporary political philosophy: An introduction* (Chapter 2). Oxford, England: Clarendon Press.

Laird, J. D. (1974). Self-attribution of emotion. The effects of expressive behavior on the quality of emotional experience. *Journal of Personality and Social Psychology, 29,* 475–486.

Laird, J. D. (1984). The real role of facial response in the experience of emotion. *Journal of Personality and Social Psychology, 47,* 909–917.

Laird, J. D., Alibozak, T., Davainis, D., Deignan, K., Fontanella, K., Hong, J., & Pacheco, C. (1994). Individual differences in the effects of spontaneous mimicry on emotional contagion. *Motivation and Emotion, 18,* 231–247.

Laird, J. D., Wagener, J. J., Halal, M., & Szedga, M. (1982). Remembering what you feel: Effects of emotion and memory. *Journal of Personality and Social Psychology, 42,* 646–675.

Lanzetta, J. T., & Englis, B. G. (1989). Expectations of cooperation and competition and their effects on observers' vicarious emotional responses. *Journal of Personality and Social Psychology, 56,* 543–554.

Lanzetta, J. T., & Orr, S. P. (1986). Excitatory strength of expressive faces: Effects of happy and fear expressions and context on the extinction of a conditioned fear response. *Journal of Personality and Social Psychology, 50,* 190–194.

Latane, B., & Darley, J. M. (1970). *The unresponsive bystander: Why doesn't he help?* New York: Prentice-Hall.

Lerner, M. J., & Miller, D. T. (1978). Just world research and the attribution process. *Psychological Bulletin, 81,* 1030–1051.

Levenson, R. W., & Ruef, A. M. (1997). Physiological aspects of emotional knowledge and rapport. In W. Ickes (Ed.), *Empathic accuracy* (pp. 44–72). New York: Guilford.

Lewis, M. (1989). Cultural differences in children's knowledge of emotional scripts. In C. Saarni & P. L. Harris (Eds.), *Children's understanding of emotions.* New York: Cambridge University Press.

Lewis, M., & Brooks-Gunn, J. (1979). *Social cognition and the acquisition of self.* New York: Plenum.

Lifton, R. (1968). *Death in life: Survivors of Hiroshima.* New York: Random House.

Lindsay-Hartz, J., De Rivera, J., & Mascolo, M. F. (1995). Differentiating guilt and shame and their effects on motivation. In J. P. Tangney & K. W. Fischer (Eds.), *Self-conscious emotions: Shame, guilt, embarrassment, and pride* (pp. 274–299). New York: Guilford.

Lipps, T. (1906). Das wissen von fremden Ichen. *PsycholUntersuch, 1,* 694–722.

Lytton, H. (1979). Disciplinary encounters between young boys and their mothers and fathers: Is there a contingency system? *Developmental Psychology, 15,* 256–268.

MacLean, P. D. (1973). *A triune concept of the brain and behavior.* Toronto, Canada: University of Toronto Press.

MacLean, P. D. (1985). Brain evolution relating to family, play, and the separation call. *Archives of General Psychiatry, 42:* 405–417.

Mahler, M. S. (1974). Symbiosis and individuation: The psychological birth of the human infant. In *The selected papers of Margaret S. Mahler* (Vol. 2, pp. 149–168). New York: Jason Aronson, 1979.

Main, M., Weston, D., & Wakeling, S. (1979). Concerned attention to the crying of an adult actor in infancy. Paper presented at the biennial meeting of the Society for Research in Child Development. San Francisco.

Malinowski, C. I., & Smith, C. P. (1985). Moral reasoning and moral conduct. *Journal of Personality and Social Psychology, 49,* 1016–1027.

Markus, H. R., & Kitayama, S. (1991). Cultural variations in self-concept. In G. R. Goethals & J. Strauss (Eds.), *Multidisciplinary perspectives on the self* (pp. 18–48). New York: Springer-Verlag.

Martin, G. B., & Clark, R. D. (1982). Distress crying in infants: Species and peer specificity. *Developmental Psychology, 18,* 3–9.

Mascolo, M. F., & Fischer, K. W. (1995). Developmental transformations in appraisals for pride, shame, and guilt. In J. P. Tangney & K. M. Fischer (Eds.), *Self-conscious emotions* (pp. 64–113). New York: Guilford Press.

Mathews, J. D., (1991). Empathy: A facial electromyographic study. Unpublished doctoral dissertation, New York University.

Mathews, J. D., Hoffman, M. L., & Cohen, B. H. (1991). Self-reports and experimental set predict facial responses to empathy-evoking stimuli. American Psychological Science meetings, Washington, DC, June 13.

McGillicuddy-De Lisi, A. V., Watkins, C., & Vinchur, A. J. (1994). The effect of relationship on children's distributive justice reasoning. *Child Development, 65,* 1694–1700.

Meindl, J. R., & Lerner, M. J. (1984). Exacerbation of extreme responses to an out-group. *Journal of Personality and Social Psychology, 47,* 71–84.

Meltzoff, A. N. (1988). Infant imitation after a 1-week delay. *Developmental Psychology, 24,* 470–476.

Midlarsky, E., & Hannah, M. E. (1985). Competence, reticence, and helping by children and adolescents. *Developmental Psychology, 21,* 534–541.

Milgram, S. (1963). Behavioral study of obedience. *Journal of Personality and Social Psychology, 67,* 371–378.

Mill, J. S. (1861/1952). *Utilitarianism.* In R. M. Hutchins (Eds.), *American state papers.* 43 (pp. 445–476). Chicago: University of Chicago Press.

Miller, J. G., & Bersoff, D. M. (1992). Culture and moral judgment: How are conflicts between justice and interpersonal responsibilities resolved? *Journal of Personality and Social Psychology, 62,* 541–554.

Miller, P. A., Eisenberg, N., Fabes, R. A., & Shell, R. (1996). Relations of moral reasoning and vicarious emotion in young children's prosocial behavior toward peers and adults. *Developmental Psychology, 32,* 210–219.

Minton, C., Kagan, J., & Levine, J. (1971). Maternal control and obedience in the two-year-old. *Child Development, 42,* 1873–1894.

Modell, A. H. (1963). On having the right to a life: An aspect of the superego's development. *International Journal of Psychoanalysis, 46,* 323–331.

Modell, A. H. (1984). *Psychoanalysis in a new context.* New York: International Universities Press.

Monroe, S. (1973, February). Guest in a strange house. *Saturday Review of Books,* pp. 45–48.

Montada, L., Schmitt, M., & Dalbert, C. (1986). Thinking about justice and dealing with one's privileges: A study on existential guilt. In H. W. Bierhoff, R. Cohen, & J. Greenberg (Eds.), *Justice in social relations* (pp. 125–144). New York: Plenum Press.

Montada, L., & Schneider, A. (1989). Justice and emotional reactions of the disadvantaged. *Social Justice Research, 3,* 313–344.

Moss, H. (1967). Sex, age, and state as determinants of mother–infant interaction. *Merrill-Palmer Quarterly of Behavior and Development, 13,* 19–26.

Mowrer, O. H. (1960). *Learning theory and behavior.* New York: Wiley.

Mueller, J. H. (1979). Anxiety and encoding processing in memory. *Personality and Social Psychology Bulletin, 5,* 288–294.

Munroe, R. H., Shimmin, H. S., & Munroe, R. I. (1984). Gender understanding and sex-role preference in four cultures. *Developmental Psychology, 20,* 673–682.

Murphy, L. B. (1937). *Social behavior and child personality.* New York: Columbia University Press.

Nelson, K. (1981). Social cognition in a script framework. In J. H. Flavell & L. Ross (Eds.), *Social cognitive development* (pp. 97–118). Cambridge: Cambridge University Press.

Nelson, K. (1993). The psychological and social origins of autobiographical memory. *Psychological Science, 4,* 7–14.

Neuberg, S. L., Cialdini, R. B., Brown, S. L., Luce, C., Sagarin, B. J., & Lewis, B. P. (1997). Does empathy lead to anything more than superficial helping? *Journal of Personality and Social Psychology, 73,* 310–316.

*New Republic* (1970, November 28). Bridging the generation gap: Editors' summary of Rep. Morris K. Udall's (D. Ariz.) discussion with his "interns," pp. 11–14.

Noddings, N. (1984). *Caring.* Berkeley: University of California Press.

Okel, E., & Mosher, D. (1968). Changes in affective states as a function of guilt over aggressive behavior. *Journal of Consulting and Clinical Psychology, 32,* 263–270.

Oliner, S. P., & Oliner, P. M. (1988). *The altruistic personality.* New York: The Free Press.

O'Neil, J. (1999, April 6). A syndrome with a mix of skills and deficits. *New York Times,* pp. F1, F4.

Orwell, G. (1958). *The road to Wigan Pier.* New York: Harcourt, Brace, Jovanovitch.

O'Toole, R. & Dubin, R. (1968). Baby feeding and body sway: An experiment in George Herbert Mead's "taking the role of the other." *Journal of Social and Personality Psychology, 10,* 59–65.

Otten, C. A., Penner, L. A., & Altabe, M. N. (1991). An examination of therapists' and college students' willingness to help a psychologically distressed person. *Journal of Social and Clinical Psychology, 10,* 102–120.

Panksepp, J. (1986). The psychology of prosocial behaviors: Separation distress, play, and altruism. In C. Zahn-Waxler, E. M. Cummings, & R. Iannotti (Eds.), *Altruism and aggression: Biological and social origins* (pp. 19–57). Cambridge: Cambridge University Press.

Parens, H. (1979). *The development of aggression in early childhood.* New York: Jason Aronson.

Paris, S. G., & Carter, A. Y. (1973). Semantic and constructive aspects of sentence memory in children. *Developmental Psychology, 9,* 109–113.

Pazer, S., Slackman, E., & Hoffman, M. L. (1981). Age and sex differences in the effect of information on anger. Unpublished manuscript. City University of New York.

Pearlman, L. A., & Saakvitne, K. W. (1995). *Trauma and the therapist.* New York: W. W. Norton.

Pederzane, J. (1998, June 12). When they can't watch another patient die. *New York Times,* p. B2.

Peng, M., Johnson, C., Pollock, J., Glasspool, R., & Harris, P. (1992). Training young children to acknowledge mixed emotions. *Cognition and Emotion, 6,* 387–401.

Penner, L. A., Fritzsche, B. A., Craiger, J. P., & Freifeld, T. (1995). Measuring the prosocial personality. In J. N. Butcher & C. D. Spielberger (Eds.), *Advances in Personality Assessment* (Vol. 10). Hillsdale, NJ: Erlbaum.

Piaget, J. (1932). *The moral judgment of the child.* New York: Harcourt.

Piaget, J. (1954/1981). *Intelligence and affectivity: Their relationship during child development.* Palo Alto, CA: Annual Reviews.

Plomin, R., Emde, R. N., Braungart, J. M., Campus, J., Corley, R., Folker, D. W., Kagan, J., Resnick, J. S., Robinson, J., Zahn-Waxler, C., & DeFries, J. C. (1993). Genetic change and continuities from fourteen to twenty months: The MacArthur longitudinal twin study. *Child Development, 64,* 1354–1376.

Radke-Yarrow, M., & Zahn-Waxler, C. (1984). Roots, motives, and patterns in children's prosocial behavior. In E. Staub, D. Bar-Tal, J. Karylowski, & J. Reykowski (Eds.), *Development and Maintenance of Prosocial Behavior* (pp. 81–99). New York: Plenum.

Radke-Yarrow, M., Zahn-Waxler, C., & Chapman, M. (1983). Children's prosocial dispositions and behavior. In E. M. Hetherington (Ed.), *Handbook of child psychology: Vol. 4, Socialization, personality, and social development* (pp. 469–545). New York: Wiley.

Rashdall, H. (1907). *The theory of good and evil.* Oxford: Oxford University Press.

Rawls, J. A. (1971). *A theory of justice.* Cambridge, MA: Belnap Press of Harvard University Press.

Rawls, J. A. (1985). Justice as fairness: Political not metaphysical. *Philosophy and Public Affairs, 14,* 223–251.

Regan, D. T., & Totten, J. (1975). Empathy and attribution: Turing observers into actors. *Journal of Personality and Social Psychology, 32,* 850–856.

Reissland, N. (1988). Neonatal imitation in the first hour of life: Observations in rural Nepal. *Developmental Psychology, 24,* 464–469.

Rogers, T. B., Kuiper, N. A., & Kirker, W. S. (1977). Self-reference and the encoding of personal information. *Journal of Personality and Social Psychology, 35,* 677–688.

Rollins, B. C., & Thomas, D. L. (1979). Parental support, power, and control techniques in the socialization of children. In W. R. Burr, R. Hill, F. I. Nye, & I. L. Reiss (Eds.), *Contemporary theories about the family: Vol. 1, Research-based theories* (pp. 317–364). New York: Free Press.

Ross, H., Tesla, C., Kenyon, B., & Lollis, S. (1990). Maternal intervention in toddler peer conflict: The socialization of principles of justice. *Developmental Psychology, 26,* 994–1003.

Rossi, S. I., & Wittrock, M. C. (1971). Developmental shifts in verbal recall between mental ages 2 and 5. *Child Development, 42,* 333–338.

Rotenberg, K. J., & Eisenberg, N. (1997). Developmental differences in the understanding of and reaction to others' inhibition of emotional expression. *Developmental Psychology, 33,* 526–537.

Ruble, D. N., & Martin, C. L. (1998). Gender development. In W. Damon (Ed.), *Handbook of Child Psychology: Vol. 3, Social, emotional, and personality development* (pp. 933–1016). New York: Wiley.

Sacks, O. W. (1995). *An anthropologist from Mars.* New York: Knopf.

Sagi, A., & Hoffman, M. L. (1976). Empathic distress in the newborn. *Developmental Psychology, 12,* 175–176.

Samenow, S. E. (1984). *Inside the criminal mind.* New York: Random House.

Sanna, L. J., & Turley, K. J. (1996). Antecedents to spontaneous counter-factual thinking. *Personality and Social Psychology Bulletin, 22,* 906–919.

Sawin, D. B., and Parke, R. D. (1980). Empathy and fear as mediators of resistance-to-deviation in children. *Merrill-Palmer Quarterly of Behavior and Development, 26,* 123–134.

Schachter, S., & Singer, J. E. (1962). Cognitive, social, and physiological determinants of emotional state. *Psychological Review, 69,* 379–399.

Schaffer, H. R., & Crook, C. K. (1980). Child compliance and maternal control techniques. *Developmental Psychology, 16,* 54–61.

Scheler, M. (1913/1954). *The nature of sympathy.* London: Routledge & Kegan Paul.

Scherer, K. (1982). Methods of research on verbal communication: Paradigms and parameters. In K. R. Scherer and P. Ekman (Eds.), *Handbook of methods in nonverbal behavior research* (pp. 136–198). New York: Cambridge University Press.

Schmidt, G., & Weiner, B. (1988). An attribution-affect-action theory of behavior: Replications of judgments of help-giving. *Personality and Social Psychology Bulletin, 14,* 610–621.

Schmitt, M., Bauerle, C., & Domke, E. (1989). Toward differentiating existential guilt and sympathy over responsibility induction: A film experiment. *Zeitscrift für Experimentelle und Angewandte Psychologie, 36,* 274–291.

Schneider, M. E., Major, B., Luhtanen, R., & Crocker, J. (1996). Social stigma and the potential cost of assumptive help. *Personality and Social Psychology Bulletin, 22,* 201–209.

Schoggen, P. (1963). Environmental forces in the everyday lives of children. In R. G. Barker (Ed.). *The stream of behavior: Explorations of its structure and content* (pp. 42–69). New York: Appleton-Century-Crofts.

Schroeder, D. A., Penner, L. A., Dovidio, J. F., & Piliavin, J. A. (1995). *The psychology of helping and altruism.* New York: McGraw-Hill.

Schwartz, S. (1970). Moral decision-making and behavior. In J. Macaulay & L. Berkowitz (Eds.), *Altruism and helping behavior* (pp. 127–141). New York: Academic Press.

Shantz, C. U. (1987). Conflicts between children. *Child Development, 58,* 283–305.

Shaw, L. L., Batson, C. D., & Todd, R. M. (1994). Empathy avoidance: Forestalling feeling for another in order to escape the motivational consequences. *Journal of Personality and Social Psychology, 67,* 879–887.

Sherrill, R. (1974, October 20). What Grand Rapids did for Jerry Ford and vice versa. *New York Times,* p. 9

Sigelman, C. K., & Waitzman, K. A. (1991). The development of distributive justice orientations: Contextual influences on children's resource allocations. *Child Development, 62,* 1367–1378.

Simmel, G. (1902). The number of members as determining the sociological form of the group. *American Journal of Sociology, 8,* 1–46.

Simmons, H., & Schoggen, P. (1963). Mothers and fathers as sources of environmental pressure on children. In R. G. Barket (Ed.), *The stream of behavior: Explorations of its structure and content* (pp. 70–77). New York: Appleton-Century-Crofts.

Simner, M. L. (1971). Newborn's response to the cry of another infant. *Developmental Psychology, 5,* 136–150.

Smetana, J. G. (1984). Toddlers' social interactions regarding moral and conventional transgressions. *Child Development, 58,* 1767–1776.

Smetana, J. G. (1989). Toddlers' social interactions in the context of moral and conventional transgression in the home. *Developmental Psychology, 25,* 499–508.

Smith, A. (1759/1976). *The theory of moral sentiments.* Oxford, England: Clarendon Press.

Spiro, M. (1993). Is the Western concept of the self "peculiar" within the context of the world's cultures? *Ethos, 21,* 107–153.

Starr, P. (1974, October 13). Rebels after the cause: Living with contradictions. *New York Times Magazine,* pp. 31–32, 100–113.

Staub, E. (1996). Responsibility, helping, aggression, and evil. *Psychological Inquiry, 7*, 252.

Stern, D. (1985). *The interpersonal world of the infant.* New York: Basic Books.

Stein, H. (1994, September 13). Deficit reduction, chapter and verse. *New York Times*, editorial page.

Stipek, D. J., Gralinski, J. H., & Kopp, C. B. (1990). Self-concept in the toddler years. *Developmental Psychology, 26*, 972–977.

Stotland, E. (1969). Exploratory investigations of empathy. In L. Berkowitz (Ed.), *Advances in experimental social psychology* (Vol. 4, pp. 271–314). New York: Academic Press.

Stotland, E., Matthews, K., Sherman, S., Hansson, R., & Richardson, B. (1979). *Empathy, fantasy, and helping.* Beverly Hills: Sage.

Stowe, H. B. (1860/1966). *Uncle Tom's cabin.* New York: Signet.

Strack, F., Martin, L. L., & Stepper, S. (1988). Inhibiting and facilitating conditions of the human smile: A nonobtrusive test of the facial feedback hypothesis. *Journal of Personal and Social Psychology, 54*, 768–776.

Strayer, J. (1993). Children's concordant emotions and cognitions in response to observed emotions. *Child Development, 64*, 188–201.

Sullivan, H. S. (1940). *Conceptions of modern psychiatry.* London: Havistock Press.

Tangney, J. (1991). Moral affect: The good, the bad, and the ugly. *Journal of Personality and Social Psychology, 61*, 598–607.

Tangney, J., & Fischer, K. (1995). *Self-conscious emotions: Shame, guilt, embarrassment, and pride.* New York: Guilford.

Tangney, J. P., Marschall, D., Rosenberg, K., Barlow, D. H., & Wagner, P. (1996). Children's and adult's autobiographical accounts of shame, guilt, and pride experiences. George Mason University.

Tangney, J. P., Wagner, P. E., Burggraf, S. A., & Fletcher, C. (1991, June). Children's shame-proneness, but not guilt-proneness, is related to emotional and behavioral maladjustment. Poster presented at the meeting of the American Psychological Society, Washington, DC.

Termine, N. T., & Izard, C. E. (1988). Infants' responses to their mothers' expressions of joy and sadness. *Developmental Psychology, 24*, 223–229.

Thompson, R., & Hoffman, M. L. (1980). Empathy and the development of guilt in children. *Developmental Psychology, 16*, 155–156.

Trivers, R. L. (1971). The evolution of reciprocal altruism. *Quarterly Review of Biology, 46*, 35–57.

Tulkin, S. R., & Kagan, J. (1972). Mother–infant interaction in the first year of life. *Child Development, 43*, 31–42.

Tulving, E. (1972). Episodic and Semantic Memory. In E. Tulving & W. Donaldson (Eds.), *Organization of memory* (pp. 301–403). New York: Academic Press.

Turiel, E. (1966). An experimental test of the sequentiality of developmental stages in the child's moral judgments. *Journal of Personality and Social Psychology, 3*, 611–618.

Turiel, E. (1983). *The development of social knowledge: Morality and convention.* Cambridge, England: Cambridge University Press.

Turiel, E. (1998). The development of morality. In W. Damon (Ed.), *Handbook of Child Psychology: Vol. 3, Social, emotional, and personality development* (pp. 863–932). New York: Wiley.

Twain, M. (1884/1977). *Adventures of Huckleberry Finn.* New York: W. W. Norton.

Vitz, P. C. (1990). The use of stories in moral development: New psychological reasons for an old education method. *American Psychologist, 45,* 709–720.

Vorrath, H. H., & Brendtro, L. K. (1985). Positive peer culture (2nd ed.). New York: Aldine.

*Webster's Ninth New Collegiate Dictionary.* (1985). Springfield, MA: Merriam-Webster.

Weiner, B. (1982). The emotional consequences of causal attribution. In M. S. Clark & S. T. Fiske (Eds.), *Affect and cognition* (pp. 185–210). Hillsdale, NJ: Erlbaum.

Weiner, B. (1985). "Spontaneous" causal thinking. *Psychological Bulletin, 97,* 74–84.

Weiner, B., Graham, S., & Chandler, C. (1982). Pity, anger, and guilt: An attributional analysis. *Personality and Social Psychology Bulletin, 8,* 226–232.

Weiner, B., Graham, S., Stern, P., & Lawson, M. E. (1982). Using affective cues to infer causal thoughts. *Developmental Psychology, 18,* 278–286.

Weiss, R. F., Boyer, J. L., Lombardo, J. P., & Stitch, M. H. (1973). Altruistic drive and altruistic reinforcement. *Journal of Personality and Social Psychology, 25,* 390–400.

Wellbank, J. H., Snook, D., & Mason, D. T. (1982). *John Rawls and his critics: An annotated bibliography.* New York: Garland Publishers.

Wender, I. (1986). Children's use of justice principles in allocation situations. In H. Bierhoff, R. Cohen, and J. Greenberg (Eds.), *Justice in social relations* (pp. 249–266). Plenum Press: New York.

Wetstone, H. (1977). About word words and thing words: A study of metalinguistic awareness. Paper presented at the second annual conference on language development, Boston.

Williams, C. (1989). Empathy and burnout in male and female helping professionals. *Research in Nursing and Health, 12,* 169–178.

Williams, C., & Bybee, J. (1994). What do children feel guilt about? Developmental and gender differences. *Developmental Psychology. 30,* 617–623.

Wilson, B. J., & Cantor, J. (1985). *Journal of Experimental Child Psychology, 39,* 284–299.

Wolff, R. P. (1977). *Understanding Rawls: A reconstruction and critique of a theory of justice.* Princeton: Princeton University Press.

Wright, H. F. (1967). *Recording and analyzing child behavior.* New York: Harper & Row.

Zahn-Waxler, C., Radke-Yarrow, M., & King, R. (1979). Childrearing and children's prosocial initiations toward victims of distress. *Child Development, 50,* 319–330.

Zahn-Waxler, C., Radke-Yarrow, M., Wagner, E., & Chapman, M. (1992). Development of concern for others. *Developmental Psychology, 28,* 126–136.

Zahn-Waxler, C., & Robinson, J. L. (1995). Empathy and guilt: Early origins of feelings of responsibility. In K. Fischer & J. Tangney (Eds.), *Self-conscious emotions: Shame, guilt, embarrassment, and pride* (pp. 143–173). New York: Guilford Press.

Zahn-Waxler, C., Robinson, J. L., Emde, N. E., & Plomin, R. (1992). The development of empathy in twins. *Developmental Psychology, 28,* 1038–1047.

Zajonc, R. B. (1968). Attitudinal effects of mere exposure. *Journal of Personality and Social Psychology Monograph Supplement, 9,* (2, Pt. 2), 1–27.

Zajonc, R. B. (1980). Feeling and thinking: Preferences need no inferences. *American Psychologist, 35,* 151–175.

Zillman, D., & Cantor, J. R. (1977). Affective responses to the emotion of a protagonist. *Journal of Experimental Social Psychology, 13,* 155–165.

# Author Index

# Subject Index

CPSIA information can be obtained at www.ICGtesting.com
Printed in the USA
LVOW11s1734301115

464716LV00002B/284/P